W9-CLA-430

ASSAULT
RIFLE

TKB-0111
G.A.Korobov

TKB-0146
I. Ya. Stechkin

TKB-0136
N.M. Afanasiev

AEK-971
S.I. Koksharov

AS
G.N. Nikonov

AKB
V.M. Kalashnikov

ASM
G.N.Nikonov

ASSAULT RIFLE

Maxim Popenker and Anthony G. Williams

The Crowood Press

First published in 2004 by
The Crowood Press Ltd
Ramsbury, Marlborough
Wiltshire SN8 2HR

www.crowood.com

British Library Cataloguing-in-Publication Data
A catalogue record for this book is available from the British Library.

ISBN 1 86126 700 2

Frontispiece: *5.45mm assault rifles, submitted to the 'Abakan' trials in 1984.*

Designed and typeset by Focus Publishing, 11a St Botolph's Road, Sevenoaks, Kent TN13 3AJ

Printed and bound in England by CPI Bath

Contents

Acknowledgements

Particular thanks are due to Richard Jones, the Custodian, and the staff of the MoD Pattern Room whose extensive library and weapon collection were consulted in the preparation of this book.

Others who have provided illustrations, other material or assistance were: Alejandro Albertengo (Argentine), Alexandre Beraldi (Brazil), Arne Brennan, Jonathan Cohen, Ladislav Findorak, Sami Jumppanen (Finland), Bojan Kavedzic (Yugoslavia), Steve Lasday, John C. Lubbers (USA), Ken Melendy, Vladimir Nenadovic (Yugoslavia), Miroslav Novak (Czech Republic), Christian Overgaard, Olof Petersson (Sweden), Paul Quimby (USA), Jakub Uchytil, Dmitry 'Lis' Salakhov (Russia), Dmitry Shiryaev (Russia), Vadim Sigalov (Israel), Paul Smith (Canada), Romeo Streigner (Croatia), Simon Tan (Malaysia), Pierangelo Tendas (Italy), Dick Venema (Netherlands), Oleg Volk (USA), Gene Whitehead, Bhaskoro Aji Wibowo (Indonesia) and Bill Woodin.

The authors also thank the many companies who made illustrations and details of their products available.

Part I

INTRODUCTION

Left *Current military rifle cartridges (from left to right): the full-power 7.62 × 51 NATO; 7.62 × 39 Russian; 5.56 × 45 NATO; 5.45 × 39 Russian.*

Below *The Fedorov Avtomat*
(courtesy MoD Pattern Room).

Chapter One

ASSAULT RIFLES: A BRIEF HISTORY

DEFINITIONS

The term 'assault rifle' is in common use to describe modern military rifles. However, there is no officially agreed definition of the term, so this book must necessarily commence by defining its subject.

The broadest definition likely to secure agreement is along the lines of: 'a standard infantry rifle with selective fire'. The phrase 'standard infantry rifle' excludes such weapons as sub-machine guns (SMGs) or light machine guns (LMGs). Compared with a traditional SMG, an assault rifle fires more powerful cartridges, has a longer barrel and a much longer range. Compared with an LMG (which typically uses the same ammunition), it is lighter and is normally hand-held rather than fired from a bipod; it is also always magazine-fed rather than (sometimes) belt-fed. 'Selective fire' means that it has the option of fully automatic fire: the weapon keeps firing for as long as the trigger is pressed or until the ammunition runs out. This therefore excludes those self-loading rifles which offer only semi-automatic fire (that is, they fire only one shot for each press of the trigger), although it would include burst-fire weapons which fire a predetermined number of rounds – usually two or three – for each press of the trigger.

This broad definition has been used as the basis for this book. However, it has to be admitted that it is not perfect for three reasons. First, some weapons have been made in both semi-automatic and selective fire versions, with some nations choosing only the semi-auto version; for the sake of completeness, these have been included. Secondly, the term 'assault rifle' should arguably be applied only to those weapons which are capable of controlled, fully-automatic fire from the shoulder; this would rule out those selective-fire rifles which chamber the traditional full-power (FP) 7.62 or 7.92mm rifle and MG cartridges (currently, only the 7.62 × 51 NATO) because their recoil is too heavy to permit this: the muzzle rises rapidly under recoil so that

all shots after the first will tend to fly over the target. Using a narrower definition to specify 'controlled automatic fire from the shoulder' would include only those weapons chambered for the less powerful 'intermediate' cartridges, so-called because they are intermediate in power between pistol/SMG and FP rifle rounds. However, some weapons have been made which can be chambered for either FP or intermediate rounds, so it has been decided (again for the sake of completeness) to include FP rifles as well, while noting that they do not make satisfactory assault rifles. Finally, some very short-barrelled assault rifles have been produced to take over the role of the traditional SMG; these are also included, since, apart from barrel length, they are essentially the same weapons.

Among the intermediate cartridges used in assault rifles two different types can be distinguished: full calibre and reduced calibre. The full calibre rounds have the same calibre as the standard FP rifle/MG ammunition, but use a shorter case holding less propellant to fire a lighter bullet, which generates much less power and recoil. The principal examples of this type are the first two purpose-designed assault rifle cartridges to see service: the 7.92 × 33 of the German MP 43/44/StG.44 of the Second World War and the 7.62 × 39 of the famous Soviet Kalashnikov AK 47 of the 1950s. (These designations follow the standard method of identifying military cartridges: 7.92 is the bore diameter – slightly narrower than the bullet – 33 is the length of the cartridge case, both measurements being in millimetres.)

The reduced calibre rounds use a smaller calibre to minimize recoil while increasing the muzzle velocity to achieve an improved target effect and/or longer range. Until recently, the only reduced calibre rounds to achieve service were the American 5.56 × 45 and the Russian 5.45 × 39, but they have now been joined by the Chinese 5.8 × 42. The full calibre assault rifle

(FCAR) rounds have maximum effective ranges in the region of 300m (330yd); double that of an SMG, and considered to be the acceptable minimum for an infantry rifle. While the reduced calibre (RCAR) rifles can hit more distant targets, at long range the little bullets are significantly less effective than those of the FP 7.62mm weapons.

EARLY HISTORY

The elements of an assault rifle were in place surprisingly early in the history of automatic weapons. Semi-automatic rifles were developed before the end of the nineteenth century and the first selective fire rifle using an intermediate cartridge was probably the Italian 6.5mm Cei-Rigotti, developed between 1900 and 1905, but this was not adopted. The First World War saw some use of FP semi-automatic rifles, especially by Germany, and mainly carried by aircrew since they were considered unsuitable for general infantry use. In addition, some of the Winchester self-loading carbines saw action, chambered for their proprietary .351 and .401 ($8.9 \times 35SR$ and $10.3 \times 38SR$) large-calibre, medium-power cartridges. These were primarily used by France, where there was also interest in the semi-automatic Ribeyrolle, which fired an $8 \times 35SR$ cartridge consisting of a standard 8mm rifle bullet inserted into a necked-down Winchester .351 case, but neither this nor a post-war 7mm version achieved service status.

The first service weapon which can be identified as conforming to the specification of an assault rifle dates back to the First World War – the Russian Fedorov Avtomat of 1916. This was a selective fire weapon using a short-recoil action and was chambered for a military rifle cartridge of intermediate calibre and power – the $6.5 \times 50SR$ Arisaka – large quantities of Japanese rifles in this calibre having been acquired by Russia. This was an excellent choice since the cartridge combined moderate recoil with good long-range performance, but only about 3,000 Avtomats were made. They were used in action in the Russian Civil War and thereby earned their place in small-arms history.

Elsewhere at this time, the prevalence of trench warfare and the associated close fighting had focused attention on short-range, automatic weapons, in complete contrast to the pre-war obsession with accurate, long-range rifle fire. This resulted in several lines of development: pistols modified with longer barrels and stocks and sometimes adapted to fully-automatic fire, purpose-designed SMGs, and the Pedersen Device, which replaced the bolt in the US Springfield rifle with a mechanism to fire small .30in (7.62×20) cartridges, no more powerful than pistol rounds – it was never used in anger.

Pistol-based carbines were a natural extension of the occasionally recurring fad for equipping pistols with detachable shoulder stocks in order to permit more accurate aiming. Longer barrels further extended the effective range (partly through increased velocity, partly because of the longer sight base), and so weapons such as the Mauser C96 ('Broomhandle') and P08 ('Luger') produced carbine derivatives, usually capable of only semi-automatic fire. These were relatively expensive to make, however, so the future in short-range automatics lay with the much simpler API (advanced primer ignition) blowback SMG. The first of these, if you discount the curious, twin-barrel Villar Perosa, was the Bergman MP 18 in 9×19 Parabellum (Luger) pistol calibre. This was the ancestor of the American Thompson, the German MP 38/40, the British Sten gun, the Soviet PPSh and others.

Attempts to improve the power and range of the small automatics, such as the use of the 9×25 Mauser Export round in the Swiss Solothurn and Hungarian Kiraly SMGs (which saw some service), did not catch on. Even less success attended the Mannlicher Carbine in 7.62×32 and various Swiss experiments to produce an FCAR cartridge, such as the 7.65×35 of the early 1920s and the 7.65×38 produced (under mysterious circumstances) just before the Second World War. Danish automatic rifles, known as the Weibel or the Danrif, were demonstrated in France in 1936, chambered for a 7×44 cartridge, firing an 8g bullet at 660–700m/s (123gr. at 2,165–2,300ft/s). The mechanism was based on the Winchester SL previously mentioned, which resulted in a violent action, and no orders were forthcoming.

In fact, despite the evidence that most shooting during the First World War was at short range, armies continued to show an interest in FP rifle/MG rounds. The USN had already dispensed with their 6mm Lee rifle and cartridge, which were really ahead of their time. The Japanese Army planned to replace their $6.5 \times 50SR$ cartridge with a new 7.7×58 calibre, although they never completed the changeover. The Italians were similarly caught at the start of World War 2 part way through a change from their 6.5×52 Carcano rifle to a 7.35×51 calibre.

Why was this? Partly because the existing 6–6.5mm cartridges were found to be less effective than was hoped, which was, in fact, more a function of the bullet design than the calibre. It was probably also because

Cartridges for self-loading weapons up to World War 1 (from left to right): 6.5mm Arisaka (6.5 × 50 SR); 6.5mm Italian Carcano (6.5 × 52); .351 Winchester SL (8.9 × 35 SR); .401 Winchester SL (10.3 × 38 SR); 9mm Parabellum (9 × 19); .30 Pedersen (7.62 × 20). 7.62 × 51 NATO for scale.

the need for a fully automatic rifle was generally resisted on the grounds of economy. Automatic rifles were much more expensive and required more maintenance than bolt-action ones, and there was also the fear that soldiers would just spray ammunition around at a great rate, causing increased cost and supply problems. This latter concern was, of course, fully justified, but it has been addressed by improving supply arrangements. So even the one nation wealthy enough to afford an automatic rifle – the USA – restricted the M1 Garand to semi-automatic fire, and FP rounds biased towards MG use prevailed. Incidentally, the USA did have the FP Browning Automatic Rifle in service, but that was too heavy to be a rifle replacement and was used as a light machine gun.

There had been some official efforts towards considering intermediate calibres, with the US Ordnance Department in the late 1920s sponsoring comparative trials of the effectiveness of different rifle cartridges using anaesthetized pigs and goats to assess the wounding effectiveness. They concentrated on a .25 inch (6.35 mm) – a rimmed ballistic test round firing an 8.1 g bullet at 808 m/s (125 grain at 2,650 fps) – a .276 (7 × 51) and the existing .30-06 (7.62 × 63)

rifle / MG round. The .25 most impressed the testers, but the Department chose the Garand rifle chambered for the .276 Pedersen cartridge which would have made an effective assault rifle round. The British were seriously interested, even manufacturing .276 ammunition in quantity between 1929 and 1933 in order to test the Pedersen rifle and also the British gas-operated White rifle in the same calibre. At this point, General Douglas MacArthur, the Army Chief of Staff, insisted on the new rifle being chambered for the .30-06 cartridge, mainly because of the large quantity of ammunition available in that calibre but also due to concerns about the performance of the .276, especially at long-range, so the Garand was duly converted to .30-06 and another opportunity was lost. British interest was also ended by this decision.

In 1930, the noted Russian gun historian, V.E. Markevich, then working at the Red Army's Weapons Scientific and Research Range, suggested to the Army weapons command that:

The new 'pistol carbines' [the designation of SMGs then in development] should not be built around pistol cartridges, because of range limitations; instead, such carbines should use a cartridge intermediate in power between the pistol and rifle cartridges. It is ridiculous to simply shorten the current rifle cartridge case and use the current (7.62mm) bullet for such cartridge, because of the rainbow-shaped trajectory and increased recoil. A true intermediate cartridge should be of 6.5mm calibre, and such a cartridge is already available in the form of American commercial .25 Remington cartridge [7.58g at 650m/s; 117gr. at 2,125ft/s]. The carbine for such cartridge should be lightweight, have a magazine capacity of 20–30 rounds, and be effective at ranges of between 100 and 300 metres [109–330yd].

Like all such theorists at the time, he was ignored by the military. This is particularly ironic as the .25 Remington shares the same case dimensions as the .30 Remington being used as the basis for the 6.8 × 43 Remington SPC, the latest experimental military cartridge now under test in the USA.

There was one rather odd American development not followed by any other country – the M1 Carbine. This was a light, semi-automatic rifle chambered for an intermediate, straight-cased 7.62 × 33 round. When developed in 1941, it was not originally intended for front-line troops but more as a self-defence weapon for second-line units, on the sensible grounds that it was much easier to shoot it accurately than a pistol. The M2

version came with a full-auto option, and thereby comes close to our definition of an assault rifle; but the cartridge was rather weak and the light, blunt-nosed bullet lost its modest velocity too quickly to be effective at the required 300m range. It was really a halfway stage between the SMG and the assault rifle. The use of the .30 carbine cartridge has recently been revived by the Israeli company IMI, which chambers it in the Magal SMG.

THE SECOND WORLD WAR AND ITS AFTERMATH

The modern line of assault rifle development started with the Germans, with the MP 43/44, later renamed StG.44, for *Sturmgewehr* or assault rifle – the first weapon to be so designated. The round for this followed the FCAR route, shortening the usual 7.92 × 57 K98 rifle/MG case to 33mm, and loading a lighter bullet at a reduced velocity. The gun was intended to replace both the 9mm SMGs and the K98 bolt-action rifle. Keeping the same calibre as the rifle was a matter of production convenience; it had previously been calculated that a 7mm calibre would be ideal. Despite initial opposition from Hitler, this was the weapon the Army wanted to back up their MG 42 GPMGs, and it was produced and used in quantity, with some 450,000 being made. However, the end of the war stopped

Some early intermediate cartridges (from left to right): 7.62mm Mannlicher Carbine (7.62 × 32); 7.65mm Swiss (7.65 × 35); 7.65 Swiss MP (7.65 × 38, with bullet unloaded); .25 Remington commercial round (6.35 × 52); .276 Pedersen (7 × 51); .30 Carbine (7.62 × 33) and 7.62 × 51 NATO for scale.

StG.44 rifle. (courtesy Dick H. Venema)

the direct line of development of this significant weapon.

One blind alley which also saw German service was the FG 42 *Fallschirmjäger Gewehr* (paratroop rifle) of 1942, which offered selective fire but was chambered for the FP 7.92 × 57 cartridge and thus proved uncontrollable in automatic fire. It saw limited service, about 7,000 being made.

Next to see service was the Soviet Simonov SKS, made in large numbers in several countries but now almost forgotten due to the fame of its successor, the Kalashnikov AK 47. Both weapons were chambered for a new 7.62 × 39 M1943 cartridge, closely comparable in performance to the 7.92 × 33; but the SKS was

not an assault rifle, being capable of semi-automatic fire only, while the AK 47 offers selective fire. There is still some sensitivity about the connection between the AK 47 and the StG.44, but two things are clear: despite the apparent similarity, the AK 47 was not a direct copy as it uses a quite different mechanism, but, on the other hand, Kalashnikov and his team must have known about the StG.44 and it is difficult to believe that they were not influenced by it.

The AK 47 and its ammunition (also used in the RPD light MG) so dominated the assault rifle field until the late 1960s that it is sometimes difficult to remember that there were other developments too, one of which saw service. This was the Czech vz52 rifle

The Russian AK 47.

chambered for their 7.62 × 45, a superior cartridge to the AK-47's in terms of range, but it was soon replaced by the vz52/57 (chambered for the 7.62 × 39) in the interests of commonality with the rest of the Warsaw Pact. The vz52 was only semi-automatic, but the Czechs were working on a selective fire weapon based on this round when the changeover to the Russian calibre took place; this assault rifle was the vz58.

Some interesting late-war experiments took place in Finland, with selective-fire rifles by Lahti and Lilja with various short-case cartridges (9 × 40, 9 × 41, 9 × 35 and 7.62 × 35) being tested, but these did not reach production. Much development activity also took place in France immediately after the war, resulting in the MAS 1948 and the MAS 1949 'automatic carbines' chambered for a 7.65 × 35 cartridge, but these did not see service. Neither did any of the several late 1940s Swiss weapons in 7.65 × 35 and 7.5 × 38 calibres (the latter firing a 8.0g – 124gr. – bullet at 670m/s, 2,200ft/s), nor the Danish Otterup rifle of the 1950s, chambered for a 7 × 36 cartridge, made by cutting down the .30-06 case, and offered to Finland (they chose the AK 47 instead).

A weapon which very nearly did see service was the British EM-2 rifle developed in the late 1940s. Unlike the AK 47, which continued to be supplemented by the full-power 7.62 × 54R Nagant cartridge in MGs and sniper rifles, this was a carefully judged attempt to produce a weapon which could replace both the 9mm SMG and the full-power .303 rifle in one package, by combining a new .280 (7 × 43) intermediate cartridge with a compact 'bullpup' layout. A GPMG based on the Bren LMG mechanism but with belt feed, the TADEN, was also developed to use this round and replace both the Bren and probably the Vickers MG. It appears to have been very successful and other NATO countries (particularly Canada and Belgium) were interested in the concept. The United Kingdom even formally adopted the EM-2 in 1951.

However, as described in Chapter 4, the intermediate cartridge concept was rejected by the USA which insisted on NATO's adopting a common round which had to be of .30in (7.62mm) calibre and powerful enough to replace the .30-06 in MGs – which, despite the American starting point of requiring selective fire, meant, by definition, that it would be too powerful to be controllable in fully automatic fire from a shoulder-fired rifle. The British, Belgians and Canadians made great efforts to meet the objections of the US Army, who thought the .280 was not powerful enough, by developing more powerful cartridges, one of which –

the 7 × 49 – actually saw service with Venezuela in the FN FAL rifle. It was all in vain; although the prototype .30 calibre rifles demonstrated poor hit probability in fully-automatic fire, the 7.62 × 51 was duly selected. Apart from being ½in (12mm) shorter than the .30-06 cartridge, it represented ·no progress whatsoever over this fifty-year old design. The British were forced to reverse their decision to adopt the EM-2 and subsequently (along with most other NATO countries) chose the FN FAL in 7.62 NATO, but the USA again went its own way, eventually adopting a rifle based on the existing M1 Garand, the M14.

THE MODERN ERA

Frustratingly for the intermediate-calibre supporters, while one branch of the US military was perfecting what became the M14, other parts were carrying out critical investigations of what actually happened in rifle combat, rather than what senior officers thought happened. There were several outcomes from this, leading to a number of development programmes during the 1950s and the 1960s. One was that the hit probability with rifles in combat was very low but could be dramatically improved if several shots could be fired simultaneously, as opposed to sequentially as in an automatic rifle. This led to Project SALVO (also described in more detail in Chapter 4), which initiated a series of experiments, including the multi-bullet loadings of conventional cartridges, multiple flechette loadings of shotguns and, ultimately, the abortive SPIW programme based around high-velocity, single flechette rounds.

Another outcome of American research was the realization that the actual ranges for rifle combat were far lower than had been thought, typically being 75–100m (77–109yd), with 90 per cent of all fire-fights taking place within 300m (330yd). This led to a proposal for a high-velocity .22 (5.56mm) calibre rifle which could match the lethality of the .30 calibre at short range but be more controllable in automatic fire and use much lighter ammunition. The eventual outcome of this was the ArmaLite AR-15 rifle and its tiny .223in (5.56 × 45) cartridge, developed from the Remington .222 commercial hunting round, which had been designed for shooting small game. It was first seen as a weapon for export to the USA's Asian allies and was tested in combat by the South Vietnamese Army in the early 1960s. There were glowing reports of its performance, and its light weight and small size were also much appreciated by the Vietnamese.

The M14 proved unsatisfactory for several reasons

The M16A1.

and its production was stopped in 1963. A small batch of AR-15 rifles was purchased (and designated M16) to tide the US Army over until the SPIW was perfected. As the flechette weapons never were perfected, more M16s were bought and it gradually took over as the Army's standard rifle. Much controversy arose as a result of the American experience in Vietnam, particularly over the effectiveness of the rifle in stopping a determined enemy, and it was clear that the long-range performance of the original light bullet (designated M193) was poor.

In the next competition for a new NATO rifle cartridge held in the late 1970s, the 5.56 × 45 was duly adopted, but in the new Belgian SS109 loading (M855 being the American version), which has a heavier bullet at a lower muzzle velocity and thereby achieves a better long-range performance. The M16 rifle in updated form, together with the more compact M4 carbine version, remains the USA's standard military rifles, despite earlier competition from the ArmaLite AR-18 and the Stoner modular weapon system.

Rather surprisingly, considering that they already had a satisfactory assault rifle cartridge, the Russians followed suit in the 1970s and adopted a new 5.45 × 39 7N6 cartridge for their next-generation rifle, the AK 74. This is no more powerful than the 5.56 NATO, although it does have a long bullet with a particularly good aerodynamic shape, and it is understood that, in some quarters, the older AK 47 7.62mm round is still preferred.

The Russians have also gone to the other extreme in adopting a 9 × 39 cartridge – essentially the 7.62 × 39 necked-out to take a larger bullet – albeit for the special purpose of being used in silenced weapons. It is loaded to a muzzle velocity just below the speed of sound and has the advantage that the large, heavy bullet retains

considerable hitting power even at this low velocity, by comparison with subsonic pistol rounds.

More recently, the Chinese have begun to introduce a 5.8 × 42 calibre for their new Type 95 assault rifles and LMGs. The ballistics seem little different from those of the 5.56mm and the 5.45mm weapon, although it is claimed that it outperforms both of them, with a penetration superior to that of the SS109, a flatter trajectory and a higher retained velocity and energy downrange. Any advantages are likely to be marginal, however.

The 5.56 × 28 FN cartridge has achieved some sales in both the FiveSeven pistol and the P90 SMG. However, as with other small PDWs (Personal Defence Weapons) such as the Heckler & Koch MP7 in 4.6 × 30, the cartridge is really only a 9mm pistol round replacement, so such weapons do not qualify as assault rifles and will not be considered further.

Despite the domination of the 5.56mm NATO round in much of the world and that of the Kalashnikov family in most of the rest, experiments with new assault rifle and ammunition concepts have, of course, continued, even with the occasional competition being held. Some of the experiments have been with conventional ammunition; others have been more exotic. These will be described later in the book.

The latest designs of assault rifles are relatively conventional, with the main point of controversy being whether they should have a traditional or a shortened 'bullpup' layout. The current market leader in international sales is probably the Heckler & Koch G36, despite, or in some cases perhaps because of, its traditional layout; the US Army favours a derivative of this, the XM8, for future adoption and will be testing it thoroughly during 2004. Other modern weapons with the traditional layout include the Swedish AK5 and the

F2000 rifle. (courtesy: FN Herstal)

Russian AN-94, although the latter is unusual in that the mechanism offers an extremely fast burst-fire mode which maximizes the chance of keeping the rounds on target.

Recent bullpup designs include the Israeli Tavor (recently adopted by Israel, and also by India to complement its own 'traditional' INSAS rifle), the Chinese Type 95, the Singaporean SAR-21 (adopted by Singapore), the new South Korean DAR-21 and the Belgian FN F2000. All of these weapons are chambered for the 5.56 × 45 NATO cartridge, except for the AN-94 (5.45 × 39) and the Type 95 (5.8 × 42).

These small-calibre cartridges bring great benefits in reducing recoil and also the weight of the ammunition to be carried. However, their effectiveness in stopping determined adversaries remains controversial and has led to a search for more effective loadings and even new more powerful cartridges, particularly in the USA. At the time of writing, the new 6.8 × 43 Remington SPC was receiving much publicity; time will tell whether it will provide sufficient advantages to enter service.

Other experiments are focusing on a different approach to small arms, featuring self-loading grenade launchers firing airburst shells. The US Army has been developing the OICW (Objective Infantry Combat Weapon), also known as the SABR (Selectable Assault Battle Rifle) and the XM29. This combines a short-barrelled 5.56mm with a self-loading, low-velocity,

shell-firing gun (initially in 20mm calibre). The heart of the weapon is a laser rangefinder coupled to a fire-control computer linked to optronic sights and an electronic fuse-setter. This complex and extremely expensive fire-control system means that the gunner can fire an HE shell to explode directly over the target at anything up to 1,000m (1,100yd) range. At the time of writing, weight problems have led to this being shelved in favour of the separate development of the 5.56mm XM8 and the XM25 (with calibre increased to 25mm), which may be combined later if the weight can be reduced from the XM29's 8.2kg to the target of 6.8 (18 to 15lb).

The French are experimenting with a similar (and even bulkier) system, the PAPOP, which has a 35mm grenade element, while another proposal is based on the Australian 'Metal Storm' technology, in which the grenade shells are stacked within the barrel. Such systems are undoubtedly impressive, but whether the complex electronics will still work when they are several years old, especially after having being kicked around a combat zone in all weathers for a few weeks, remains to be seen.

In the long run, it seems likely that current cartridge technology will be replaced by something quite different, although it is not immediately apparent what this might be. Flechette rounds have been tried and rejected, at least for now. Caseless ammunition has also been tried and rejected, at least for now. We may see some-

Above *The XM29 OICW*

Right *20mm and 5.56mm cartridges for the OICW.*

Protoype of the French PAPOP.

thing more radical – perhaps a large-calibre weapon following on from the current grenade projects and capable of firing a cluster of flechettes, an HE shell or a variety of other lethal or non-lethal natures. Looking even further ahead, perhaps someone will crack the energy supply problem and deliver an electromagnetic weapon capable of extremely high velocities at an acceptable size and weight. For the present, however, it seems that the conventional assault rifle and its 'intermediate' ammunition will be around for a long time to come.

Chapter Two

TECHNICAL BACKGROUND: THE WEAPONS

CONFIGURATION

An assault rifle consists of the following principal elements: barrel, action, pistol grip, buttstock, trigger group, receiver, magazine and sights. It may also be fitted with accessories such as a sling, a bayonet or a grenade launcher. There are two major variations in the layout of an assault rifle – traditional and bullpup – as shown in the illustrations below.

The 'traditional' system (so-called because it emerged first) has the magazine and action ahead of the trigger and the pistol grip. This is really a hangover from the days of bolt-action rifles, in which the bolt handle needed to be close to the trigger for rapid operation; this inevitably meant that the magazine and action were in front. This became the accepted layout for a rifle, although it should perhaps be noted that the

bullpup layout was first tried in bolt-action rifles, for instance, the Thorneycroft carbine of 1901. The origin of the bullpup layout as applied to automatic weapons is somewhat uncertain. There were various experimental designs, such as a bullpup pistol patented by the Frenchman Henri Delacre in 1936, and the concept was being considered for automatic rifles during the Second World War. The derivation of the term 'bullpup' is also obscure, but it may relate to the stubby, short-nosed, bulldog puppy.

In bullpup rifles the action and the magazine are located behind the trigger, within the buttstock, thereby producing a much shorter weapon for the same barrel length as in the traditional type. There are certain disadvantages to bullpups. In most cases, fired cartridge cases can be ejected only to the right-hand

An M16 (top) with an L85A2. The barrels are of similar length, but the bullpup L85 has the action and magazine behind the pistol grip, significantly shortening the total length. (courtesy MoD Pattern Room)

side of the gun, which means that they cannot be fired left-handed since the cases would hit the firer's face (most can be adapted for left-handers, but that takes time). This means that users cannot switch shoulders to fire round the corner of a building, for instance. Magazine changes may also be more awkward. The necessarily straight-line stock means that the firer cannot sight along the top of the barrel, so if iron sights are used they have to protrude high above the barrel and the firer therefore has to expose more of his head 'above the parapet'. Proponents of bayonet fighting will also point to the shorter length of the weapon, which means that it is necessary to get closer to the enemy. Bullpups have the action by the firer's head, which some find uncomfortable, and short-barrelled versions have the muzzle quite close to the firer, which means that muzzle blast can be more of a problem.

There are, of course, counter arguments. The lack of the ability to switch shoulders may be more theoretical than real, since this may, in practice, be little used by ordinary soldiers as opposed to special forces. Most soldiers in combat have enough trouble hitting the target when firing from their usual shoulder let alone from their 'wrong' side, so many armies train in shooting from only one shoulder. The magazine change is not necessarily more difficult, and some users prefer the 'inboard' location as it makes it easier to change magazines when travelling in an open vehicle, for example. Military rifles are also increasingly being issued with optical sights, so the iron sights objection is now less important. In any case, military rifles of traditional layout also have high-mounted sights now because they generally have straight-line stocks, in which the top of the buttstock continues in a straight line from the barrel, instead of being angled downwards as it is in most older rifles. This is because the recoil thrust in a straight-line stock goes into the shoulder direct, whereas in an angled stock it goes over the shoulder and hence tends to rotate the gun upwards. Bayonets are now too irrelevant to modern combat situations for their length to matter.

Most significantly, bullpup proponents will point out that the increasing deployment of troops in cramped helicopters or armoured vehicles, together with the needs of urban combat, put a premium on compactness. Traditional rifles can match a bullpup's short length only by using stocks which can be folded alongside the barrel, or sometimes over the top of it, giving the choice between a long weapon or a short one which cannot be fired accurately. The only other option is to reduce significantly the length of the barrel, to the detriment of ballistics and effectiveness, especially at longer ranges. These folding stocks are commonly of the 'skeleton' type (that is, they consist of an open framework) and may be made of metal or plastic. They are usually less rigid and comfortable to shoot with than fixed stocks. Not all rifles are able to use folding stocks anyway because the action may extend into the stock (as in the M16). In such cases telescoping stocks may be used instead, but these do not deliver such a reduction in length as a folding stock and cannot match the compactness of a bullpup. Finally, firers used to the traditional layout often criticize the different, more rearward, weight balance of a bullpup, but that is, of course, a matter of what one is used to.

What is certain is that the debate between proponents of the traditional and the bullpup layout can become heated and rely more upon emotion than logic. It is also worth noting that the use of bullpup rifles has been gradually spreading, with the majority of recent assault rifle designs being of this type, and that the latest of them – the Belgian FN F2000 – overcomes the principal objection by being genuinely 'ambidextrous' without any modifications or adjustments being required.

The materials from which assault rifles are made have changed over the decades. Most obviously, the 'furniture' (buttstock and hand grips or guards) used to be wood but this has now almost entirely been replaced by plastics. More subtly, there was a contest between machining or milling many of the metal parts from solid steel (solid, but heavy and expensive to make) or stamping them from metal sheet (cheap and light, but can be flimsy). In modern designs, newer technologies for forming the metal parts are employed to achieve solidity with lower costs, and the use of plastics is being extended to include parts previously made from metal, such as magazines.

Most assault rifles were commonly designed specifically for their purpose, but it is now normal for them to have a 'modular' design, which enables a range of weapons to be assembled from common components. The originator of this concept was probably the American designer Eugene Stoner, who developed the Stoner 62 and 63 systems during the early 1960s. Weapons ranging from a sub-machine gun to a belt-fed GPMG were all based on common components. This was found to be perhaps going too far, resulting in some versions being unnecessarily heavy or complex, but it is now standard for new weapons to be available with different barrel lengths and stocks, in some cases including a heavy barrel with bipod version for the LMG role. The Steyr AUG, Heckler & Koch G36 and the derived XM8 all offer this.

ONE WEAPON — FOUR VARIANTS

The XM8 is designed as a modular weapon that fires 5.56 x 45mm NATO ammunition. Different barrels and other modules can be swapped quickly depending on operational requirements. The XM8 will be lighter and more reliable than the existing M4 carbine and M16 rifles. If approved, the Army could field 900,000.

XM8 BASELINE CARBINE
• 12.5" barrel
• common modular assemblies

• side loading 40mm grenade launcher

XM8 Carbine with add-on XM320 grenade launcher

COMPACT CARBINE
• short 9" barrel
• butt cap receiver cover
• personal defense applications

SHARPSHOOTER VARIANT
• 20" barrel
• advanced optical sight (all variants)

AUTOMATIC RIFLE
• heavy 20" barrel for sustained fire
• integral folding bipod
• 100-round drum magazine

handguard with integral bipod

handguard

compact carbine handguard

multi-function red dot sight

removable carry handle

carbine barrel

common XM8 receiver

100-round drum magazine

30-round box magazine

automatic rifle barrel and gas system

adjustable buttstock positions

compact carbine barrel and gas system

butt cap

quick detachable X320 40mm grenade launcher

The variants of the XM8 family. (Heckler & Koch, USA)

Modern weapons also facilitate the fitting of accessories and commonly feature the American 'Picatinny Rail', a mounting fitted to the top of the weapon which allows a range of different sights to be installed and exchanged at short notice. The latest designs go further, with the FN F2000, for example, not only having the facility to fit various types of sight above the barrel, but other accessories (notably a grenade launcher) below.

The development of hybrid rifle/self-loading grenade launcher, such as the XM29 and the PAPOP, produces major problems in assembling the components, including the complex sighting system, into a compact and usable package. The XM29 uses the bullpup configuration for the grenade launcher, then fits a short-barrelled rifle in front of the pistol grip. The Australian Metal Storm system, which is well suited to short, fat projectiles and has the benefit of not requiring an autoloading mechanism, appears to be an attractive option in providing the grenade element in hybrid weapons.

ACTION TYPES

The most important aspect of the design of any automatic weapon is the firing cycle: the means whereby the mechanism loads a cartridge into the chamber,

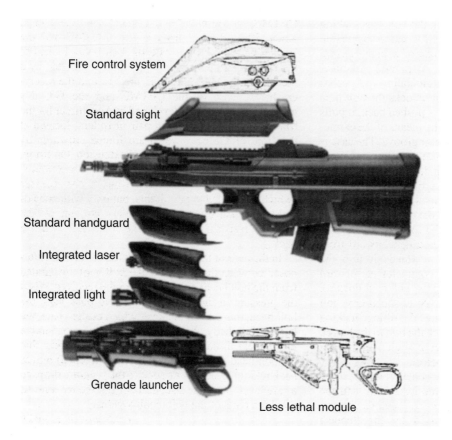

Fire control system

Standard sight

Standard handguard

Integrated laser

Integrated light

Grenade launcher

Less lethal module

The FN F2000 modular system showing the interchangeable sights above, with hand guard, torch or laser pointer below.

fires it, extracts the fired case from the chamber, ejects the fired case away from the gun and then reloads the next round. This is the most complex aspect of weapon design and the most likely source of unreliability. The most common type of mechanism used in assault rifles today is gas-operated, although some use retarded blow-back. Others, such as short recoil, have been tried, but have not survived in this application.

The gas-operated mechanism taps a small quantity of gun gas (from the burning propellant) from the barrel after the bullet has passed and uses this to drive the firing cycle. Commonly, the gas transfers from the barrel via a small hole into a cylinder lying above or below the barrel. The gas pressure pushes a piston within the cylinder and this piston drives the mechanism via an operating rod. There is a distinction between long-stroke pistons (in which the piston is attached to the rest of the mechanism and travels the full length of the recoil stroke) and short-stroke actions (in which the piston travels only a short distance, giving a 'kick' to send the rest of the mechanism on its

way). In some designs (most notably the M16) there is no piston; the gas travels down the cylinder to act on the mechanism direct. This results in a simpler and lighter action, but with a greater risk of the mechanism fouling due to a build-up of deposits of propellant residue.

In a gas-operated gun the bolt or breechblock is mechanically locked to the barrel at the instant of firing in order to prevent the chamber pressure from forcing it open. Once the bullet has left the barrel and the pressure has dropped to an acceptable level, the bolt is unlocked and driven back by the operating rod (or gas pressure in the case of the M16) against the pressure of a return spring. The methods by which the bolt is locked to the barrel vary. A common type is a rotary bolt, like that of a bolt-action rifle. The bolt, which is contained within a bolt carrier, has a series of lugs projecting to each side at the front. To lock the mechanism, the bolt carrier is pushed forward until the breech is closed and the bolt is fully forwards, at which point the final forward movement of the bolt carrier rotates the bolt (usually by means of a stud on the bolt running in a spiral groove in the carrier), the bolt lugs locking into place in radial slots within the barrel extension. When the gun is fired (by means of a long, spring-driven striker or firing pin, or a pivoting hammer hitting a shorter firing pin), the operating rod pushes back the bolt carrier, which first unlocks the bolt then carries it to the rear. As the bolt is pushed back, it pulls the fired case from the chamber by means of the extractor hooked into the case's extractor groove. The case is then knocked out of the ejection port by an ejector (usually a fixed stud of some kind, which the case hits on its way back). As the bolt carrier reaches the bolt stop at the end of its rearward travel, it cocks the firing pin or hammer ready for the next shot. The return spring then pushes the bolt carrier forward. As the bolt goes forward, it slides a fresh cartridge forward from the magazine and 'chambers' it (feeds it into the chamber); the bolt carrier then completes its forward movement, rotating and locking the bolt as it does so.

The most common alternatives to the rotary bolt locking system involve sliding or tilting locking pieces, which, when in place, lock the bolt to the barrel. The bolt carrier pushes these out of alignment, freeing the bolt to travel rearwards as before.

The retarded blow-back type of action was used by some early weapons, such as the Ribeyrolle and the Danish Weibel rifle described in the previous chapter. More recently, it has been used by the Spanish CETME, the German G3 (and most other Heckler & Koch rifles) derived from it, the SIG 510 and the French FAMAS. In this case the bolt is not locked to the barrel, but its rearward movement is resisted by a mechanism connected to both the bolt and the receiver. In the case of the CETME and the G3, this mechanism (originally developed by Vorgrimler for the Mauser StG.45) consists of pair of rollers, located at the front of the bolt, which are forced outwards by springs into recesses in the barrel extension. On firing, the chamber pressure pushes the bolt backwards, forcing these rollers inward and out of the recesses (which are angled to permit this, but only with considerable resistance); once the rollers are out of the recesses, resistance drops and the bolt is free to move back.

In the case of the FAMAS, a two-arm lever is interposed between the bolt head, the bolt body (separated from the bolt head) and an insert in the receiver. When the pressure in the chamber begins to push back the bolt head, this acts on the lever which pushed back the heavier bolt body at a faster rate (due to considerable mechanical disadvantage), this process ensuring that the bolt head (with the cartridge case attached) moves back relatively slowly. As soon as the pressure drops to a safe level, the lever disconnects from the receiver so that both parts of the bolt recoil together.

continued on page 28

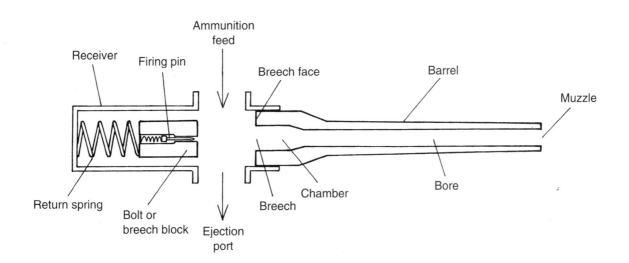

Basic elements of a gun action.

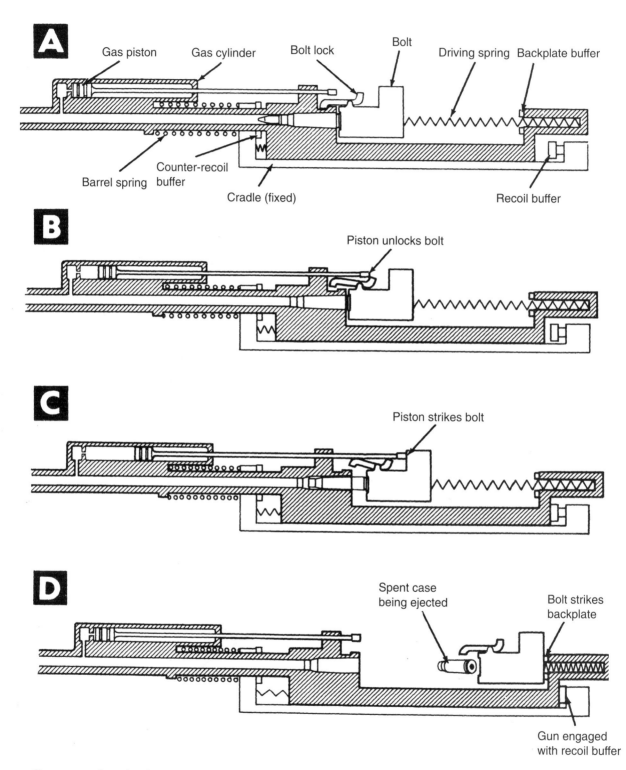

Gas-operated mechanism. (BuOrd, USN)

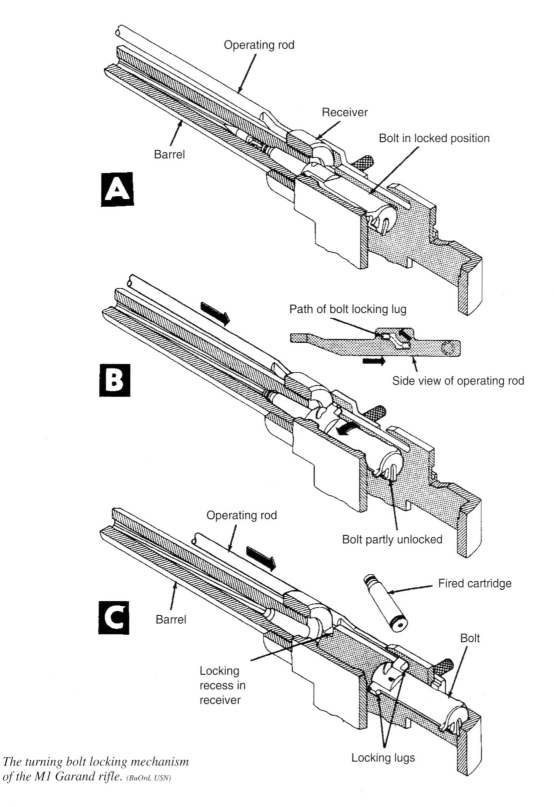

Operating rod

Receiver

Bolt in locked position

Barrel

A

Path of bolt locking lug

Side view of operating rod

B

Bolt partly unlocked

Operating rod

Fired cartridge

C

Barrel

Bolt

Locking
recess in
receiver

Locking lugs

*The turning bolt locking mechanism
of the M1 Garand rifle.* (BuOrd, USN)

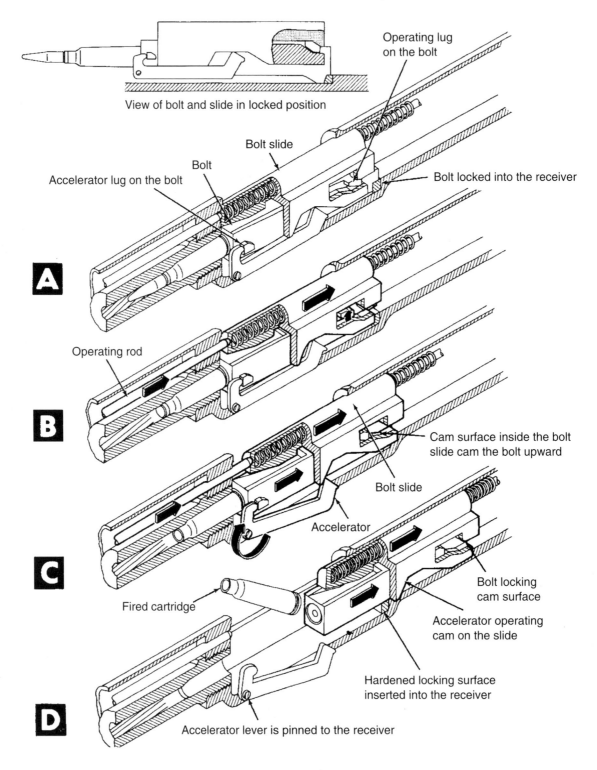

View of bolt and slide in locked position

Operating lug
on the bolt

Bolt slide

Bolt

Accelerator lug on the bolt

Bolt locked into the receiver

A

Operating rod

Cam surface inside the bolt
slide cam the bolt upward

Bolt slide

B

Accelerator

C

Fired cartridge

Bolt locking
cam surface

Accelerator operating
cam on the slide

Hardened locking surface
inserted into the receiver

D

Accelerator lever is pinned to the receiver

A propped breech locking system, patented by D. Saive (the FN designer) in 1950. (BuOrd, USN)

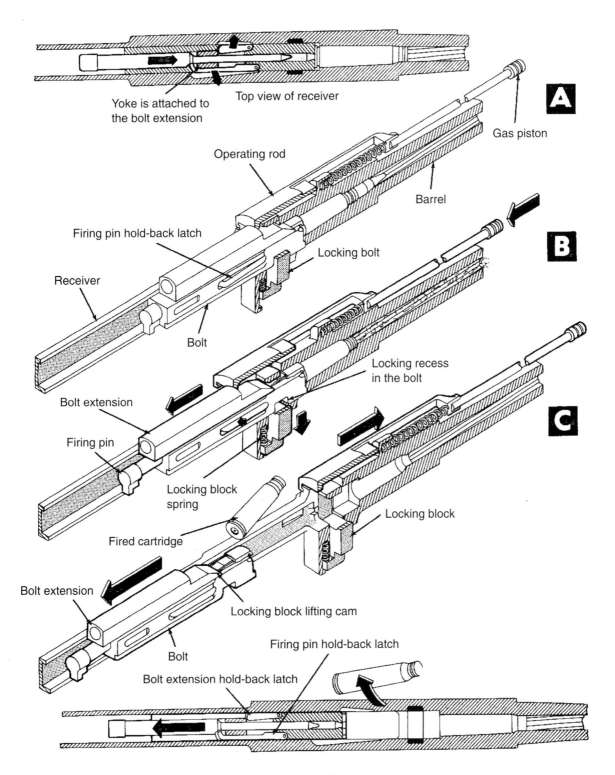

A locking block mechanism, from the Simonov automatic rifle. (BuOrd, USN)

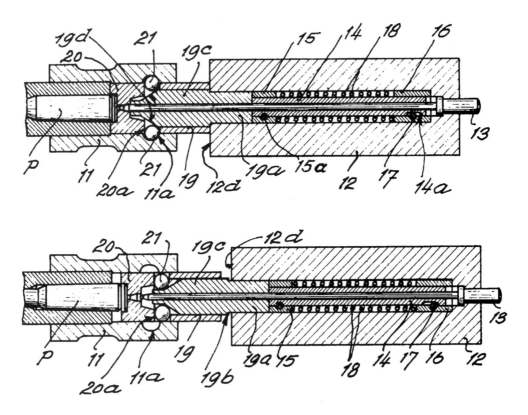

StG.45 action, showing the construction of the two-part breechblock and retarding rollers. (from a post-war patent granted in the FRG to Ludwig Vorgrimler)

Regardless of the type of retarded blow-back mechanism, the significant point is that the entire firing cycle is driven only by the pressure on the base of the cartridge case, which pushes the bolt back. This means that there is no 'primary extraction'; the fired case is not pulled from the chamber. This entails the risk that friction between the case and the chamber wall, caused by the chamber pressure, may overcome the rearwards pressure on the case, preventing it from extracting or (much worse) pulling the case apart, leaving the case body stuck in the chamber – not a quick job to correct. For this reason, blow-back-type actions have frequently used waxed or oiled cartridge cases to provide some lubrication. Nowadays the preferred solution is to use a 'fluted chamber' – a series of longitudinal grooves in the chamber wall which allow some gun gas to filter back past the case, 'floating' it free of the chamber. There is another issue, which is recoil management; users of the roller-locked 7.62mm G3 have noted a significantly harder recoil than with equivalent gas-operated weapons, probably because gas operation

bleeds off some of the gas which would otherwise add to the recoil impulse. This is less of an issue with 5.56mm guns since they have a very light recoil.

Gas operation is more complex, but it does present another benefit apart from positive primary extraction and lighter recoil. The quantity of gas allowed through to the cylinder can often be adjusted by a simple valve to meet different circumstances (although this is uncommon in 5.56mm weapons). Not all ammunition has the same pressure characteristics. Furthermore, in very cold weather propellants generate less pressure and so more gas can be allowed through to drive the mechanism. The same solution can be used if a gun starts to become clogged up but there is no time in which to clean it. The valve also usually has a fully closed position, so that the mechanism does not operate when rifle grenades are fired. The fact that Heckler & Koch, who utilized the retarded blow-back principle for many years, have switched to a gas-operated system for their latest model, the G36, indicates where the balance of advantages lies.

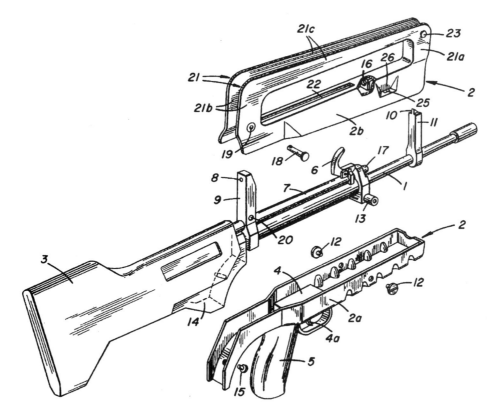

The French FAMAS.

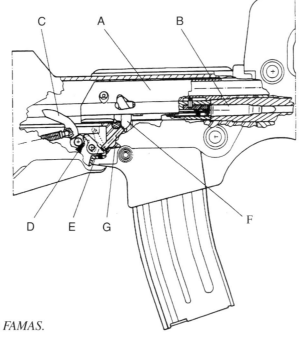

A – bolt carrier
B – cartridge in the chamber
C – hammer (cocked)
D – sear
E – auto-sear
F – retarding lever
G – auto-sear pusher

Diagram of the action of a FAMAS.

For the sake of completeness, it is worth mentioning some other action types no longer used. the most significant of these is the short-recoil, which featured in the first assault rifle (the Russian Federov Avtomat) and the American Johnson, which saw some use in World War II. In this case, the bolt is locked to the barrel, as in the case of gas operation, and by an equal variety of mechanisms. However, the barrel is free to recoil a short distance in the receiver. On firing, the bolt group and barrel recoil together for a few millimetres until the bullet has left the muzzle, at which point the bolt is unlocked from the barrel (which is then stopped) and continues its rearwards path through its momentum, usually aided by a mechanical accelerator (a lever acting on the bolt which is pushed by the barrel as it reaches its limit of rearwards movement). The problem with this system, which is still employed effectively in some MGs and automatic cannon, is that a rapidly moving barrel is an unwelcome complication in a hand-held weapon, and is also not conducive to accuracy. Rather surprisingly, this method of operation is being revived in the experimental Brazilian FA-1 (rifle) and CA-1 (carbine) bullpup 5.56mm rifles, apparently in the search for low production costs. The long-recoil mechanism, which differs from the short-recoil in that the barrel recoils all the way back with the barrel group before it is unlocked, is even less suitable for an assault rifle, although very good at absorbing the recoil impulses of a heavy cannon.

Other actions which are still used in other applications include the delayed blow-back, in which the bolt is locked to the barrel until unlocked by gas or recoil, at which point blow-back takes over (principally of use in achieving a very high rate of fire, and often used in automatic cannon). There is also the advanced primer ignition (API) blow-back, which has no locking or delay mechanism but achieves the necessary delay in breech opening by firing each cartridge as the bolt is still travelling forward at maximum speed, so the recoil has to stop this movement before it can drive it back again (wonderfully simple but not high-performance and requires firing from an open bolt). This system is still the most common one used in SMGs.

Then there is 'floating firing', otherwise known as the soft or differential recoil action, which is really a way of mounting the action rather than an operating mechanism. This is similar to the long-recoil action, except that the barrel group is held back at the maximum recoil position before firing. On firing, the barrel group moves forward and the cartridge is fired just before it reaches the fully-forward position, so the recoil must first overcome its momentum before

pushing it back again. This is excellent for smoothing out the recoil impulses of automatic cannon and HMGs, but has obvious disadvantages in an assault rifle. Despite this, at least one experimental attempt was made to use the system in the .27 Broadway Trust Company rifle being unsuccessfully developed in 1944–45.

Finally, there are the externally powered mechanisms such as the chain guns or modern rotary Gatlings, which are very reliable but are driven by an electric motor and therefore require a power supply to make them work. Despite the heroics of over-muscled, Hollywood film stars, this does not make them a sensible choice for an assault rifle – somehow the trailer carrying the necessarily large battery pack or generator (not to mention the huge quantity of ammunition required) never seems to appear in the films.

One of the most important issues in a military rifle is reliability, and it has proved surprisingly difficult to achieve this. The conditions experienced in training – shooting on a firing range with plenty of time to clean weapons – do not necessarily exist in combat, and recent experience of action in desert conditions (especially in the type which produces very fine dust) has shown how quickly a rifle can become inoperative unless it is properly looked after. Some possible causes of unreliability – faulty ammunition or damaged magazines – are not the rifle's fault, but others are.

The characteristics of a weapon which best ensure its reliability are: a powerful operating mechanism, which can still drive the action even when it is hindered by dirt; a heavy reciprocating bolt group, which again helps to overcome friction; loose tolerances between the internal moving parts to stop them from becoming jammed with dirt; a design which prevents the entry of dirt into the mechanism as much as possible and facilitates its removal if it does get in, and finally a rugged construction which will tolerate much abuse without damage. These characteristics are possessed to a high degree by the Kalashnikov AK 47 and the weapons derived from it and account for its legendary reputation for keeping on firing almost regardless of neglect and abuse. The penalty is greater weight and less accuracy than most Western 5.56mm rifles.

RATES OF FIRE AND THEIR CONSEQUENCES

In fully automatic fire, the gun will fire its next shot the instant the bolt is locked or in place again. In semi-automatic fire, the firing pin or hammer is not released until the trigger is released and pressed again. Burst-fire controls include a mechanical counting mechanism which interrupts the automatic cycle after a set number of rounds (usually three) has been fired. The reason for this is that, even with a low-recoil RCAR weapon, only the first two or three shots are likely to be on target, with the remainder going astray and so burst fire prevents wasted ammunition. The counter argument is that this can be a disadvantage if a soldier is suddenly surprised by the enemy at short range, and troops can (and should) be trained to fire in short bursts anyway.

There is another reason for firing in short bursts only, and that is to avoid the barrel's overheating. The barrels of assault rifles are quite thin and rapidly overheat in automatic fire owing to the pressures and temperatures generated by the burning propellant. This brings with it the risk of excessive barrel wear, and more dramatically that of 'cook-offs', in which the propellant in the cartridge in the chamber is heated up to the point of detonation.

In machine guns this is commonly avoided by ensuring that the gun fires from an 'open bolt', which means that each burst of fire stops with the bolt held back and the chamber empty. This is also a necessary part of the operation of most SMGs, except for the few which do not use the API blow-back system. The problem with this is that there is a long 'lock time' – pressing the trigger does not immediately fire the gun because the bolt first has to travel forward and chamber the cartridge. This leads to inaccurate shooting and is therefore not used in assault rifles. There may also be a problem in leaving the chamber open in that unwanted objects might fall inside. It is worth noting that some automatic weapons, such as the German FG 42 rifle, have fired from a closed bolt in semi-automatic mode but switched to open-bolt firing in fully automatic, thereby enjoying the best of both worlds.

A common way of minimizing the problem of overheating and the resulting excessive wear is to treat the chambers and bores by chrome plating them or lining them with a heat-resistant material such as Stellite. The rate at which barrels heat up also obviously depends on the rate of fire (RoF) – the time it takes to complete the firing cycle. The optimum RoF is generally agreed to be between 500 and 750 rounds per minute (rpm); this is obviously the theoretical or 'cyclic' rate, which might more realistically be expressed as from eight to twelve rounds per second. A higher speed than this, not only heats up the barrel even more quickly, it also wastes more ammunition and increases the total recoil, making it more likely that shots will fly off target. This can be a problem in some of the light, small-calibre weapons; the M16 RoF has been measured at 1,100 rpm, significantly higher than the figure usually stated. However, a high RoF does have the benefit of putting several rounds into the target area before the target can take cover, improving the chance of scoring a hit.

At least two designs (the German HKG 11 and the Russian AN-94) have attempted a different approach, with a very fast (about 2,000 rpm) burst-fire capability, coupled with a barrel group free to recoil in the stock. This is so arranged that the initial recoil impulse is taken up by the movement of the barrel group. Only after the last shot of the burst has left the barrel does the barrel hit the stop, transmitting the combined recoil force to the firer's shoulder. This means that all of the shots in the burst will be clustered together. This not only improves the hit probability at long range, it also improves effectiveness at short range, an important factor in the light of the continuing controversy over the effectiveness of the little RCAR bullets.

Another means of minimising the effect of recoil is to fit a recoil reducer or muzzle brake. This is a device fitted to the muzzle which traps some of the gun gas and deflects it to the side or rear. In a typical high-velocity rifle cartridge, the rapid expansion of the gun gas leaving the muzzle behind the bullet generates between 30 and 40 per cent of the total recoil, and so diverting some of this can have a worthwhile effect. A variation on the muzzle brake is the 'compensator', which directs all the diverted gas upwards to counteract the tendency of the muzzle to rise under recoil. Muzzle brakes and compensators are sometimes combined with a flash suppressor, usually consisting of several forward-facing prongs (which does exactly what the name suggests), which may also act as the launcher for firing rifle grenades. There is a penalty to the use of muzzle brakes, however – they divert high-velocity gas back towards the firer, making him unpleasantly aware of the muzzle blast. The more efficient the muzzle brake in diverting gas, the worse the effect on the firer, potentially to the detriment of his shooting accuracy.

Another popular muzzle attachment is a suppressor (as opposed to a flash suppressor), which is a cylinder surrounding the barrel into which the gun gas is allowed to escape before the bullet leaves the muzzle. This reduces the firing signature – the muzzle blast and flash – and therefore makes the gun more comfortable to shoot, as well as making it more difficult for the enemy to locate. A larger and more effective version of the suppressor is the silencer, which is used with subsonic ammunition so the 'crack' of a supersonic bullet does not alert the enemy.

MAGAZINES

A key element of the modern military rifle – and a common source of problems – is the magazine. This performs the dual function of holding the ready-use ammunition on the gun and presenting each cartridge at the correct angle to be picked up by the bolt and loaded into the chamber. The cartridges are pushed into the magazine against the pressure of a spring, which holds them firmly against the retaining magazine lips, parts of the sides of the magazine which are folded over the open end. This means that cartridges have to be slid lengthwise in and out of the magazine. The precise position of the lips is vital in presenting each cartridge at the correct angle, yet they are commonly made of thin metal and easily damaged (by being used to remove the top from a bottle, for example, for which task they are unfortunately well-shaped).

The vast majority of magazines are of the 'box' type, in which the rounds are stacked in a double column. As all current assault rifles have the magazines hanging below the gun, their capacity is limited by the practicable maximum length: too long, and the soldier will be unable to fire the gun when lying prone. In effect, this means a maximum capacity of thirty rounds for a RCAR, while magazines for those weapons using 7.62 × 51 NATO ammunition generally hold only twenty.

However, box magazines are not the only type available. Where a larger capacity is needed without excessive length, a drum magazine may be used. This is of cylindrical shape, with the cartridges coiled within it; 5.56mm versions can contain up to sixty rounds, or, if more still are needed, then a double-drum is available holding 100 rounds. This consists of two drums side-by-side, each feeding rounds in turn. This is not exactly a new idea, being basically the same as the seventy-five-round saddle drum which was standard fitting for the 7.92mm MG 17 used by the Luftwaffe in the Second World War. However, these drum magazines are bulky, and an alternative approach is to design the gun to accept two or more box magazines clipped together. Only one is feeding the gun at any one time; when this is empty, the linked magazines are slid sideways, putting the fresh magazine into the feeding position. The problem with this is that it leaves the top of the 'spare' magazine open to the elements, and anything else which might want to drop in.

NATO does have a STANAG (standardization agreement) covering 5.56mm magazines which should make them interchangeable between different weapons. However, it should not be assumed that this is always the case, although the M16 type is increasingly seen as the standard for compatibility. Not all magazines are metal; the Steyr AUG, for instance, is one which uses see-through plastic, enabling the number of rounds remaining to be easily checked. The HK G36 magazines are also made of tough plastic, and, as this feature has been retained in the US XM8 rifle derived from it, these may in due course replace the M16 type.

SIGHTS

Perhaps the greatest influence on the effective accuracy of a rifle, apart from the training of its users, are the sights, and this is one area which has seen considerable change in recent years. Originally, the preferred sights for early assault rifles consisted of the traditional two-element 'iron sights' (that is, without any glass lenses), with an open rear sight mounted some distance from the shooter's eye, and a post foresight near the muzzle. This is often known as the 'leaf type', since the rear sight consists of one or more flat pieces of metal with a notch in the top, which is lined up with the foresight; 'leaves' of different heights can be flipped into position for different ranges. This has the virtue of being simple and quick to use, and the disadvantage of being the least accurate type. A variation of this is the so-called tangent rear sight, which incorporates a single, vertical piece with notch, mounted on a vertically adjustable ramp, with the position 'range setting' being controlled by a slider with several settings. This type usually offers more range settings than a typical leaf sight.

A more accurate form of iron sights retains the same foresight but uses a rear aperture sight at the back of the action, close to the eye, which provides a small hole through which the firer looks at the foresight. Simple versions are known as peep sights, more sophisticated ones, capable of various adjustments, as diopter sights. They are more accurate than the leaf type, partly because they permit the aiming eye to be placed more accurately, partly because of the longer sight base between the front and rear sights, but they can take slightly longer to use.

In recent years, optical sights have become more common. Perhaps the first assault rifle to be designed to use one as standard was the EM-2, making a virtue out of the problem of mounting sights high above the barrel by combining the sight with a carrying handle. The first one to see service with a standard optical sight was the Steyr AUG, followed by the Enfield SA80. The EM-2's sight did not magnify – the lens system was there to ensure that the target and the aiming reticule were both in focus – while the Steyr features a 1.5 power magnification sight and the SA80's SUSAT is a 4x telescope. Clearly, the higher the magnification the more precise the long-range shooting, but the downside is a narrower field of view, making it more difficult to pick up the target, and also magnifying any unsteadiness on the part of the shooter. A high-power scope is therefore generally held to be better for careful and deliberate aiming rather than snap shooting at close range.

An alternative form of sight is the 'red dot' type. This is usually of unit (1×) magnification, with the sighting element being a bright red dot, usually battery-powered so that it may also be used at night. The idea is to aim the weapon with both eyes open, thereby maintaining the full field of view as well as seeing the aiming mark. This is very fast in use, but less accurate at long range than a telescopic sight. The HK G36 provides the option of fitting both telescopic and red dot sights, one above the other. Optical sights may be supplemented by laser pointers, which project a red dot actually on to the target (with considerable psychological effect if the target notices), and there are several types of night sight using light intensifiers or thermal imagers, but these are for special purposes. The future is predicted to lie in video sights, in which a camera on the gun transmits a sighting picture to a head-up display attached to the firer's helmet. This has the advantage of allowing the user to fire accurately from behind cover, exposing only the gun and its camera, as well as incorporating zoom telescopic power to suit the circumstances, and night-viewing capability.

ACCESSORIES

The basic elements of an assault rifle have now been described, but it may also be fitted with a range of accessories. Some (such as the FAMAS) are fitted with a folding bipod for steadier long-range shooting in the prone position, although these are more generally associated with the light support versions of these weapons. These LSWs may also be known as SAWs (squad automatic weapons) or LMGs, and are also fitted with longer and heavier barrels to permit more sustained and accurate fire.

The carrying sling is still an important element of a weapon since it can determine how easy it is to carry the gun on extended patrols. A well-designed sling can also be wrapped around the left arm (for right-handed shooters) to add extra support and steadiness when firing the rifle.

Finally, most modern assault rifles have the capacity to launch grenades against targets meriting an application of high explosive. There are two approaches to this: rifle grenades, which simply slip over an appropriately-shaped launcher fitted to the muzzle and

The adjustable peep rear sight of an M16.

are fired by pulling the rifle's trigger in the usual way, or grenade launchers which are effectively separate, short-barrelled, single-shot guns fitted under the rifle barrel and fired with a separate trigger. Projectiles for both types usually have a fuse which prevents detonation until the grenade is a safe distance from the firer. Rifle grenades have the advantages that they add no size nor weight to the rifle, and they have a large warhead offering considerable destructive effect. In World War II these needed to be fired using a special blank cartridge, which was rather inconvenient. Modern types use standard ammunition, and either trap the bullet and use its energy to project the grenade (helpfully known as the 'bullet trap' type) or have a hole down the centre through which the bullet escapes (the 'bullet through' type), and use the gun gas expanding from the muzzle as a propellant. The latter loses something in energy, but gains through not having to switch the gas operation valve to 'closed' first.

The problem with a rifle grenade is that, when ready to fire, it effectively blocks the standard operation of the rifle. That means that, if the shooter with a grenade in place has to fire his rifle in an emergency (for instance, if an enemy appears in front of him), he should first either remove or fire the grenade, which

The Austrian Steyr AUG with a rifle grenade ready to fire.

will take time and may cost him his life. The underbarrel launchers do not block the rifle, but add a significant penalty in the bulk and weight of the combined weapon. Also, typical grenades for under-barrel launchers have warheads much smaller in size and weight, limiting their effectiveness.

The most recent trend in this field is the use of time-fused grenades in conjunction with a fire-control computer, mounted on the rifle and coupled with the sights. This unit incorporates a laser rangefinder, ballistic computer and a means for programming the warhead before the shot. Before firing, the shooter determines the range to the target by using the laser rangefinder and the computer automatically corrects the sights to achieve the appropriate trajectory and preset the time fuse, so the warhead will explode when it reaches the target. This allows the engagement of targets in defilade (when they are hiding behind cover) by using air-burst fragmentation warheads. At the present time there are several projects that attempt to achieve such an effect, including the American XM29 OICW system and the French PAPOP. The Belgian F2000GL system offers a less costly alternative, with non-programmable grenades, but with an electronic sighting unit which allows much more accurate long-range fire.

CONCLUSIONS: THE IDEAL RIFLE?

From all of the above it is possible to draw up a specification for the characteristics of an 'ideal' rifle, common to all calibres and even regardless of whether the preferred type has a traditional or a bullpup layout, as follows:

1. Maximum reliability, even under the most adverse conditions. This also includes durability, tolerance of the kind of rough treatment common in warfare. Reliable functioning requires an action which is protected as far as possible from the ingress of dirt and designed to expel any dirt which does get in. There should be a surplus of power available to drive the action and positive extraction, which implies a piston-type gas operation (preferably with an adjustable valve). Cleaning equipment should be provided in a compartment somewhere on the rifle.

2. Maximum ease of use for both right- and left-handed users (few weapons score well at this). All controls should be 'ambidextrous', and all fall readily to hand and be operated in an instinctive way. It is common to combine the safety catch with the single shot/automatic fire selector, but this is arguably not ideal; a safety catch needs to be instantly and silently flipped on and off without moving the hand from the firing position and is best given just that function to do. (It could perhaps be a spring-loaded flap located within the trigger guard which has to be pushed to one side before the trigger can be pulled; it is then unnecessary to have to remember to switch it on and off.) The fire selector should be different, perhaps the ideal being the Steyr AUG's trigger control; normal pull for single shots, heavy pull for automatic fire; again, no switches to remember. The magazine release catch needs to be convenient to use by the hand grasping the magazine, but must not be easily hit by accident. The magazine should also be easy to locate in the magazine well and click into place with a simple, vertical push, without needing to be rocked from side-to-side or front-to-back.

The AUG with an M203 40mm grenade launcher.

3. Compactness for use in vehicles and in street-fighting, combined with a long enough barrel to provide the ballistics required to retain maximum effectiveness out to at least 300m (330yd). This implies either a bullpup layout or a folding/telescoping stock. In the latter case, care needs to be taken to ensure that the stock is quickly and easily extended, but is comfortable to use and remains rigid despite much use and abuse.

4. A flexible sight-mounting system, which can accept a standard telescopic sight or night sights, but also has simple iron sights for emergencies. The ability to fit a range of accessories such as grenade launchers, torches and laser pointers is also important.

5. Other issues include:
   - A magazine hold-open device, which holds the bolt back when the last shot has been fired. This would seem obvious, but an astonishing number of weapons do not have it; the German G3, HK rifles generally, SIG and the original FAMAS are among the culprits (the later FAMAS has it). Their users only discover that the magazine is empty when they pull the trigger and nothing happens.
   - A trigger pull, light and crisp enough to permit accurate firing on semi-automatic (unimportant in fully automatic fire, which should be for short-range emergencies only; in most circumstances, a trained rifleman will score more hits with rapid semi-automatic fire).
   - A charging handle (accessible to both hands, of course) which can also be used to force home a reluctant cartridge or to kick a stuck case out of the chamber.
   - A trigger guard which permits the use of mittened hands; either one which can be pushed out of the way or a full-hand guard like the Steyr AUG and the latest FAMAS.
   - A forward hand guard shielded from heat build-up.
   - A design which enables the gun to be quickly and easily field-stripped for cleaning, without the risk of losing small parts or reassembling them in the wrong order.

There is another important factor which is difficult to describe objectively, and that is the general handling of the weapon. The pistol grip and the hand guard should be well shaped to provide a good grip, and the stock should provide a comfortable cheek rest. The gun should feel well-balanced and come up to the aim naturally. The problem is that people differ in their views on this and, in particular, proponents of traditional rifles dislike bullpups, and vice versa. Finally, and bearing in mind that it is increasingly common to fit accessories of various types, thereby adding noticeably to the weight, the weight of the basic rifle should be kept as low as is compatible with durability.

Chapter Three

TECHNICAL BACKGROUND: AMMUNITION DESIGN AND BALLISTICS

INTRODUCTION

Ammunition usually receives little attention in books about weapons, yet an understanding of its characteristics and performance is essential to an appreciation of the factors which have driven, and still drive, the development of the assault rifle. A cartridge is a unit or round of ammunition consisting of a projectile, propellant which, when burned, generates gas to thrust the projectile from the gun, a primer to ignite the propellant and a cartridge case to hold it all together. The projectile – known in small arms as a bullet – is the most important element as the whole purpose of a rifle is to get a bullet to hit the target.

The study of ballistics may be divided into three: internal, external and terminal. Internal ballistics concerns what happens between the cartridge's being fired and the bullet's leaving the muzzle. External ballistics is concerned with the flight of the bullet from the muzzle to the target. Terminal ballistics describes what happens when the target is hit.

As we have seen, an important aspect of performance is recoil since this determines how controllable the rifle will be. An assault rifle cartridge, like any other aspect of weaponry, is a compromise between conflicting requirements and this chapter is concerned with explaining those which arise and the ways of addressing them. There are necessarily some formulae required to explain what is happening, but these have been kept to a minimum.

THE BULLET

The basic type of military bullet is known as 'ball' ammunition. This was named after the round lead balls which were the standard small arms projectiles until the nineteenth century. The name is still applied to standard rifle ammunition, in which the bullet consists of a jacket (originally copper, now a variety of alloys) normally enclosing a lead core. Lead is still used because it has a high density (which helps the ballistics) and is relatively cheap, although steel is sometimes used as an alternative. It is enclosed in a jacket of a harder material, primarily to prevent it from being torn apart by the rifling as it passes up the barrel, because this not only ruins the accuracy of the bullet, it also leaves an unwelcome deposit in the bore. Fully jacketed bullets also avoid any accusations of illegality since, unlike soft-point hunting rounds, they do not expand on impact to maximize the wounding effect.

Bullets in assault rifles usually have pointed noses in order to reduce air resistance and thereby reduce the rate at which they lose velocity. This means that their centre of gravity is behind their mid point, so that, left to themselves, they would naturally travel base first. To prevent this, they are spun by the barrel's rifling, which provides stability. Many bullets are also given tapered rather than flat bases (also known as 'boat-tailed' or 'streamlined' bullets) as this further reduces the aerodynamic drag, particularly at subsonic velocities.

The other type of bullet sometimes used in assault rifles is armour piercing, or AP. In these bullets much of the lead core is replaced by hard steel or in some cases by tungsten carbide which is harder and more dense for greater effectiveness, but at higher cost. They are therefore sometimes called APHC, for armour piercing hard core, to distinguish them from other AP types. In the past, AP bullets have mainly been used by full-power MGs or HMGs against vehicles, but the recent and rapid development of individual body armour protection for infantry is raising AP performance up the agenda even for assault rifles. The use of body armour by US troops in Iraq in 2003 has reportedly had a significant effect in reducing the number of casualties. Perhaps because of this trend, the NATO standard 5.56×45 'ball' round, the SS109 or M855, actually has a semi-armour piercing (SAP) bullet, with a small, hard, steel element close to the bullet tip and achieves good penetration out to long range.

Tracer bullets are also sometimes used, but more often in light MGs. These are hollow at the base to contain a chemical which burns in flight to reveal the trajectory of the bullet and indicate whether the shooting is on target. However, the bullet tends to be lighter (and gets lighter still as the chemical burns) and the gas emitted by the tracer also affects the bullet drag, so no tracer can provide exactly the same trajectory as a ball or AP round.

Rifle bullets other than the standard ball round are often identified by differently coloured tips. Several colour schemes have been used in different places and at different times, but a black tip usually indicates an AP bullet and a red tip a tracer. Other colours are much less predictable; for example, the USA used a green tip to indicate the 7.62×51 M198 Duplex ball loading, but it is now used for the M855 SAP, which is their current standard 5.56×45 round.

PROPELLANT AND PRIMER

There are three different types of smokeless propellant used in modern ammunition, known as single-base, double-base and triple-base. All are based on nitrocellulose with nitroglycerine (or an equivalent) and nitroguanidine as other major components in the more complex versions, triple-base including all three.

The increasing complexity of the propellants is due to the constant search for the ideal combination of characteristics. These include maximum power for a high muzzle velocity, moderate pressure and temperature to minimize the stresses and erosive effects on the gun, as little fouling and corrosion as possible and a minimum of smoke and flash at the muzzle. Many of these desiderata are mutually exclusive and so each propellant is a compromise. Propellants must also be insensitive to rough treatment, provide consistent performance over a wide range of climatic environments and be tolerant of storage for long periods in poor conditions.

Propellants are generally prepared in the form of grains or small pellets. The precise chemical composition and the size and shape of the grains will vary from one cartridge to another in order to provide the power

Sectioned 5.56×45 NATO AP cartridge, showing the hard core (silver coloured) and the lead tip filler.

and pressure characteristics suited to the gun. The fact that this is an important issue was famously illustrated by the problems accompanying the introduction of the American M16 rifle in Vietnam in the 1960s: the gun and ammunition were developed using a particular type of powder which was very clean burning; when the ammunition was mass-produced, the propellant was replaced by a different type which was not as clean burning. This proved disastrous because the pistonless action of the gas system was particularly susceptible to fouling, with the result that many guns jammed in action until the problem was identified and solved.

All current service ammunition for assault rifles is of the 'centrefire' type. This uses a percussion cap known as a primer, which produces a flash of flame when struck by the firing pin. It is housed centrally in a cavity known as the primer pocket, in the head or the base of the case. The flame reaches the propellant via a central hole or holes in the cavity. Once fired, the primer can be knocked out of the case, which can then be reloaded.

The performance of a given cartridge depends upon the maximum pressure which the gun is designed to accept. Pistols and shotguns, for example, are usually intended to work only at relatively low pressures, while rifles, machine guns and cannon are generally much stronger, so cartridges for them can be loaded to higher pressures, yielding higher velocities. Guns differ and some can take much higher pressures than others. This is usually determined by the strength of the mechanism which locks the bolt or the breech-block to the breech at the instant of firing. However, modern gun designs are usually so strong that the limiting factor tends to be the ability of the ammunition to sustain the pressure without the metal of the cartridge case sticking to the chamber walls and preventing extraction, or the primer being pushed back on to the firing pin with such force that it is punctured. Military rifle ammunition is typically loaded to around 3,500kg/sq cm (50,000lb/sq in, or psi).

THE CARTRIDGE CASE

The cartridge case has two major functions: first, it holds together all the active components of the cartridge – projectile, propellant and primer – in a waterproof container which is rugged enough to withstand the rough handling which tends to occur in automatic weapons; second, when the gun is fired, the cartridge case expands by the pressure against the walls of the firing chamber, forming a gas-tight seal which prevents any propellant gas from seeping back into the gun mechanism – and possibly into the firer's face. It also has a further benefit, which is to carry heat away from the chamber as the case is ejected, thereby reducing the risk of a round left in the chamber 'cooking off'; a newly-fired case is very hot.

The second function explains why brass is still the most popular material for small-arms cartridge cases, despite its weight and cost. Standard cartridge brass (70 per cent copper, 30 per cent zinc) has exactly the right characteristics in that it expands instantly to form a seal without splitting open, then contracts slightly to

facilitate extraction. Other materials have been used, however, and even more experimented with. Steel has seen some use in assault rifle cartridge cases; particularly the 7.92×33 – wartime production of which was all steel – and the 7.62×39, which may be of steel or brass. Steel is lighter and cheaper than brass, both of these being significant benefits. However, it requires more protection against corrosion and, being less resilient, forms a less perfect seal on firing. Light alloy, based on aluminium, has even more attractions as it can save between 25 and 38 per cent of the total weight of a cartridge. For a long time it proved difficult to achieve satisfactory results with this material and it has so far achieved service status only in aircraft cannon ammunition. A unique problem is the risk of 'burn through', caused by the tendency of aluminium to catch fire, with disastrous results for the gun. This has led to special precautions being taken with experimental ammunition. For example, the American 6mm SAW (squad automatic weapon) project of the early 1970s was designed around a 6×45 steel case. A light alloy version had to be made longer, at 50mm, to allow enough space for a fireproof silicon lining inside the case. A plastic material is potentially an even more interesting one since it is lighter still and very cheap. However, it does not have the strength to replace metal in conventional actions and those experimental plastic-cased rounds which have been developed have had to adopt a radically different cartridge shape. A compromise is the two-piece round with a metal base (where the stress is greatest) and a plastic body. These have been successfully developed in the USA and may well yet see military use. Apart from cost and weight, other advantages claimed are that a plastic is a natural insulator (so the chamber does not get as hot), retains its shape when mishandled instead of denting, and that any ruptured cases are much more easily removed.

The ultimate in weight saving would be to dispense with the cartridge case altogether. Rather surprisingly for such a radical concept this was perfected and, as we will see, nearly made it into service in the HK G11. It may yet return in some form.

Cartridge case design is a science in itself. There are certain basic requirements – the case must locate the projectile in precisely the correct position in the firing chamber (with the exception of advanced primer ignition [API] blowback guns, which fire as the case is moving forwards), it must be easy to extract once fired and it must function well in automatic weapons – but there are several methods of achieving these aims.

Before proceeding further, it is desirable to be clear about the nomenclature of cartridge cases. The elements are shown in the illustration. Cases usually have an identifying headstamp around the primer pocket, which may contain information about the cartridge, the manufacturer and the year of production. Rimless cases need an extractor groove and 'bottleneck' cases also have a shoulder, where the case is reduced in diameter down to the neck in cartridges in which the calibre is significantly smaller than the case diameter. Some cases have a belt – an annular projection – just above the extractor groove.

In modern small-arms cartridges the inside neck diameter is made fractionally smaller than that of the bullet, thereby ensuring that the bullet is gripped firmly until it is fired.

Accurate location in the firing chamber is essential to the ignition of the primer; the cartridge needs to enter the chamber, but not too far or the firing pin will not touch the primer. It is also important in the internal ballistics of the gun because the projectile must be in the same place, relative to the conical section leading to the rifling, to achieve consistent pressure characteristics. The distance between the face of the bolt and the part of the chamber which locates the cartridge is known as the 'headspace'.

The earliest method of achieving accurate location was by means of a rim around the head of the case. This remains outside the chamber or in a recess so that it is flush with the breech face. The rim also provides something for the extractor to hook on to in order to pull the fired case from the chamber. Rimmed cases are still used in small arms (for instance, the Russian 7.62 × 54R) but not in assault rifles, because in spring-loaded magazines the rims can foul each other if improperly loaded. Stacking rimmed ammunition in a box magazine also produces an excessive curve in the magazine.

By far the most common military case type is the rimless, in which the rim is reduced to the same diameter as that of the case so that the cartridges in magazines can be stacked on top of each other and slide forward without the risk of jamming. To give the extractor something to hook on to, an extractor groove is cut into the case just above the rim. There have been a few examples of semi-rimmed (or semi-rimless) cases in which the rim is only fractionally wider than the case and is combined with a small extractor groove, but these have not proved to be a particularly successful compromise.

Blow-back weapons do not strictly require case extractors to function since the fired case is pushed out of the chamber by gas pressure. Some early designs for such weapons accordingly used cartridges without

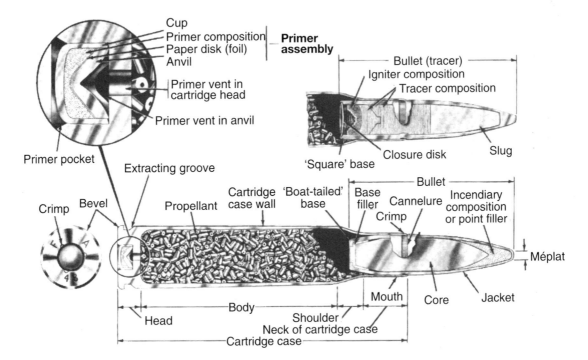

Sectioned drawings of a cartridge loaded with an AP bullet, with a tracer bullet shown separately.

rims or extractor grooves. This was soon proved to be a bad idea because the only way of unloading an unfired cartridge was to poke a stick down the barrel.

Rimless cases need a method of accurate location in the chamber and this is normally achieved by using a bottleneck case, in which the headspace is determined by the contact between the shoulder of the case and the matching part of the chamber. With straight or strongly tapered cases this becomes more difficult to achieve and so such cases often have a projecting belt just in front of the extractor groove to provide positive location. Belted cases in small-arms calibres are mainly associated with commercial hunting rifle ammunition and have not been used in assault rifles. Note the risk of confusion with the term 'belted ammunition' which may also be referring to cartridges linked by a long belt in belt-fed guns, as an alternative to box magazines. Small arms ammunition may be provided in belts for use in LMGs where more sustained fire is required, but belt feed is not used in assault rifles.

With any rimless cartridge case of a given propellant capacity there is a choice to be made between a 'short fat' case and a 'long thin' one (or something in between). Short fat cases permit a shorter action which can cycle more quickly and also result in a slightly shorter gun, but fewer of them can be fitted in a given length of box magazine.

As we have seen, military cartridge designations are usually given in metric case measurements of the calibre and case length. The 7.92mm Kurz is therefore described as the 7.92×33, since the calibre is 7.92mm and the case length is 33mm. Note that this is not the same as the total cartridge length including the bullet; in the 7.92mm Kurz this is around 47mm. Letters may be added after the numbers to denote some variation from the military standard rimless head, the most common being R for rimmed or SR for semi-rimmed, although B for belted may be encountered as well.

INTERNAL BALLISTICS

Some of the issues involved in internal ballistics have already been touched on. The relationship between the calibre and the weight of the projectile, and the weight, form and chemical composition of the propellant, together with the barrel length, will determine the pressure exerted on the chamber and gun barrel by the expanding propellant gas, the rate of acceleration of the projectile up the barrel and the velocity achieved at the muzzle.

As soon as the primer ignites the propellant, gas is

generated which rapidly builds up a considerable pressure. This pushes the projectile out of the case and up the barrel. The characteristics of propellant powders are such that the peak gas pressures are generated almost immediately, as the projectile begins its trip up the barrel (more precisely, when it is slowed by hitting the rifling). That is why the barrel steel is thickest at this point. As the projectile accelerates up the barrel, it makes space for the gas to expand and so the pressure falls. It is still significant when the projectile leaves the muzzle, resulting in a rapid expansion into the open air causing the characteristic 'bang' of a gun firing. This final expansion, coupled with the end of the friction between the projectile and the barrel, results in a final boost to the projectile so that its maximum velocity is attained just beyond the muzzle, although 'muzzle velocity' is usually measured at several metres past the muzzle.

The muzzle velocity achieved by any given cartridge will clearly depend on the projectile weight, and this may vary considerably. It is therefore usual for the power of cartridges to be described in terms of their muzzle energy, to enable comparisons between cartridges to be made. Muzzle energy may be measured in joules (metric) or foot-pounds (ft lb). This is calculated as follows (note that, although the correct term is 'mass', 'weight' has been used instead for easier comprehension; mass is a constant regardless of gravitational pull, whereas weight depends on gravity, however, on the earth's surface the two are effectively the same):

joules: multiply the projectile weight in grams (g) by the square of the muzzle velocity in metres per second (m/s), then divide the result by 2,000; so a 40g projectile fired at 800m/s will generate: $(40 \times 800 \times 800)/2,000 = 12,800J$

foot-pounds: multiply the projectile weight in pounds by the square of the muzzle velocity in feet per second (ft/s), then divide the result by 64; note that there are 7,000 grains (gr.) in a pound, so for bullet calculations you can enter the weight in grains then divide the resulting calculation by 7,000

to convert *foot-pounds* to *joules*, multiply by 1.348

to convert *joules* to *foot-pounds*, multiply by 0.742

15.432gr. = 1g; 2.205lb = 1kg and 3.281ft = 1m

Note that in developing muzzle energy, muzzle velocity is much more important than projectile weight. Doubling the muzzle velocity of a projectile quadruples its energy, whereas doubling the weight only doubles its energy.

The muzzle energy which is generated by a given amount of propellant will depend on the calibre of the gun. Think of the barrel as the cylinder of an engine and the bullet as a piston. In a small-calibre weapon, the gas has a very small piston area – the base of the bullet – on which to work. Since the pressure it can generate per square millimetre of 'piston area' is limited, it can apply only a certain amount of force to the bullet. In a larger calibre weapon, the piston area is greater so the same amount of propellant can do more work. This explains why, in the case of a rifle cartridge made in several different calibres (for instance, the .30-06, also made in .25, .27 and .35 calibres), there is usually a direct relationship between the calibre and the muzzle energy generated: the bigger the calibre, the higher the muzzle energy.

For a given calibre, there is a practical limit to the amount of propellant which can be used. The law of diminishing returns applies, and to use bigger cartridge cases holding more propellant will achieve ever-smaller increases in velocity from the extra propellant. A cartridge which is so big as to be unable to use all of its propellant efficiently is described as 'over-bore'. Such cartridges have very unpleasant firing characteristics, with high levels of muzzle flash and blast and usually wear out barrels quickly. They also need long barrels to give the necessarily slow-burning propellant time to generate a high velocity, which can be inconvenient. Incidentally, in any given cartridge different projectile weights may produce different energy levels; typically, an 'average' weight for the calibre produces the highest energy, with unusually light or heavy projectiles doing less well. This may in part reflect the characteristics of the propellant, although these are adjustable; heavier projectiles need slower-burning (and usually bulkier) powders to keep the pressure peak down, whereas light projectiles need faster-burning powders to accelerate them quickly enough to reach a high velocity. Very heavy projectiles may protrude deeper into the case, thus reducing the space for propellant.

What is the maximum velocity which a projectile can be pushed to? This is ultimately limited by the expansion rate of the gas from the burning propellant. In rifles, the practical limit is around 1,200m/s (nearly 4,000ft/s) achieved in small-calibre guns which need only light bullets (plus a couple of seriously over-bore Second World War 7.92mm anti-tank rifles). The highest velocities currently achieved are in tank guns firing APFSDS shot, which is extremely light for the calibre and allows velocities to be pushed up to 1,800m/s (nearly 6,000ft/s), which is close to the theoretical limit for conventional powder propellants. To go much faster would require a different technology. In assault rifles, however, the optimum balance of characteristics is achieved at lower velocities of around 800–900m/s (2,600–2,950ft/s).

Barrel length can be a significant issue affecting ballistics, particularly in assault rifles where there is strong motivation to reduce the size of the gun. Typically, a bullet will accelerate rapidly up the barrel at first, then the acceleration will gradually fall until ultimately the gun gas pressure will drop below that necessary to overcome the friction of the bullet in the bore, and the bullet will begin to slow down. For any cartridge there is therefore an optimum barrel length for achieving the maximum muzzle velocity, but this is not especially critical and barrels 10 per cent shorter or longer than this will have little effect on the velocity. Problems begin when the barrel is shortened to significantly below this level. Not only does the muzzle velocity begin to fall away – which can have a noticeable effect on both the external and the terminal ballistics – but the propellant has insufficient time to burn completely, resulting in increased muzzle flash and blast.

EXTERNAL BALLISTICS: SECTIONAL DENSITY AND BALLISTIC COEFFICIENT

Just two key factors determine the external ballistics of a projectile: the muzzle velocity and the ballistic coefficient. The latter is significant because it determines the rate at which the projectile slows down, and, in conjunction with the muzzle velocity, this decides the maximum range (at any given elevation) and the time of flight to any particular distance. The time of flight in turn determines the amount by which the projectile drops downwards since this happens at a constant rate due to gravity. The curved path of the projectile which results from the muzzle velocity, the ballistic coefficient and gravity drop is called the trajectory.

A high muzzle velocity is almost always regarded as desirable in direct-fire weapons (as opposed to mortars and howitzers which can lob shells over hills to hit unseen targets). It provides a flatter trajectory and a shorter time of bullet flight. This minimizes the effect of any misjudgement by the shooter of target range, cross-wind strength (which causes 'wind drift') or target speed, thereby making it easier to hit distant targets. It also results in the projectile's striking the target at a high velocity and therefore with greater effect. Armour penetration, for example, is directly related to the striking velocity, other things being equal.

The problem is that a high muzzle velocity carries penalties. To achieve a significant increase in velocity with a given bullet, far more propellant is needed, which requires a larger and heavier cartridge case and a bigger and heavier gun. A longer barrel is usually required to give the projectile time to accelerate to its higher speed. Recoil, muzzle blast and barrel wear will all be much worse, and a magazine of a given size will hold fewer cartridges. As we have seen, there is also a practical limit to how high the velocity of any given projectile can be pushed. To make the most of the muzzle velocity, we need to achieve a high ballistic coefficient.

There are two elements which decide the ballistic coefficient (BC): the sectional density (SD) and the form factor (FF). The SD is a simple calculation as it is the ratio between calibre and projectile weight. The formula is:

for metric measurements: multiply the projectile weight in grams by 1.422, then divide the result by the square of the calibre in millimetres; so for a 7mm bullet weighing 9g: $(9 \times 1.422)/(7 \times 7)$ = an SD of 0.261

for imperial measurements: divide the projectile weight in pounds by the square of the calibre in inches (if bullet weights are in grains, divide the result by 7,000)

What the SD measures is the weight (or momentum, when moving) behind every square millimetre of the projectile calibre (that is, the cross-sectional area of the projectile). The higher the SD, the better the velocity retention. If projectiles were solid cylinders, then for a given SD they would all be of the same length regardless of their calibre. In practice, of course, the length varies with the calibre; a 10mm projectile will be about twice the length of one of 5mm, and will therefore have about double the SD value. This explains why artillery shells travel much further than rifle bullets, no matter how fast or streamlined. Other things being equal, the bigger the calibre, the longer the range and the shorter the flight time to any given range.

Other things are, of course, far from equal, which is where the form factor comes in. The FF measures the aerodynamic efficiency of the projectile's shape, and is much more complicated to calculate; without access to the manufacturer's data, only approximate estimates can be made. The SD multiplied by the FF provides the ballistic coefficient (BC), which, along with the muzzle velocity, determines the ballistic performance of the bullet. It is obvious that a projectile with a pointed nose will encounter much less air resistance than a simple cylinder and it will therefore have a better FF; but problems arise when one tries to become more specific.

The first problem is that the FF is different at subsonic and at supersonic velocities, because shapes which work best at subsonic speeds are not the best at supersonic ones. At subsonic speeds, the drag caused by the low-pressure area created at the back or base of the projectile is significant and major reductions in drag can be made by tapering this to some extent (giving boat-tailed or streamlined bullets). At supersonic speeds it is the nose shape that is critical; finely pointed noses are needed, but the back end does not matter so much. Some taper towards the base is still useful, but the optimal taper angle is different from that at subsonic velocities. The benefit of boat-tailing at very long range can be demonstrated by two .30-06 bullets, both weighing 180gr. (11.7g) and fired at 2,700ft/s (823m/s). At sea level, the flat-based bullet will travel a maximum of 3,800m (4,160yd), the boat-tail 5,200m (5,690yd).

It is possible to obtain some idea of typical FFs by comparing manufacturers' BC data with the calculated SDs for the same projectiles. In the case of small-arms bullets, this provides the following approximate FFs (each figure should be multiplied by the SD to give the BC):

flat-nose lead: 0.8
round-nose lead: 0.9
round-nose jacketed: 1.0
semi-pointed, soft point: 0.9–1.1
pointed, soft point: 1.2–1.6 (depending on the sharpness of point)
pointed, full-jacket: 1.5–1.8
pointed, full-jacket, boat-tailed: 1.9–2.0

Most military rifle bullets will have form factors in the 1.6–2.0 range.

Comparing the BCs with ballistic tables for the ammunition gives the following results. These figures show the approximate percentage velocity loss over 100m for supersonic projectiles (900m/s) with the following BCs:

BC	0.15	0.20	0.25	0.30	0.35	0.40	0.45	0.50
v loss %	25	18	14	11.5	9.5	8	7	6.5

The next table gives typical results showing the velocity loss from military cartridges at different range.

What the table demonstrates is that: the 5.45 × 39 bullet has a good FF by comparison with either of the 5.56mm bullets since it retains a relatively high percentage of its initial velocity considering its SD; similarly, the 5.56 × 45 bullets have a better FF than the 7.62 × 39; and neither the RCAR (5.56 × 45) nor the FCAR (7.62 × 39) can match the FP round (7.62 × 51) in velocity retention because of its better SD.

It is important to note that the calibre measurements are notional; they usually refer to the diameter of the bore (ignoring the rifling grooves), but alternatively may refer to the diameter of the bullet or to some convenient figure reasonably close to either. It must therefore not be assumed that a projectile from one '7.62mm' cartridge can necessarily be used in another; in all Western cartridges this is the bore measurement and the appropriate bullet diameter for this calibre is 7.82mm, but the Russian '7.62mm' bullet diameters are around 7.9mm. The third table of rifle calibre measurements shows some of the common cartridge designations of each calibre.

Velocity Losses of Rifle Bullets

Cartridge	Bullet weight[1]	Muzzle velocity[2]	v at 200m[3]	v at 400m[3]
5.45 × 39	53/3.43 (.156)	2,950/900	2,340/713 (79%)	1,800/550 (61%)
5.56 × 45	55/3.56 (.156)	3,200/975	2,410/735 (75%)	1,710/522 (54%)
5.56 × 45	62/4.0 (.176)	3,050/930	2,430/740 (80%)	1,880/574 (62%)
7.62 × 39	123/7.97 (.182)	2,330/710	1,795/547 (77%)	1,310/399 (56%)
7.62 × 51	150/9.72 (.226)	2,800/853	2,325/709 (83%)	1,895/578 (68%)

Notes
1 = in grains/grams (and SD)
2 = in feet per second/metres per second
3 = in feet per second/metres per second (and percentage of muzzle velocity remaining)

Rifle Calibre Measurements

Bullet diameter (mm/in)	Bore diameter (mm/in)	Cartridge designation
5.60/.221	5.5/.217	5.45mm Russian
5.69/.224	5.59/.220	5.56mm, 5.6mm, .218, 219, .22, .220, .221, .222, .223, .224, .225, .226
6.2/.244	6.0/.240	6mm, .240, .243, .244
6.53/.257	6.35/.25	6.35mm, .25, .250, .257
6.71/.264	6.55/.258	6.5mm, .256, .260, .264
7.04/.277	6.85/.270	6.8mm, .270, .277
7.21/.284	7.0/.276	7mm, .275, .276, .280, .284
7.82/.308	7.62/.300	7.5mm, 7.62mm, 7.63mm, 7.65mm, .30, .300, .307, .308
7.90/.311	7.7/.303	7.62mm (Russian), 7.65mm (Belgian), 7.7mm, .303, .311
8.20/.323	7.92/.312	7.92mm, 8mm (most, but not all)
8.59/.338	8.38/.330	8.58mm, .33, .330, .338, .340

BULLET STABILITY AND RIFLING

An important element in external ballistics is bullet stability. If an ordinary pointed bullet were fired from a smooth-bore gun, it would start to tumble before travelling base first since that is its naturally stable orientation, thereby ruining its aerodynamics and accuracy. To avoid this, the bullet is made to spin rapidly, which ensures that it remains stable in flight, pointing towards the target. This is achieved by cutting spiral grooves into the barrel, called rifling (the surface of the bore which remains between the grooves being known as the 'lands'). As we have seen, the diameter of a bullet is slightly more than that of the gun. This is so that the lands can grip the metal jacket of the bullet to make it spin. Modern rifle bullets are spun extremely rapidly, typically at around 200,000 rpm.

The rate of twist of the rifling is traditionally described in terms such as 1 in 10, which means that the bullet will rotate through 360 degrees after it has travelled through 10in (254mm) of barrel. For any given calibre, the longer the bullet, the tighter the rate of twist needs to be to achieve stability. The most famous case in which this became an issue was probably that of the 5.56×45 cartridge. In its original American loading, this fired a 55gr. (3.56g) bullet (the M193) for which the M16A1's 1 in 12 barrel twist was adequate. It is widely believed that the rather marginal stability of the bullet increased its readiness to tumble on hitting the target, thereby enhancing its lethality. In fact, this is not a significant factor as any pointed bullet, with a centre of gravity well to the rear, will tumble when passing through a dense medium such as flesh since no amount of spinning would be sufficient to overcome its basic instability.

When NATO decided to adopt the 62gr. (4.0g) Belgian SS109 bullet (US designation M855) and, in particular, its rather longer accompanying M856 tracer, it was found that the rifling twist was no longer adequate, leading to the bullet's tumbling after leaving the muzzle. These loadings are therefore authorized only for use with the M16A1 in an emergency, at ranges of less than 100m (110yd). In the M16A2 version the rifling twist was accordingly increased to 1 in 7. Rifles in this calibre are now found with a variety of twists from around 1 in 7 to 1 in 9. These can also fire the original 55gr. bullet satisfactorily.

TRAJECTORY AND SIGHTS

The trajectory is the curved path taken by the bullet from the muzzle to the target. As we have seen, it is caused by gravity but its shape is determined by the muzzle velocity and the ballistic coefficient of the bullet. The trajectory is not a symmetrical curve; for any given calibre, a light, high-velocity bullet will initially have a flat trajectory but, as it slows down quickly, the curve will steepen markedly at longer ranges. If a heavy, streamlined bullet is fired at a lower velocity from the same gun, its curve will initially be steeper than with the lighter bullet but, as it will lose velocity more slowly, the trajectory curve will not steepen at such a high rate. This is partly why heavier bullets are preferred for long-range shooting: by retaining more of their velocity at longer ranges, combined with their greater weight and SD, they also retain more energy to hit the target.

Rifle sights needed to be adjusted (zeroed) so that the bullet strikes exactly where the sights are aiming at a particular range. At shorter ranges, the bullet's trajectory will be above the line of sight; at longer ranges it will fall increasingly below. The maximum height above the line of sight is known as the 'vertex height', 'mid-range trajectory' or 'maximum ordinate'. The chosen range for zeroing the sights will be carefully selected to match the characteristics of the trajectory, so that within the likely firing range the trajectory will not be too far above nor below the line of sight. Because the trajectory steepens with increasing range, the zero distance will be relatively close to the expected maximum firing range.

Taking all of this into account, the typical zero distance for an assault rifle is likely to be in the region of 250m (274yd) since this will ensure that the bullet will strike within a few centimetres of the sight line at any distance between the muzzle and 300m (330yd).

The table on the next page gives some trajectory information for common military rifle cartridges.

Military sights (except for snipers) are not usually intended to be rapidly adjusted in the field for firing at different ranges. For shooting at longer ranges, the assault rifle user with optical sights may be given some help in the form of markings on the reticle. Some optical sights also provide an aid to range estimation, usually by indicating the height of an average man at certain distances.

SUBCALIBRE AMMUNITION

As we have seen, the higher the SD figure (the heavier the bullet in a particular calibre), the better the velocity retention, assuming equal form factors. Heavy AP bullets have better armour penetration, other things being equal, and, since they slow down less, this advantage will increase with range. The disadvantage

Bullet Trajectory Data

Cartridge	Bullet weight[1]	Muzzle velocity[2]	Drop (mm) 200/400m[3]	Elevation (mils) 200/400m[4]	Vertex (mm) 200/400m[5]
5.45 × 39	53/3.43	2,950/900	296/1,416	1.53/3.68	82/420
5.56 × 45	55/3.56	3,200/975	260/1,290	1.33/3.38	73/393
5.56 × 45	62/4.0	3,050/930	281/1,296	1.41/3.37	75/382
7.62 × 39	123/7.97	2,330/710	668/2,338	2.68/6.27	120/700
7.62 × 51	150/9.72	2,800/853	317/1,455	1.60/3.77	85/418

Notes
1 = bullet weight in grains/grams.
2 = muzzle velocity in feet per second/metres per second.
3 =.distance below the sight line that the bullet drops, if the sight line is along the bore
4 = angle of elevation in mils needed for the bullet to strike the target at each range
5 = maximum height of the trajectory above the sight line when zeroed at these ranges.

of heavy projectiles is that they require much more work to accelerate up to a high muzzle velocity. These conflicting demands explain the interest in subcalibre ammunition, which is extremely light for its calibre in the barrel (that is, the calibre of the sabot) but extremely heavy for its very narrow calibre once the sabot has dropped away. There is a penalty in that the energy used to accelerate the sabot is wasted and so this is made as light as possible.

Subcalibre projectiles have been tested many times in small arms but have seen only limited use. They are of two types: discarding sabot (DS) and fin-stabilized discarding sabot (popularly known as 'flechette'; *fléchette* is the French for 'little arrow') rounds. These have seen most use as the primary armour-piercing ammunition of automatic cannon and tank guns, in which application they are known as APDS and APFSDS, respectively. What they have in common is that the projectile has a significantly smaller diameter than the bore, which makes it lighter and therefore can be fired at a higher velocity, to the benefit of both ballistics and armour penetration. The space between the projectile and the bore is filled with a 'sabot' (the French for shoe), which wraps around the projectile in the barrel but falls away from it as soon as the projectile has passed the muzzle.

The difference between DS and flechette rounds is that in the former type the projectile is essentially a small bullet which is stabilized by being spun by the rifling. However, rifling no longer works once the length of the projectile exceeds five or six times its diameter, so the very long, thin flechette rounds have to have small fins added to the tail, like the tail feath-

ers of an arrow, and for exactly the same reason. Such projectiles are disturbed by rifling (it causes them to yaw – the long axis of the projectile adopts an angle to its line of flight) and work better from a smooth-bore barrel. Both DS and – especially – flechette rounds lose some accuracy over full-calibre bullets because the flight of the projectiles is disturbed by sabot separation. However, this is offset by the much higher velocity, providing a flat trajectory and short flight time and thereby improving the hit probability at long range.

The only service application at present is in 7.62 × 51 calibre sniper rifles fielded by the Swedish Army, which fire 4.81mm diameter, 3.4g (52gr.) tungsten alloy DS bullets at 1,340m/s (4,400ft/s). By comparison with the standard 7.62 × 51 military ball loading, this reduces the time of flight to 1,000m (and therefore the susceptibility to wind drift) by one-third, increases the terminal velocity at that distance by 58 per cent and reduces the vertex – the height of the bullet trajectory above the sight line – by the same amount. The combination of short flight time and flat trajectory minimizes the effects of errors in estimating range and wind drift and thereby increases the hit probability at that range by between two and four times.

The several experimental efforts to introduce flechette rounds in assault rifles will be discussed in the next chapter.

RECOIL

Recoil is an important issue in the design of assault rifles and their ammunition, because one of the major problems associated with them is how to combine the striking energy required to be effective against personnel at ranges of several hundred metres with a recoil light enough to permit controlled automatic fire.

The recoil force generated by firing a cartridge has two components: the momentum of the projectile and that of the escaping gas. Projectile momentum is easy to compare between loadings – multiply the projectile weight by its muzzle velocity (so a cartridge firing a 10g bullet at 1,000m/s will have the same bullet momentum and recoil impulse as one firing a 20g bullet at 500m/s). Note that this is a different calculation from muzzle energy, since bullet weight and muzzle velocity are of equal value. In the example above, the 10g loading develops twice as much energy; for the 20g bullet to produce the same energy, it would have to be fired at just over 700m/s, and would then generate 40 per cent more recoil. This explains why, in different bullet-weight loadings of the same cartridge which generate the same muzzle energy, the heavy bullet loading will produce the heavier recoil.

The recoil caused by the escaping gas – a kind of rocket effect – is not quite as straightforward since there is no simple ratio to indicate exactly what proportion of the recoil is generated by the escaping gas as opposed to that from the projectile. However, a good approximation can be made, based on the weight of the propellant multiplied by the velocity of the gun gas compared with the weight multiplied by the velocity of the projectile. In empirical tests, the velocity of the gas escaping from the muzzle of a rifle has been determined to be 1,200m/s (4,000ft/s) plus or minus 10 per cent. It is therefore fairly simple to work out what

proportion of the recoil impulse is generated by the escaping gas. In a small-calibre, high-velocity rifle, such as the 5.56mm NATO model, it is in the region of 35–40 per cent. In a medium-velocity rifle, such as the 7.62mm NATO, it is more like 30 per cent, and for the low-velocity 9 × 19 SMG/pistol round it is perhaps 10–15 per cent.

The percentage will vary depending on the barrel length. A gun with a shorter barrel than standard for the calibre will develop a lower muzzle velocity (hence a reduced bullet momentum) but the gas will escape at a higher pressure, so increasing the 'rocket effect' – as well as muzzle flash and blast.

This information may be used to compare the recoil impulse generated by several military small arms cartridges, as shown in the table below.

What this chart shows is that the 7.62 × 51 cartridge generates approximately double the recoil impulse of the 5.56 × 45. In guns of the same weight, this means that the 7.62mm gun will travel backwards at twice the speed of the 5.56mm version. It will therefore generate four times as much recoil energy (the square of the velocity), which is what the shooter experiences, and explains why assault rifles in this calibre are so much harder to control in fully automatic fire. Reducing the weight of the weapon also increases the perceived recoil. The gun's recoil momentum with a given cartridge remains the same, but the recoil velocity of the lighter gun will increase. Halving the weight of the gun will double the recoil velocity and the perceived recoil. The results of all of this for common military rifles are shown in the table on the next page.

Recoil Impulse Generated by Cartridges

Cartridge	Bullet weight[1] [BW]	Muzzle velocity[2]	Bullet momentum[3] [BM]	Propellant weight[1] [PW]	Gun gas velocity[2]	Gun gas momentum[3] (PM)	Total momentum[3] (BM + PM)
5.45 × 39	3.43	900	3.09	1.5	1,200	1.8	4.89
5.56 × 45	3.56	975	3.47	1.78	1,200	2.14	5.61
5.56 × 45	4.0	930	3.72	1.6	1,200	1.92	5.64
7.62 × 39	7.97	710	5.66	1.7	1,200	2.04	7.70
7.62 × 51	9.75	853	8.32	2.98	1,200	3.58	11.90

Notes
1 = weight in grams (propellant weight estimated where not known); 2 = velocity in metres per second; 3 = a notional momentum value, for comparison purposes only, calculated by multiplying the weight by the velocity in kilometres per second, i.e. mps/1,000.

Recoil Energy of Rifles

Gun	Gun weight unloaded (kg)	Cartridge	Cartridge recoil impulse	Gun recoil velocity (m/s)	Gun recoil energy (J)
AK74	3.86	5.45 × 39	4.89	1.27	3.1
M16A1	2.89	5.56 × 45	5.61	1.94	5.4
M16A2	3.77	5.56 × 45	5.64	1.50	4.2
AK47	4.3	7.62 × 39	7.70	1.79	6.9
M14	3.88	7.62 × 51	11.90	3.06	18.2

The only way of reducing the recoil force generated by a cartridge, while maintaining the muzzle energy, is to reduce the effect of the escaping gas by diverting some of it, either to one side or (preferably) to the rear. As we have seen in the previous chapter, a device to achieve this is known as a muzzle brake. The extent to which a muzzle brake can reduce the recoil obviously depends upon the proportion of the recoil impulse generated by the propellant gas; it gives the greatest benefit in very powerful, high-velocity weapons. An efficient muzzle brake can reduce the recoil impulse of a high-velocity cartridge by up to 30 per cent, thereby reducing the gun recoil energy by about 50 per cent. Higher figures are possible, but only by using brakes which are so large that they would be impracticable. Some military weapons are fitted with a suppressor, which is intended to reduce the muzzle flash and blast to make the firer harder to locate. By tapping off gas before the bullet leaves the muzzle and allowing it to escape more slowly, these also reduce the recoil force, although to a lesser extent than muzzle brakes.

Of course, a specially designed, recoilless gun deflects most of the gas directly behind the weapon, to ensure that the rocket effect precisely balances the projectile momentum. However, this requires the use of several times as much propellant as with a conventional gun of the same muzzle energy, so the ammunition is bulky and expensive. The firing cycle is also more complex and therefore this approach has not been adopted for assault rifles.

Self-loading weapons, particularly if gas-operated, tend to reduce the perceived recoil because some of the energy is used to drive the reloading mechanism. As already mentioned, the shape of the rifle can also affect the perceived recoil; a 'straight' or 'straight-line' stock which directs the recoil impulse into the shoulder causes less barrel jump than a dropped or angled stock, which has the thrust line over the shoulder. More subtle variations, such as an absorbent buttstock and even the shape of the stock and the handgrips, can also affect the perceived recoil, weapons with narrow, sharp grips and stocks appearing to kick harder.

TERMINAL BALLISTICS

There are two aspects to terminal ballistics: what happens when a bullet strikes armour and what happens when it penetrates a body.

Figures quoted for the thickness of armour penetrated by particular AP ammunition need to be treated with caution as they are affected by several variables. One is obviously range, since performance reduces in line with velocity. Another is the type of armour being attacked, some being more resistant than others (complicated by the fact that body armour may consist of layers of artificial fibre, metal and ceramics, to each of which bullets react in different ways). The third main variable is the angle at which the bullet strikes the armour. The further from the perpendicular the bullet strikes, the less it will penetrate, although the extent of this depends on the bullet design.

Two of these variables are normally dealt with in the standard way of describing penetration, which is to list the thickness penetrated at a given range and striking angle, as in 10mm/300m/60 degrees. An unwelcome complication is that there have been two differing conventions for describing the striking angle: from the horizontal or from the vertical. A hit perpendicular to the armour surface (the optimum for penetration) is described in NATO terminology as being at 90 degrees, but in the past it has sometimes been described as being at 0 degrees.

To give an idea of the performance of which AP bullets are capable, the Swedish Carl Gustav 5.56 × 45 APHC round can penetrate 15mm/100m/90 degrees; the FP 7.62 × 51 version can manage this at 300m. It is usual for the material penetrated in such tests to be a homogeneous steel plate of specified hardness. The US tungsten-alloy cored M995 5.56 × 45 AP bullet is claimed to penetrate only 12mm at 100m, but it is unclear whether the same hardness of armour was used.

It is generally true that, if matters such as bullet design and velocity are constant, then the longest bullet with the highest SD (which has the greatest weight behind each square millimetre of frontal area) will penetrate best. This tends to favour larger calibre weapons, as their bullets are usually longer. However, FCAR bullets, such as the 7.62 × 39, are poorer penetrators than RCAR rounds such as the 5.45 × 39, because they are much the same length and have a lower muzzle velocity. The best penetrators are subcalibre projectiles, especially the long, thin flechettes. There is some question, however, about the effectiveness of flechettes on the people inside the armour once they have penetrated. When applied to the effect on a human body, terminal ballistics is a rather gruesome subject. However, it cannot be glossed over as it is vital to the debate about the effectiveness and optimum calibre of assault rifles. It is worth at the start dealing with one common myth; that military bullets are designed to wound but not kill, the theory being that a wounded man will also take out of the fight a couple of his comrades while they help him to safety. Apart from the fact that soldiers are generally instructed to leave the wounded to the medics and press on, this defies logic. It takes relatively little power to inflict a lethal wound – the weak .22 rimfire target cartridge has killed thousands – but a lot more to quickly disable an opponent, which is what the military is interested in. All of the current military rifle cartridges are more than powerful enough to kill; the argument is over how quickly they are able to disable opponents so that they can't fight back.

When a bullet passes through a human body, it creates both permanent and temporary wound channels. The permanent one is slightly wider than the bullet and is the source of most of the injury; the temporary one is wider still but usually closes quickly without causing much damage. The first generation of jacketed military rifle bullets at the end of the nineteenth century had rounded noses and parallel sides and were quite stable, following a straight path through the body. This created a very narrow wound channel, with a strong probability of the victim's making a quick recovery, provided that no vital organs were seriously damaged, and this earned such bullets a reputation for ineffectiveness.

However, as we have seen, modern pointed bullets are inherently unstable because their centre of gravity is much closer to the base than the tip. They will therefore tumble end-to-end on entering a body, before settling down to travelling base first. This tumbling creates a far wider, permanent wound channel (widest where the bullet is travelling sideways in mid-tumble) and is responsible for most of the injury caused. In contrast, commercial hunting bullets are designed to expand on impact, which greatly increases the size of the wound channel, but these are illegal for military use; tumbling achieves a similar effect in a different way. The rate at which a bullet tumbles depends on a number of factors, mainly concerned with the size, the shape and the composition of the bullet. The British .303in Mark VII ball round, used in rifles and MGs in both World Wars, had a light alloy tip filler, thereby producing a stronger rearward weight bias which caused more rapid tumbling. This was the subject of criticism from Germany, who argued that it was against the spirit of the international Hague Convention of 1907, which banned bullets calculated to cause unnecessary suffering.

Other things being equal, small-calibre bullets tend to tumble faster than larger ones, which partly accounts for the reputation for effectiveness achieved by the 5.56 × 45 NATO round. Both M193 and M855 bullets usually start tumbling about 10cm (4in) after penetration and take another 15cm to complete the manoeuvre. The 7.62 × 51 M80 ball tumbles more slowly, starting at around 15cm and taking a further 25cm to complete. The rate of tumbling for the 7.62 × 39 varies considerably depending on the type: the Russian steel-cored ball at first just yaws between 25 and 30cm and does not complete tumbling until about 50cm after impact, whereas the Yugoslav M67 bullet, which has a lead core with a hollow tip (and therefore a stronger rearward weight bias) tumbles much more quickly, starting after only 10cm. The 5.45 × 45 ball (which also has a hollow tip) follows a similar pattern to the Russian 7.62 × 39, except that it begins yawing after penetrating only about 5cm and has finished tumbling after about 40cm. It must be stressed that these are all average figures when fired into a homogeneous ballistic gelatine designed to mimic accurately the response of human flesh. What actually happens when bullets strike the decidedly non-homogeneous human body may vary considerably, and there have been combat reports of 5.56mm bullets passing straight through a body without tumbling.

Incidentally, it is often stated that the 5.45mm's hollow tip is designed to bend on impact to encourage tumbling, and this has been demonstrated when the bullet is fired into plasticine (and sometimes occurs when it hits a human target). However, this does not happen when it is fired into ballistic gelatine. The hollow tip is probably there to keep the weight down despite the bullet's having a long, slender nose for external ballistic reasons. It also provides a useful rearward weight bias. One experimental bullet type specifically designed to encourage fast tumbling was the *Löffelspitz* or spoon tip, invented by Dr Voss when working for CETME, which has an asymmetric tip; this does not affect the external ballistics.

If the bullet hits an unprotected body, it is likely to be most effective if it completes tumbling within about 30cm, as this is similar to the average thickness of a torso. This may appear to favour the small-calibre rounds, which generally tumble within this distance. However, if the bullet hits something else first (for instance, the enemy's arm) then the bullet will start tumbling before hitting the body and in these circumstances the 7.62mm bullets are likely to perform better. Furthermore, small-calibre bullets are more easily stopped by obstacles such as ammunition magazines kept in chest pouches, as has been demonstrated in tests. In any case, the basic wound channel created by the bigger bullet will clearly be larger than with the small calibres, other things being equal.

A further degree of injury occurs with bullets which break up under the stress of tumbling, the multiple fragments going in different directions and adding significantly to the wounding effect. Most bullets do not break up, the most famous ones which do being the 5.56 × 45 loadings, both the M193 and the M855. The US M80 7.62 × 51 does not break up, but the German equivalent has a thinner jacket with a cannelure (a knurled ring around the centre) which does break up and probably inflicts the most severe wounds of any modern military rifle bullet. It should be noted that bullets which strike bone may also cause much more serious injuries since bone fragments can act in much the same way as bullet fragments.

The importance of fragmentation to the effectiveness of the 5.56mm bullets has a bearing on some of the criticism aimed at the current short-barrelled US M4 carbine. Fragmentation occurs only at high impact velocity. The barrel of the M4 is only 14.5in (368mm) long, rather than the 20in (508mm) barrel of the standard M16A2, which reduces the muzzle velocity to the point where fragmentation occurs only at very short range. In the normal 510mm (20in) barrel the maximum fragmentation distance is around 150–200m (164–220yd; the longer distance being for the M193),

but in the short carbine barrels it can be as low as 50–100m (55–110yd). However, fragmentation is an accidental effect rather than a specific US military requirement, and it appears that different bullet production batches may perform differently, with some failing to fragment; serious criticisms were expressed about the effectiveness of the M855 'green tip' bullets used during the American action in Somalia. There are also reports from Iraq of combatants continuing to fight despite being hit in the body several times by 5.56mm bullets at very short range.

The controversy over the effectiveness of the M4 appears to have stimulated the development of improved loadings. The heavy (77gr./5.0g) Mk 262 5.56mm loading was originally designed for accurate, long-range target shooting, but has been found to tumble well and fragment at much lower velocities than the current service rounds. It was used by US Special Forces and the Marine Corps in Iraq in 2003, and may well be adopted more widely. More radically, a new 6.8 × 43 cartridge is being considered, described below.

It is often believed that 'hydrostatic shock' caused by the high velocity impact of a bullet has a significant disabling effect on the victim. However, this is disputed by others, who state that the damage caused by the wound channel is the only cause of injury. It is undoubtedly true, as demonstrated by recent experience in Iraq, that people can be shot at point-blank range by high-velocity rifle bullets yet still carry on fighting, clearly not disabled by shock. Some tests indicate that people hit by bullets or fragments travelling in excess of the speed of sound in flesh (around 1,500m/s or 4,900ft/s) suffer far more serious injuries because of the shock wave travelling through their bodies, although this too is disputed by others. This could become a significant issue if flechettes were to be reconsidered since they remain stable in flesh and create extremely narrow wound channels; without some added wounding mechanism, they are likely to prove ineffective. One flechette design, for the Winchester XM258 shotgun round, had an annular groove around the middle to encourage it to break in two on impact, but it is not known how effective that would be.

Finally, people do react differently to being shot depending on the circumstances. A soldier who is 'psyched up' for battle, with adrenaline surging through the bloodstream, will be much harder to disable than the same man when relaxed. Despite what Hollywood may sometimes portray, it appears that the only way to be sure of an 'instant knockdown' in battle is to achieve a hit on the central nervous system – the brain or the spine. Regardless of the calibre or bullet type, a hit anywhere else may not take immediate effect and the victim is likely to be capable of fighting back for at least a short time. The argument about whether a tumbling and fragmenting small-calibre bullet is a better route to achieving this than a bigger and more powerful round is likely to continue for the foreseeable future.

THE SEARCH FOR THE PERFECT CALIBRE

It will by now be appreciated that the designer of ammunition for an assault rifle has a difficult set of problems to solve: recoil light enough to permit controlled fully-automatic fire is essential; it is also valuable to reduce ammunition size and weight as much as possible so that an infantryman can carry more of it (it is one of the unwritten laws of the infantry that lighter equipment never results in a reduced load to carry – only in a larger quantity). These considerations argue in favour of a RCAR cartridge, and the smaller and less powerful the ammunition, the better.

On the other hand, there is no point in reducing the power of the cartridge to the point where it is no longer effective in achieving the rapid disabling of enemy personnel. As we have seen, small, high-velocity bullets carefully designed to maximize the wounding effect (without, of course, infringing international law) can be effective at short range, although their performance tends to be erratic. Such bullets lose velocity quickly and therefore lose effectiveness at long range. This may not matter if the troops are sent in to undertake urban warfare, but if in the following week they find themselves in open country then it matters a great deal. It is also usually a requirement that the LMGs

carried by infantry sections should chamber the same ammunition as the rifles, which emphasizes the need to provide a better long-range performance than is strictly required of an assault rifle. It would, of course, be better still from the viewpoint of logistics to use one cartridge to replace both assault rifle and full-power MG rounds, as the British planned in the late 1940s with the 7×43. It is not difficult to outline the characteristics of such a cartridge, which would be intermediate in power between the 5.56×45 and the 7.62×51 (or, in Russian service, the 5.45×39 and the $7.62 \times 54R$) and capable of replacing both.

Such an ideal cartridge would need to combine long-range effectiveness similar to that of the 7.62mm, with recoil light enough to permit controlled, fully automatic fire. There are three elements to this which operate together: calibre, bullet sectional density and muzzle energy. To obtain any advantage in reduced recoil over the 7.62mm would require an upper calibre limit of 7mm; to gain a useful performance increase over the 5.56mm would indicate a lower calibre limit of 6mm; to match the long-range performance of the 7.62mm would require a bullet sectional density at least as great. The 9.72g (150gr.) standard bullet of the 7.62mm has an SD of 0.226, while the long-range 5.0g (77gr.) bullet available for the 5.56mm has an SD of 0.219. This suggests an SD of 0.230. Finally, muzzle energy: the maximum should be 2,500J to provide the right balance of power and recoil. This would be needed at the top end of the calibre range, but, since smaller calibres need less energy to penetrate armour, this provides a range of choices in common calibres, as shown in the table below. Clearly, the figures for each calibre are only indicative as the bullet weight and muzzle velocity could vary to some degree, but the ones shown all have the same SD of .230.

Characteristics of Some 'Ideal' Cartridges

Calibre (mm/in)	Bullet weight	Muzzle velocity	Muzzle energy (J/ft lb)	Recoil factor (est. moment)
6mm/.24	6.2g/96gr.	831m/s/2,726ft/s	2,140/1,590	7.8
6.35mm/.25	6.9g/106gr.	811m/s/2,660ft/s	2,270/1,675	8.2
6.5mm/.258	7.3g/113gr.	797m/s/2,615ft/s	2,320/1,725	8.5
6.85mm/.270	8.0g/123gr.	781m/s/2,562ft/s	2,440/1,800	8.9
7mm/.276	8.4g/130gr.	772m/s/2,533ft/s	2,500/1,860	9.1

Note
The 'recoil factor' is calculated in the same way as for the table in the previous section, and assumes a propellant weight of around 2.2g in each case.

The muzzle energy to achieve the same penetration varies in direct proportion to the calibre. The energy which can be extracted from a given cartridge case also varies in direct proportion to the calibre, so the case diameter and the length would be similar for all of the cartridges in the table. How big would the case need to be? Intermediate in diameter between the 7.62 and 5.56mm (around 10.5mm), and about 45mm in total length.

The recoil energy of weapons chambered to fire these cartridges, assuming an empty gun weight of 3.8kg (8.4lb), would range from 8J for the 6mm, to 11J for the 7mm; roughly intermediate between the 5.56 × 45 and the 7.62 × 51 weapon, as would be expected.

All of the above cartridges would deliver what is required; the choice between them would be a question of deciding between lighter recoil and ammunition weight on the one hand, or greater hitting power on the other. The midpoint calibre of 6.5mm seems to offer the best all-round compromise. Ironically, this specification is not dissimilar to some of the 6.5mm military rifle cartridges in use until the end of the Second World War, including the 6.5 × 50SR Arisaka, used in the very first assault rifle, the Federov Avtomat. However, they generally fired heavier bullets at a lower muzzle velocity. Improvements in powder technology would also allow the required performance to be extracted from smaller cases. It is interesting to note that the proposed new American military 6.8 × 43 Remington SPC described in the next chapter has a performance similar to that of the 6.85mm round listed above, but firing a slightly lighter bullet at a higher velocity.

The history of post-war military small-arms cartridge development has been a tussle between the conflicting requirements of power and controllability. The 'holy grail' of many weapons developers has been the general-purpose cartridge, capable of reaching out to long range in MGs and sniper rifles, while having the light recoil to permit controlled automatic fire in shoulder-fired assault rifles. As we have seen, such cartridges are quite feasible and have indeed existed for decades, but, for a variety of reasons, have not so far succeeded in being adopted post-war by any major military power. The rather sorry tale of what actually happened is described in the next chapter.

Chapter Four

THE DEVELOPMENT OF THE ASSAULT RIFLE CARTRIDGE

It should by now be understood why the designers of assault rifles have from the beginning sought to adopt or develop ammunition which, while remaining effective at the normal maximum range for rifle combat (around 300m; 330yd), has a significantly lighter recoil than full-power rifle and MG cartridges. However, the search for the ideal assault rifle cartridge has sometimes been influenced by a desire to simplify ammunition supply by using the same round to replace the traditional full-power rifle/MG cartridge. This made the task of the designers more difficult, as it pushed the range requirement up to 1,000m (1,100yd) or more.

THE FIRST ASSAULT RIFLE CARTRIDGES

At the start of the Second World War there was a substantial power gap between pistol/SMG ammunition and rifle/MG cartridges. The most popular pistol/SMG round (then and now) was the 9×19, also known as the Parabellum, although the more powerful 9×25 (Mauser Export) saw some use in SMGs, and a smaller calibre cartridge from which it was derived, the 7.63mm Mauser (also known as the 7.62×25 Tokarev) was used in the USSR. The USA was unusual in retaining a larger calibre in the .45in (11.5×23) Automatic Colt Pistol round, also used in the Thompson and later SMGs. The muzzle energy of these pistol/SMG rounds was within the range 400–600J (300–450ft lb) which in conjunction with the short, wide, blunt-nosed bullets reduced the effective maximum range in SMGs to about 150m (165yd).

Most of the rifle/MG cartridges then in service were broadly comparable in calibre and power: the main ones being the 7.92×57 (German Mauser), the $7.62 \times 54R$ (Russian), the $7.7 \times 56R$ (.303in British) and the 7.62×63 (American .30-06). Their muzzle energies are in the 3,000–4,000J range (2,200–3,000ft lb),

providing a maximum range limited by the weapon and its users rather than the ammunition. As we have seen, such power generates noticeable recoil in a rifle.

There were some smaller rounds in service, notably the 6×60 (USN Lee rifle of 1895, which was really ahead of its time), the 6.5×52 (Italian Carcano) and the $6.5 \times 50SR$ (Japanese Arisaka) which produced around 2,200–2,500J (1,600–1,850ft lb). Had they been developed in appropriate loadings they would have made an excellent basis for an assault rifle, but, apart from the brief appearance of the Russian Federov Avtomat in $6.5 \times 50SR$ twenty years earlier, they were never given the chance. Another military cartridge common in Scandinavia, the 6.5×55 Swedish, was significantly more powerful than these at 2,800J (2,100ft lb). The straight-cased American .30 M1 Carbine cartridge (7.62×33) was used in a selective fire weapon, but this generated only 1,200J (890ft lb), which, while better than the SMG cartridges, was not enough to provide the 300m + effective range requirement.

The first of the purpose-designed assault rifle cartridges to enter service was the German 7.92×33 (Kurz), which emerged after experiments with various case lengths and shapes. Polte and DWM both developed 7mm cartridges before Polte concentrated on several options during 1939–40, with case lengths of between 30 and 45mm, which all retained the same calibre and case diameter as the 7.92×57 so that they could be made by using existing machinery. The chosen 7.92×33 finally became a production item early in 1942 with an order for 10 million rounds. The shorter case reduced the propellant capacity and muzzle energy by half (about 2,000J/1,500ft lb) and had a similar effect on the recoil, making it feasible to control the fire of the selective fire rifles designed for the cartridge, while still preserving an effective range of at least 300m. Bullets of 7, 7.5 and 8g (108, 116 and 124gr.) were tested before a final decision in favour of

Early World War 2 pistol, SMG and rifle cartridges (from left to right): .45 ACP (11.5 × 23); 9mm Parabellum (9 × 19); 9mm Mauser Export (9 × 25); 7.62mm Tokarev (7.62 × 25); .30 Carbine (7.62 × 33); .30-06 (7.62 × 63); 7.62mm Russian (7.62 × 54 R); .303 British (7.7 × 56 R); 7.92mm Mauser (7.92 × 57).

an 8.1g steel-cored bullet fired at 690m/s (125gr. at 2,260ft/s), as measured in British tests using captured weapons.

This was followed by the second of the FCAR cartridges, the Soviet 7.62 × 39 Model 1943, which also develops around 2,000J/1,500ft lb (the case being slimmer as well as longer than that of the 7.92 × 33). This was not derived from an existing cartridge, but since the contemporary Soviet SMG and rifle/MG rounds both had the same calibre, it must have been thought convenient to retain it. The only other FCAR cartridge to see service was the Czech 7.62 × 45 (originally produced in 7.5 × 45, firing a 8g bullet at 750m/s), which, being a lengthened version of the Model 1943, was a little more powerful with 2,230J/1,650ft lb, but was again easily controllable.

Next in the field came the British, who in 1945 set up the Small Arms Calibre Panel in order to determine

the optimum cartridge for a lightweight rifle. After many calculations and experiments mainly involving rounds of between .25 to .27in calibre (6.35–6.8mm), they reported in 1947 in favour of further development of two alternative designs. One was a .27in (6.8 × 46) firing a steel-cored 100gr. bullet at 2,750–2,800ft/s (6.5g at 840–850m/s), which still retained 81ft lb (109J) of energy at 2,000yd (1,830m), a significant figure since the estimated energy required to inflict an injury to an unprotected man is around 60ft lb (80J). The other was a .276 (7 × 43; later redesignated .280 to avoid confusion with earlier cartridges) which was tested with bullets weighing between 8.4 and 9g (130–140gr.) at between 747–710m/s (2,450–2,330ft/s). The 130gr./2,450ft/s loading had a retained energy of 100ft lb at 2,000yd (135J at 1,830m). Eventually a loading of a Belgian-designed 9g bullet at 736m/s (140gr. at 2,415ft/s) was decided on. The .280 calibre (actually 7mm, with a .276in bore and .284 bullet) was a little larger than was thought ideal but it was selected for further development, reportedly in order to try to meet American preferences for good long-range performance. For the same reason, the original case rim diameter was increased slightly to match that of the American .30-06 to make it possible to rebarrel existing guns more easily, leading to a change in designation to .280/30.

In conjunction with the .280, two new rifles were developed, the EM-1 and the EM-2 bullpups, described in more detail in the section on the United Kingdom in Part II. It is important to note that, unlike the FCARs described above, the .280 was intended to replace entirely both the 9mm SMG and the .303in rifle/MG rounds. It was envisaged that the rifle would normally be used in semi-automatic mode at ranges in excess of about 150m, with fully-automatic fire being used in short bursts at shorter ranges. The .280/30 cartridge was formally adopted in August 1951 as the '7mm Mk 1Z', at the same time as the EM-2 was adopted as the 'Rifle, No.9 Mk 1'. But fate was about to disturb these careful plans.

Towards the end of World War 2 the USA had also begun thinking about replacing the .30-06 cartridge and associated weaponry and had developed the concept of a selective-fire 'Lightweight Rifle'. What they really wanted was the selective-fire .30 M2 Carbine but with the hitting power of the .30 Garand, at a weight of 3.2kg (7lb). It was rather ambitiously hoped that this one weapon would replace the M1 Garand and the .30 Browning Automatic Rifle (both in 7.62 × 63), the M1/2 Carbine in 7.62 × 33 and the M3 SMG in .45 calibre (11.5 × 23). The Lightweight Rifle was intended to chamber a shorter cartridge than the 7.62 × 63, but still with a reasonable long-range performance so that it could entirely replace the older round; it was required to have 'a stopping and wounding power which shall not be less than that of the standard calibre .30 ammunition [7.62 × 63] fired from the M1 at ranges of 400, 800, 1,200 and 2,000 yards [up to 1,830m]'. Many experiments followed but, contrary to all of the logic of ammunition design, the US Ordnance Department decided that they wanted to retain the .30in calibre. The Americans accordingly ended with what was simply the .30-06 case shortened from 63 to 51mm, but with a very similar performance at around 3,500J (2,600ft lb) muzzle energy (made possible by improvements in propellant technology) and therefore a very similar recoil. Inevitably, this meant that the planned new selective-fire rifle would prove uncontrollable in fully-automatic fire, and so it proved, years

before the M14 (based on the old .30-06 M1 Garand) finally entered service.

Interestingly, American opinion on this subject was far from united. The EM-2 and its .280 cartridge were thoroughly tested in the USA in 1950 alongside the FN FAL in the same calibre (the Belgians being enthusiastic supporters of the British concept) and in comparison with the American T25 prototype rifle. This was chambered for the original 'T65' cartridge, a 7.62 × 47 round which was the first stage in the development programme which eventually led to the FAT1E3 casein the T65E3 loading, later adopted as the 7.62 × 51 NATO. Testing took place at Fort Benning where the US Army Infantry Board was based, and the tests were expected to result in the choice of a new standard rifle cartridge for NATO.

At Fort Benning, the Trials Board reported on the cartridges as follows: 'That the T65 Cal .30 is not satisfactory because of its excessive recoil, blast, flash and smoke. That the Cal .280 is not satisfactory because of its comparatively high trajectory. That of the two basic types of rounds submitted for test the British calibre .280 is preferred.' The detailed findings from the tests showed that, while the T65 had a flatter trajectory and produced more severe wounds at ranges of less than 1,000yd (900m), the British round became more effective at longer ranges because of its superior ballistic coefficient. At 1,000yd the .280 could penetrate body armour 70 per cent of the time, compared with 60 per cent for the .30. The British cartridge also produced considerably less flash and smoke. Most significantly, while the T25 was found to be the more accurate rifle and achieved more hits per minute when fired from a bipod, the EM-2 was far superior in this respect when fired from the shoulder.

Clearly, the British designers had achieved all that they had aimed for, but the Trials Board's recommendation to focus development on the .280 cartridge was rejected by the Chief of Staff of the US Army. This was due to the clear preference of the Ordnance Department and the American military, political and industrial establishment in favour of a full-power .30 calibre rifle of American origin.

The British felt that the Aberdeen trials should have settled the matter and so did not give up easily. They set about meeting the American objections by producing more powerful versions of their cartridge, with the support of Belgium and Canada. The first change was to upload the 43mm case to 2,550ft/s (777m/s) with the 140gr. (9g) bullet, to meet the criticism of the trajectory and also to address complaints that the low temperatures of Arctic conditions reduced the performance to an unacceptable level. This raised the energy remaining at 2,000yd to 126ft lb (170J). However, the British cause was severely damaged by a change of government, which led early in 1952 (reportedly followed a meeting between President Truman and Winston Churchill, the new Prime Minister) to a decision to rescind the adoption of the EM-2 and its 7mm cartridge before any had been issued.

Despite this setback, Britain, Belgium and Canada combined (in the 'BBC Committee') to make one last attempt to develop a new 7mm round which would be acceptable to NATO. Several lengthened cartridges with such designations as 'Optimum', 'High Velocity', 'Compromise' and 'Second Optimum' were developed, mostly with 49mm cases, although the final attempt was simply the 7.62 × 51 necked-down to 7mm. Muzzle velocities were in the range 2,750–2,800ft/s with the 140gr. bullet (9g at 840–850m/s). However, the Americans would not be convinced. In any case, the recoil had by this time increased significantly and the balance of the original EM-2 concept had been lost. At the end of 1953 the BBC Committee reluctantly bowed to American pressure and the 7.62 × 51 was formally adopted as the new NATO cartridge. The only result of all of this effort was a 7 × 49 cartridge, known as the 7mm Medium, which saw service in an FN FAL selective-fire rifle which was sold to Venezuela.

THE HALL AND HITCHMAN REPORTS, PROJECT SALVO AND THE SPIW

While the .30 calibre rifle and ammunition were still being developed, a number of American research projects were coming to radically different conclusions about the requirements for a military rifle. In 1950 the Ballistic Research Laboratory (BRL), an Army unit based at the Aberdeen Proving Grounds, was asked to investigate combat rifle effectiveness. The resulting report titled *An Effectiveness Study of the Infantry Rifle* was presented by its author (Donald Hall) in 1952. This was a theoretical study of the effectiveness of different calibres, which concluded that significant improvements in hit probability could be expected of a small-calibre, high velocity cartridge owing to its flatter trajectory, and that there would also be benefits in a considerable reduction in ammunition weight. His calculations showed that at 400yd (366m) the single-shot hit probability of 0.35 expected of the .30-06 could be increased to 0.45 with a high-velocity .21 (5.3mm) round.

In parallel with this study, the civilian Operational

Research Office (ORO) of the US Army's General Staff had been considering the development of improved body armour (Project ALCLAD; the final report was delivered in 1950) and went on from there to examine what really happened in rifle combat. The resulting report on Project BALANCE by Norman Hitchman, the head of ORO's Infantry Division, emerged in 1952 a few months after the Hall report.

Hitchman's report was forthright in presenting its findings, much to the discomfiture of many staff in the Ordnance Department. Examination of World War 2 combat records and of new data emerging from Korea (over 600 soldiers were interviewed), showed that the average distance for aimed bullet hits was in the region of 75–100yd (70–90m) with 80 per cent of effective rifle and LMG fire being reported at ranges of less than 200yd and 90 per cent at less than 300yd (275m). Hits at ranges longer than this were very infrequent since even good marksmen found that terrain and visibility severely hindered their effectiveness; it was estimated that at 300m there was only a 10 per cent chance of seeing a man-sized target in most terrain conditions.

The NATO rifle cartridge trials, 1950–52 (from left to right): .30-06 for scale (7.62 × 63); .30 T65 (7.62 × 47); 7.62 × 51 NATO; 7mm/.280/30 British/Belgian (7 × 43); 7mm Medium (7 × 49).

Even worse for the Ordnance Department were the results of testing its treasured .30 cal Lightweight Rifle prototypes, duly reported by ORO. The tests involved firing controlled, five-round bursts at silhouette targets contained within a frame 6ft (1.8m) square. In repeated tests fired at a distance of just 100yd (90m), no more than one bullet from each burst even hit the frame, let alone the target. Even at 50yd (45m) not more than one bullet per burst hit the target. It was the first bullet which hit; the remainder went over the target as the muzzle rose under recoil. The inevitable conclusions of the Hitchman Report were that the .30 cal Light Rifle cartridge was vastly overpowered for its purpose and that fully-automatic fire with a powerful rifle was a waste of time and ammunition. This was just under five years *before* the M14 was officially adopted for US Army service, complete with a powerful .30in (7.62 × 51) cartridge and selective fire. Another controversial finding in the Report was that the accuracy of the rifle made no difference to the hit probability, because the typical aiming errors were so huge. The length of time that soldiers were exposed to fire, combined with the degree to which they were exposed, were far more significant in determining their probability of being hit than the marksmanship of the opposing riflemen. This led to the conclusion that a weapon capable of firing four rounds simultaneously or nearly so, with a dispersion between shots of 20in at 300yd (500mm at 275m) would be the optimum solution to maximize the hit probability, with an expected improvement over the .30-06 of more than 100 per cent. This led in 1952 to the establishment of Project SALVO which, as well as studying conventional small-calibre cartridges (described later), investigated a range of exotic ammunition options.

These included 12-bore shotgun cartridges loaded with thirty-two 'ice pick' projectiles (flechettes), developed by AAI at the behest of the Office of Naval Research. Each flechette weighed 0.84g (13gr.) and was fired at 427m/s (1,400ft/s). The flechettes showed remarkable penetration even at long range, but too much dispersion for anything except close-range work. (Multiple-flechette loadings did reach service, but only in artillery ammunition such as the notorious 105mm 'Beehive' shells, a modern version of multi-ball grapeshot or canister loadings intended to cut swaths through mass infantry attacks.)

Another idea was multi-bullet loadings of .30 cal rifle cartridges with either two (Duplex) or three (Triplex) short bullets stacked on top of each other, at first by using modified cases with lengthened necks, then standard cases. Incidentally this was not a new

idea; the .303 Greener Triplex, for instance, dated from 1918 while during World War 2 the Germans tested a 7.92 × 57 case loaded with two 8.1g Kurz bullets fired at 536m/s (125gr. at 1,760ft/s), for use at ranges of less than 300m.

Two different .30-06 cases were used: in the SALVO 1 series a special long-necked version was tried, while in SALVO 2 the standard case was used. Several loadings were tested as shown in the table.

Loading	Bullet weights (g/gr.)	Velocities (m/s/ft/s)
SALVO 1 series		
Duplex	2 × 7.1/110	768/2,520[1]
Duplex	2 × 6.2/96	800/2,630[1]
Triplex	3 × 4.3/66	805/2,640[1]
SALVO 2 series		
Duplex	2 × 6.2/96	806/2,645[1] 762/2,502[2]
Triplex	3 × 4.0/61	888/2,913[1] 839/2,754[2] 68/2,251[3]

Notes
1 = velocity of first bullet
2 = second bullet
3 = third bullet

These demonstrated hit probabilities increased by 65 or 100 per cent, respectively over the single-bullet (Simplex) rounds. One such loading was even adopted for service, although it appears to have seen little use. This was the M198 Duplex in 7.62 × 51 calibre, in which the two bullets, each weighing around 85gr. (5.5g), were fired at 2,750ft/s (838m/sec) for the front bullet and 2,200ft/s (670m/sec) for the rear one.

More exotic still were the single-flechette rounds. These promised even greater advantages because their extremely high velocity maximized the hit probability (and penetration), while the light weight of the flechette minimized recoil. Some rifles were designed with three or four barrels to allow salvo fire instead of burst fire, but they were so bulky and heavy that interest eventually focused on burst-fire, single-barrel automatic rifles. Their notional calibre was 5.6 or 5.56mm, but the flechettes measured 1.8mm (0.7in) in diameter, weighed 10gr. (0.65g) and were fired at around 4,000ft/s (1,220m/s). It is worth noting that the sabots were heavier than the flechette, at 12gr. (0.78g),

*Project SALVO
multiball loadings:
.30-06 Triplex
loading with
extended neck;
7.62mm NATO M198
Duplex, sectioned to
show the stacked
bullets.*

*Sectioned XM216 SPIW
cartridge, showing the
puller sabot surrounding
the front of the fin-
stabilized flechette.*

while the propellant weighed 15.5gr. (1.0g), which meant that bullet momentum contributed only around 27 per cent of the recoil impulse, sabot momentum 32 per cent and propellant gas 41 per cent.

Many technical problems in designing the flechette rounds had to be overcome, mainly concerned with the design of the sabot. A conventional 'pusher' sabot, with the propellant entirely behind the flechette, resulted in a cartridge which was too long and thin to be convenient, so the concept of the 'puller' sabot was invented. This gripped the front of the flechette only and pulled it up the barrel, thereby allowing most of the flechette to be buried in the case, surrounded by propellant. While this shortened the cartridge and reduced the weight (by 25 per cent in both cases), it introduced a host of technical problems concerned with ensuring that the sabot maintained its grip throughout the enormous pressure and acceleration of firing, then was released cleanly as soon as the projectile left the muzzle. Eventually, this was solved with the aid of a 'sabot stripper', a device fitted to the muzzle which cut

and spun the sabot to ensure clean separation, and patents for both the puller sabot and stripper were submitted in 1954.

The promise of the flechette led to the concept of the Special Purpose Individual Weapon or SPIW. This was the project which the US Army hoped would provide a replacement for the M14, and huge resources were devoted to its protracted development during the 1960s. It would feature not only a burst-fire flechette rifle (various cartridges were tried, all in 5.6mm notional calibre), but also a 40mm repeating grenade launcher, all for less weight than an M1 Garand; a total of 4.5kg (10lb) including 60 flechette rounds and three grenades.

An initial evaluation of the performance of the single flechette cartridge took place in 1960. This concluded that, despite a single-shot dispersion about double that of a conventional rifle, the burst fire capability and light weight of the gun and ammunition made it considerably more effective than the M14 and that development should be continued. The programme was originally designated APHHW (All-Purpose Hand-Held Weapon) and was renamed SPIW in 1962, by which time the 40mm grenade-launcher requirement had been added.

Four companies developed SPIW prototypes which were tested in 1964. These were:

- AAI, chambered for the 5.6 × 53 XM110 cartridge (using 'piston priming');
- Springfield and Winchester, both using the 5.6 × 44 XM144 round;
- Harrington & Richardson, firing its own 5.6 × 57 plastic-cased cartridge of triangular cross-section, loaded with three XM144-type flechettes.

The H&R was technically the most interesting since the triple-flechette cartridge was designed using the Dardick Tround open chamber principle, and each flechette in the case was simultaneously fired down a separate barrel. However, the three barrels made it too heavy and the mechanism was judged to be unsafe as the cases split open, thus it was rejected immediately.

SPIW flechette cartridges (from left to right): .223 for scale (5.56 × 45); XM144 (5.6 × 44); XM645 (5.6 × 57B); XM216 (5.6 × 44).

Winchester offered a gun with a barrel which recoiled in the stock as the three-shot burst was fired. This idea was later revived in the HK G11 and the AN-94, but on this occasion it was judged to be too complicated and in any case the barrel hit the buffers before the third round was fired. The Springfield Armory's offering was a bullpup using two thirty-round magazines in tandem (the others used sixty-round drums) and was found to be the most reliable and accurate. The AAI was the simplest, lightest and most durable.

The 'piston primer' was an unusually large primer which was meant to be pushed back from the case by gas pressure on firing, thereby unlocking the bolt. It was a neat system, incidentally used by John Garand in the first of his autoloading rifle projects which led to the M1 Garand; however, he used standard cartridges and primers. He had to drop the idea when it was decided to change from a quick-burning to a progressive powder for the .30-06 cartridge, and to firmly crimp the primer in place. The piston primer led to a simple gun mechanism, but the cartridge was even more expensive to make than the other flechette rounds, which were themselves several times the cost of conventional cartridges.

None of the SPIW weapons tested came close to meeting the specification. They particularly failed on reliability and durability, but all were also too heavy and inaccurate, suffered from excessive muzzle flash and blast, overheated, operated at too high a pressure and the cartridges were too fragile and easily dented. There was also concern about tiny glass fragments from the fibreglass sabots injuring the shooter's eyes. Despite this, AAI and Springfield were asked to continue development. In 1966 the survivors were tested again. By this time the XM110 cartridge had been superseded by the 5.6 × 57 XM645, and the XM144 by the 5.6 × 44 XM216, which was wider (the head diameter was increased from 7.8 to 8.5mm) to provide improved propellant capacity, but the results remained poor.

Work on the SPIW continued and resulted in 1968 in a victory of sorts; in a BRL comparison with the M14 and the M16A1 (all firing in burst fire or fully-automatic mode), the SPIW was found to be the easiest to control and produced the highest hit probability. Interestingly, it was most closely challenged in hit probability by the M14 firing the M198 Duplex round. The M16A1 came last, with an experimental two-round burst proving superior to the fully-automatic setting. In January 1969 AAI were awarded a contract to manufacture twenty 'XM19 Rifle, Primer Actuated, Flechette Firing' prototypes, to compare with two other Project SALVO concepts: a .17in sequentially fired bullet (that is, burst fire) rifle, and larger-calibre, multiple flechette loadings. These will be described later. However, the work on the SPIW was all in vain. The weight target proved impossible to meet and the flechette rounds never achieved the accuracy nor the low cost required. Furthermore, by the time the SPIW prototypes were starting to produce reasonable results, over five million M16s had been purchased and it was firmly established as the US Army's new rifle. The last of the SPIWs was the AAI XM70. After that, the project reverted to research and development status for a few years, before being eventually 'removed from immediate consideration' in 1973. This was not the end of the flechette concept, however, as we shall see.

THE SMALL-CALIBRE REVOLUTION
The costly failure of the SPIW project provided the opportunity for an alternative and much simpler approach to prosper. Even before the Hall report was published, experimenters at Aberdeen's BRL and Development and Proof Services (D&PS) had been conducting a small-calibre, high-velocity (SCHV) research programme. Their work, which was used by Hall, focused on the improvements in hit probability which could result from a high-velocity rifle of .22in (5.56mm) or smaller calibre.

From 1952 until 1956, a series of small-calibre cartridges were developed under the auspices of Project SALVO. These included the 'Homologous Series', based on the 7.62 × 51 case but with different calibres, as tabulated below.

All except the .18 were also tested with Duplex loads; in each case, the two bullets weighed more than the Simplex one and so the muzzle velocities were reduced. Even the long .30-06 case was necked to .22 calibre (5.56 × 63): it fired a 3.45g (53gr.) bullet at 1,200m/s (53gr. at 3,940ft/s), and a long-necked Duplex version was also tested firing two 3.24g (50gr.) bullets at 907m/s (2,975ft/s) for the front one and 883m/s

(2,897ft/s) for the rear. The lack of improvement of this over the .22 Homologous may be put down to the fact that the latter was already 'overbore'; there were no further increases in velocity obtainable by increasing the case capacity. At the other end of the scale, the little .22 APG (Aberdeen Proving Ground) Carbine was tested by the BRL. The 5.56 × 33 cartridge, which was developed from a cut-down .222 Remington case rather than being a necked-down .30 Carbine, fired a 2.66g bullet at 950m/s (41gr. at 3,115ft/s).

All of this experimentation resulted in 1957 in a request from the US Continental Army Command to ArmaLite (a division of the Fairchild Engine & Airplane Corporation) for a small-calibre, high-velocity rifle. ArmaLite had previously made a favourable impression with their advanced AR-10 rifle in 7.62 × 51, which had arrived on the scene too late to achieve significant sales, the M14 having been chosen by the US Army and the FN FAL having mopped up most of the rest of the world. Eugene Stoner, the most famous post-war American military gun designer, went to work on the gun and cartridge. He started with the commercial .222 Remington cartridge, introduced in 1950 for shooting small game. A boat-tailed, 3.56g (55gr.) bullet was designed, which the little case could fire at 990m/s (3,250ft/s). Some modifications to improve the case capacity and reduce the high chamber pressures resulted in the slightly longer .222 Special (later renamed .223 Remington to avoid confusion), which, after some competition with the almost identical .224 Winchester, was chosen for the new rifle.

The development of the .223 Remington, and the AR-15 rifle designed to fire it, was complete by 1958 and the Infantry Board tested it in that year in comparison with the M14. In the *Evaluation of Small Calibre High Velocity (SCHV) Rifles* report, the AR-15 was judged superior to the M14. This led to further testing by the Board and the Arctic Test Board, but the AR-15s they tried were in poor condition and did not perform well. The Ordnance Department therefore decided

Homologous Series of Cartridges

Designation	Metric dimensions	Bullet weight (g/gr.)	Muzzle velocity (m/s/ft/s)
.18 Homologous	4.5 × 52	2.24/35	1,293/4,240
.22 Homologous	5.56 × 52	3.46/53	1,200/3,940
.25 Homologous	6.35 × 52	5.24/81	1,050/3,445
.27 Homologous	6.8 × 52	6.52/100	950/3,115

Project SALVO – the conventional cartridges (from left to right): .22/30 (5.56 × 63);
.22 Homologous (5.56 × 52); .25 Homologous (6.35 × 52); .27 Homologous (6.65 × 52);
.22 APG Carbine (5.56 × 33); commercial .222 Remington (5.56 × 43); .223 Remington
(5.56 × 45); .224 Winchester E2 (5.56 × 45); .25 Winchester FA-T 116 (6.35 × 48).

against adopting the rifle and recommended instead that development of a .258in (6.35mm) round should be pursued. Frankford Arsenal, in conjunction with Winchester, did produce several 6.35 SCHV rounds based on the .25 Remington case (a popular choice, as its diameter was in between the 7.62 × 51 and the 5.56 × 45). The FA-T110 case measured 6.35 × 48 and the FA-T125 6.35 × 53. These loaded either one 4.5g (70gr.) at 1,020m/s or two 3.4g (53gr.) bullets, the latter being fired at 790m/s (2,600ft/s) for the front bullet and 747m/s (2,450ft/s) for the rear. However, the decision against the .223 was overturned by further trials in 1959, which again found the AR-15 superior to the M14 and recommended that its development should be pursued as a replacement for the 7.62mm rifle – which had been formally adopted for service only two years before.

These trials did not at first result in orders from the Army and, in fact, the US Air Force placed the first order in 1960 to replace the .30 M2 Carbine used by Strategic Air Command sentries. Adoption by the Army came about almost by accident, owing to the cancellation of M14 production and the need to find a stopgap weapon to tide the Army over until the arrival of the SPIW. A last-ditch effort by Remington to offer the .224 E5, which (like the E4) was based on the fatter .25 Remington case with a rebated rim to fit the AR-15 bolt head and with its total length reduced to fit the action, proved as unsuccessful as their other challenges. The AR-15 was duly ordered.

With the SPIW experiencing continuing and insoluble problems, the AR-15 was now unstoppable; it was redesignated M16 and formally adopted by the USAF in 1964. The US Army simultaneously chose it as a 'limited standard', formally adopting the M16A1 in February 1967. The rest of the history of 'the Black Rifle' is told in the section on American weapons below. The 3.56g ball loading for the .223 Remington cartridge was formally adopted as the 5.56mm M193. As a result of experience in Vietnam, there was much controversy about its effectiveness even at short range, in terms of its capacity to disable an opponent immediately. Stories of dramatic lethality were countered by tales of a serious lack of stopping power by comparison with the 7.62 × 51. What was agreed by all, however, was that the long-range performance of the little bullet was poor, so the 7.62mm hung on in service, primarily in MGs and sniper rifles, but the M14 was also retained by the USN.

The selection of the M16 did not end ammunition experiments. In 1962, Frankford Arsenal developed a Duplex loading for the little 5.56 × 45 cartridge, with bullets weighing 2.1 and 2.2g (33 and 34gr.) being fired at up to 810m/s (2,760ft/s). This idea never seems to go away, as it was revived in the late 1980s by Olin for the Advanced Combat Rifle trials, this time with 2.3 and 2.1g bullets (35 and 33gr.) fired at up to 880m/s (2,900ft/s). A different approach was taken in 1965 with the conversion of five XM16E1s to fire a necked-down 4.32 × 46 cartridge. Some 5.56 × 45 ammunition was also ordered with .17 calibre (4.3mm) saboted bullets for comparison. The ultimate result of this was the burst-fire AAI Serial Bullet Rifle of 1976. Its 4.32 × 46 cartridge pushed the little 28gr. (1.18g) bullet out at 4,000ft/s (1,220m/s).

The 5.56 × 45 has also been necked down in Germany to create the very similar 4.3 × 45 (although this was really to test ballistics as a stage in the development of the caseless G11), with even smaller calibres being produced experimentally. Unusual bullets have been tried, such as the South African Monad, a lightweight, high-velocity loading intended for short-range use and inspired by the French THV pistol bullets.

For many years the 5.56mm/M16 combination was used by the USA (and purchased by several other countries) but not formally adopted by NATO. The next stage in the small-calibre revolution occurred in the trials held between 1977 and 1980 to adopt a new

Micro calibres (from left to right): .12 US (3 × 47); 3.5mm FN (3.5 × 50.5); 4.3mm German (4.3 × 45); .17 US (4.32 × 46); 4.6mm HK/CETME (4.6 × 36); 4.85mm British (4.85 × 49); 5.56mm FABRL (5.56 × 38); 5.56 × 45 with MONAD bullet.

NATO cartridge to supplement the 7.62 × 51 as a second small arms round. This requirement made it effectively impossible for any intermediate general-purpose round (which might have replaced the 7.62 × 51) to be proposed, and meant that only cartridges substantially smaller than the 7.62mm would be considered. Individual weapons (that is, rifles) chambered for the new round were expected to have an effective range of 300–400m, but the same ammunition was to be used in a Light Support Weapon which needed to reach out to 800 m (875yd). Following a development programme lasting from 1970 to 1978, the British contender was chambered for a new 4.85 × 49 cartridge, which was simply the 5.56mm necked down to take a smaller, but relatively heavy, bullet in the interest of improved long-range performance: it fired a 3.58g bullet at 950m/s (56gr. at 3,115ft/s). It performed well, but not sufficiently better than the 5.56mm to prevail.

These trials resulted, to no one's surprise, in the selection of the 5.56mm as the next NATO cartridge with the designation 5.56 × 45 NATO, but in a different loading. America submitted the XM777, which had a steel tip to improve penetration but still weighed 3.53g (54.5gr.), but the Belgian SS109 bullet was chosen, which also contained a hard steel element near the tip (technically making it a semi-armour piercing or SAP round) but was heavier at 4.0g (62gr.). The muzzle velocity dropped to around 930m/s (3,050ft/s) but the loss of velocity at long range was reduced. In combination, these changes provided a better long-range performance and significantly improved penetration. The US-made version of this loading was designated M855 and remains in American service as the standard ball round to this day. The Americans achieved something of a pyrrhic victory in this competition: they had hoped to save money by being able to continue with their existing M16A1, but the heavier SS109 bullet could not be stabilized by the slow-twist rifling of their existing gun and therefore they had to introduce the modified M16A2 in any case.

Some limited use has recently been made by American Special Forces and the USMC of the 5.56 mm Mk 262 loading. This features a heavy, streamlined target bullet of 5 grams (77 grains) fired at 832 m/s (2,730 fps) from a 16 inch (406 mm) barrel, to further improve the long-range performance. It has also been discovered that this bullet fragments violently at velocities down to 610 m/s (2,000 fps), making it more lethal at any distance. From a 16 inch (406 mm) barrel it will fragment out to 300 m (250 m from the 14.5 inch – 368 mm – M4 barrel) and when zeroed at 200 m it shoots 50 mm high between 100–125 m and 220 mm low at 300 m. However, given the continuing controversy over the effectiveness of small bullets compared with larger calibres, its effectiveness will need to be clearly demonstrated in action before everyone will be convinced, and there have been some reports that performance in action has been disappointing.

The next development in the small-calibre revolution was the surprise adoption by the USSR of a new 5.45 × 39 7N6 cartridge in the Kalashnikov AK-74 series. As the designation suggests, this was introduced in the mid 1970s to replace the 7.62 × 39 round, although even in the Soviet army replacement was gradual and the older cartridge does, of course, remain in widespread service around the world. Despite the similar case length, the 5.45 is not a necked-down version of its ancestor, but uses an entirely new case with a smaller diameter (the head measures 9.97mm, as opposed to 11.30mm for the 7.62 × 39). The steel-cored, 3.42g (53gr.) bullet has a hollow tip, which allowed the designers to incorporate a long, tapered nose of excellent aerodynamic form. The muzzle velocity is 900m/s (2,950ft/s). The long bullet requires a steep 1 in 7.7 rifling twist to stabilize it and the leading edge of the rifling lands had to be given a bevelled edge to minimize the distortion of the bullet.

Some confusion was caused in the 1980s and the 1990s by the announcement of new Russian cartridges in 6mm calibre. These began with the 6 × 53, with other experimental versions in 6 × 57 and 6 × 58, but most interest appeared to have focused on a 6 × 49 which emerged around 1990. However, none of these were intended for assault rifles; they were high-power cartridges – achieving as much as 1,150m/s (3,770ft/s) with bullets of around 5g (77gr.) – meant to replace the venerable 7.62 × 54R in MGs and sniper rifles. It appears that work on these lapsed in the mid 1990s.

Some unusual developments have seen service in Russia, however, including the 9 × 39 round for a silenced assault rifle (including an AP loading which can penetrate a 6mm steel plate), and even dart-firing assault rifles for use under water, one of which can also be used on land. More details of these are included in the section on Russian armaments below.

A further surprise emerged from China in the late 1990s in the form of the Type 95 rifle and LMG in a new 5.8 × 42 cartridge, which followed much experimentation, including 6 and 6.2mm calibres. China had previously relied on weapons of Russian origin and the development of a new cartridge instead of the simple

The 9 × 39 AP round demonstrating its ability to punch neat holes through a 6mm steel plate at 100m.

adoption of the 5.45 × 39 was unexpected. This development can probably be attributed to political rather than technical factors, although the Chinese claim that their new round outperforms both the 5.45 × 39 and the 5.56 × 45, with penetration superior to that of the SS109, a flatter trajectory and a higher retained velocity and energy down range. As with the other modern, small-calibre cartridges, it is intended to be controllable in an assault rifle but also to have a good long-range performance; it is even chambered in a sniper rifle and a belt-fed GPMG. The performance of the 5.8mm is, however, much in line with that of the SS109, since it has a 4.15g (64gr.) bullet fired at 930m/s (3,050ft/s: increased to 970m/s/3,182ft/s from the longer-barrelled LMG). If the Chinese performance claims are accurate, the bullet presumably has a better aerodynamic form than the SS109, although it is unlikely to better the 5.45mm or the 5.56mm Mk 262 in this respect.

By this point Western assault rifle ammunition development appeared to have fossilised, with the

The 9 × 39 SP6 round (with AP bullet) on the right, compared with the 7.62 × 39 (left) and the 5.45 × 39 (centre).

5.56 × 45 seemingly assured of an indefinite future until replaced with some entirely different technology. However, it appears that the continuing grumbles about the effectiveness of the little cartridge have had some effect, as the American SOCOM (Special Operations Command) is investigating an entirely new cartridge to replace the 5.56 mm in at least some applications. After testing calibres ranging from 6 to 7.62 mm, they settled on a 6.8 × 43 (designated the 6.8 mm Remington SPC – Special Purpose Cartridge) as having the best blend of characteristics. The dimensions of the new round have been constrained by the need to restrict the overall length to that which will permit its use in standard 5.56 × 45 actions, as the intention is that existing weapons can be converted by changing the barrel and upper receiver. It was originally hoped to use existing 5.56mm magazines with modifications to the lips and follower and a reduction in capacity from 30 to 25 (due to the wider case diameter – the 6.8 mm is based on the .30 Remington case, like so many previous efforts), but in practice this does not seem to be satisfactory so it is likely that purpose-designed magazines will be required.

The new 6.8 × 43 fires a 7.45 gram (115 grain) bullet at 808 m/s (2,650 fps) from a 420 mm (16.5 inch) barrel for a muzzle energy of 2,430 joules (1,800 ft lbs), very similar to the 'ideal' .270 / 6.85 mm cartridge discussed in the previous chapter. The bullet weight is slightly lighter, the muzzle velocity a little higher. This may simply be due to the need to restrict the overall length of the cartridge which effectively prevents the use of long heavy bullets with a good BC. Despite this limitation, the 6.8 mm bullet's advantage over the 5.56 mm SS109 of 55% greater energy at the muzzle is extended to 84% by 550 metres. From a longer barrel it achieves 850 m/s (2,800 fps) and the trajectory matches that of the 7.62 × 51 out to 500 m. However, the main purpose of the new round appears to be to improve the terminal ballistics at typical assault rifle ranges of 300m; the bullet will reportedly fragment while tumbling at least to this range, and possibly further.

The new Chinese 5.8 × 42 between the 5.45 × 39 (left) and the 5.56 × 45 (right). (courtesy Gene Whitehead)

The 6.8 × 43 Remington SPC (right) next to a 5.56 × 45. (courtesy Gemtech)

Full-calibre assault rifle rounds – service and experimental (from left to right): 7.92 × 57 (for scale); 7.92mm Kurz (7.92 × 33); 7.62 × 39 Russian; 7.62 × 45 Czech; 7.9mm CETME Model 53 with alloy bullet (7.92 × 40); 7.62 × 51 with CETME bullet; 7mm Danish Otterup (7 × 36); 7.65mm French Model 48 (7.65 × 35); 7.5mm French CRBA (7.5 × 43); 7.5 × 38 Swiss.

At the time of writing the future of the 6.8 × 43 is unclear, as no official statement has been issued. It is being developed for Special Forces only, but if it is adopted and proves successful it is not difficult to foresee its use spreading throughout the US armed forces. This could well be followed in due course by another NATO competition which will result, to universal astonishment, in the selection of the 6.8 mm as the new NATO small arms cartridge. If that happens, the outcome will at least be a very much better rifle round than those contests which produced the 7.62 × 51 and 5.56 × 45, with the potential to replace both of these cartridges. Some developers are promoting an alternative cartridge, the 6.5 mm Grendel, which is based on the slightly fatter 7.62 × 39 case, as this permits the use of longer bullets with a superior long-range performance, even better than the 7.62 × 51. However, the development of the 5.56 mm Mk 262 loading, which can be used in unmodified weapons, may prove a serious threat to the adoption of any new round.

OTHER EXPERIMENTAL AMMUNITION

Despite the domination of the 5.56 × 45 NATO round in much of the world and of the 7.62 × 39/5.45 × 39 in most of the rest, experiments with new assault rifle ammunition concepts have continued, even with the occasional competition being held. Some of the experiments have been with conventional ammunition, others have been more exotic. The key experimental programmes which resulted (however tortuously) in the adoption of a new cartridge have been discussed earlier, so this will concentrate on abortive efforts.

An intriguing variation on conventional ammunition design emerged from Spain in the 1950s, as a result of the work of the German ballistician Dr Voss, who went to work for CETME after the Second World War. The cartridges, developed in 7.92 × 40 and 7.62 × 40 calibres, were basically standard FCAR rounds, but what was different was the use of very light bullets with aluminium (or in one case plastic) cores. Typical bullet weights were 5.2–6.8g (80–105gr.), with velocities similar to those of the standard NATO loading. These certainly delivered light recoil but would normally lose velocity and effectiveness quickly. In the Voss design this was offset by making the bullets very long and of an extremely refined aerodynamic form. The degree of success achieved is unclear, but the ammunition was not adopted.

Many different experimental but conventional cartridges for assault rifles have been developed in several countries in the endless search for some marginal advantage over existing ammunition. These were mainly concerned with calibres smaller than 5.56mm, presumably to see how small a cartridge could become while still remaining militarily useful, the advantages of light weight and low recoil proving tempting.

The experimenting countries included the USA, with the .17in (4.32 × 46) FAT 216 for the late 1960s Serial Bullet Rifle and at least two FABRL rounds of the early 1970s, the 5.56 × 38 and the 4.32 × 40 (FABRL probably originally stood for Frankford Arsenal and Aberdeen's Ballistic Research Laboratories, but was later explained as 'Future Ammunition for Burst Rifle Launch'). Reducing recoil was at a premium, so the light bullet/high velocity approach was followed, with long-range performance being provided by making the bullets highly aerodynamic, with 'spire points'. The 5.56 × 38 fired a 2.4g bullet at 1,180m/s (37gr. at 3,870ft/s).

Belgium produced a 4.5 × 44 in the 1950s (the .280 necked down) and a number of experimentals in the 1970s; this was obviously a good time for ammunition research, as it was clear that the 7.62 × 51 was due to be replaced as the standard NATO rifle calibre. These followed the usual small-calibre route and were made by necking down the 5.56 × 45 case, to 4.5, 3.5 and even 3.25mm. Germany similarly produced 4.9, 4.5 and 4.3mm versions of the same case.

Not all of the experimental cartridges were small. French experiments in the late 1940s with 7.65 × 35 and 7.65 × 42, extending into the 1950s with 7.62 × 42 and 9 × 40 rounds, have already been mentioned. These were basically similar to the existing FCAR rounds such as the AK 47's. In the early 1960s there were German experiments with a 6.5 × 43 and a 7.62 × 40, although it seems that these were just test cartridges with no weapon in mind for them (a matter for regret since the 6.5mm looked useful).

Perhaps the most interesting and instructive series of post-war experiments took place in the United Kingdom in the late 1960s and the early 1970s, when a thorough attempt was made to design an ideal military small-arms round using a lighter cartridge with less recoil than that of the 7.62 × 51. This started with calculations of the bullet energy required to inflict a disabling wound on soldiers with various levels of protection. The energy varied depending on the calibre, since a larger calibre required more energy to push it through armour; for example, it was calculated that, while a 7.62mm bullet would need 700J to penetrate contemporary helmets and heavy body armour, a 7mm would require 650J, a 6.25mm 580J, a 5.5mm 500J and a 4.5mm 420J. These figures apply at the target; muzzle energies would clearly have to be much higher, depending on the required range and the ballistic characteristics of the bullet.

A range of 'optimum solutions' for cartridges of different calibres was calculated; in all cases the trajectory needed to be at least as good as that of the 7.62 × 51. These resulted in muzzle energies ranging from 825J in 4.5mm to 2,470 in 7mm. More work led to a preferred solution: a 6.25mm calibre firing bullets from 5.9 to 7.1g (91 to 110gr.). Eventually, a bullet of 6.48g (100gr.) at 817m/s (2,680ft/s) was chosen, for a muzzle energy of 2,160J (1,600ft lb); incidentally very similar to that of the 'ideal' 6.35mm round outlined in the previous chapter. The old 7mm EM2 case was necked down to 6.25mm for live firing experiments, although, had the calibre been adopted, a new, slimmer case would probably have been designed. Ammunition was manufactured from 1969 to 1971. Tests revealed that the 6.25mm cartridge matched the 7.62 × 51 in penetration out to 600m (660yd) and remained effective for a considerably longer distance (the SD of .236 being slightly better than that of the bigger cartridge), while producing recoil closer to that of the 5.56 × 45. However, the steadily increasing use of the 5.56 × 45 round meant that the 6.25mm stood no chance of being selected by NATO, and so development effort switched to the 4.85 × 49 based on the 5.56's case.

Immediately after the British 6.25 mm experiments, the US Army identified a need for a cartridge for an LMG which could reach out further than the 5.56 mm M193. While not strictly intended for assault rifles, its use may well have spread to them if adopted. Various experiments resulted in the 6 × 45 SAW (Squad Automatic Weapon) which in its XM732 ball loading fired a relatively heavy 6.8 gram (105 grains) bullet at a medium velocity of 769 m/s (2,520 fps) for optimum long-range performance; it was still delivering 330 joules (250 ft lbs) at 915 metres (1,000 yards). The SAW was eventually abandoned in favour of the promised better long-range loading for the 5.56 × 45 (which eventually emerged as the SS109) and because fielding two similar calibres at squad level was felt to be inefficient.

The Swiss experimented with at least two assault rifle cartridges from the late 1960s before adopting the 5.56mm NATO: the 5.6 × 48 Eiger and 6.45 × 48 GP 80. The 5.56mm, developed between 1967 and 1977, fired a 3.7g bullet at 1,050m/s (57gr. at 3,445ft/s) for 2,040J (1,510ft lb), considerably more than the 5.56mm NATO. This was abandoned in favour of the 6.45mm GP 80, which managed to propel its 6.3g bullet at 900m/s (97gr. at 2,950ft/s) for 2,550J (1,890ft lb). With the benefit of hindsight, a heavier bullet at a more moderate velocity would have provided a better general-purpose loading for the 6.45mm. In the event, the GP 80 was rejected in favour of the 5.56 × 45 after extensive troop trials.

Despite concerns about the effectiveness of the 5.56 × 45, some experimenters have worked with even smaller calibres. The American .18 (4.5mm) Homologous and .17 SBR, and the British 4.85mm have already been described, and 'micro calibres' of 3.5 and 3mm (and possibly more, or less) have been tried, mainly during the 1960s and the 1970s. It is difficult to imagine that such cartridges could do anything to improve on the 5.56mm's range and effectiveness. There is also the capillary problem with the really small bores: any water which gets into the barrel will be difficult to dislodge. This is, in fact, a potential problem with any bores of less .25in (6.35mm) calibre; early .223 AR-15 barrels had to be strengthened after bursts caused by water remaining in the barrel.

One cartridge which had a weapon developed and

The search for the ideal calibre (from left to right): 5.56 × 45 (for scale); 6 × 45 SAW (steel case); 6 × 50 SAW (light alloy case); 6.25 × 43 British; 6.5 × 43 German; Swiss 5.56mm Eiger (5.6 × 48); Swiss 6.45mm GP80 (6.45 × 48).

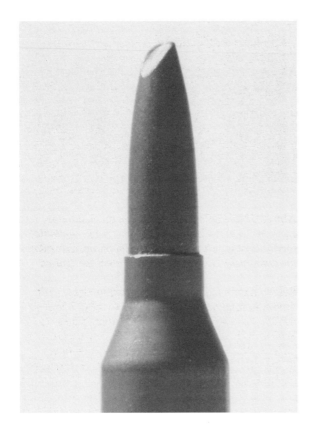

Close-up of the bullet of the 4.6 × 36 HK/CETME, showing the Löffelspitz 'spoon tip' bullet.

marketed for it was the 4.6 × 36 HK, for the HK-36 (not to be confused with the later HK G36) assault rifle. This used the *Löffelspitz* 'spoon tip' bullet developed for CETME's 4.56mm CIP-613 to encourage rapid tumbling. Bullets were a 2.7g soft core fired at 850m/s (41.7gr. at 2,789ft/s) and a 3.5g hard core at 780m/s (54gr. at 2,559ft/s). CETME manufactured the same cartridge.

THE EXOTICS

Most of the attempts to produce exotic assault rifle ammunition have taken place since World War 2, but there was one wartime experiment which deserves mention. This was the .27 BTC (Broadway Trust Company) cartridge, the Trust being set up Sir Dennis Burney (more famous for developing large-calibre, recoilless cannon and the 'squash head' shells for them), ICI and the Ministry of Supply to develop weapons for the Army. The .27 BTC was developed in 1944/45 and contained two interesting innovations. The first was the adoption of a 'high-low' pressure system, in which the propellant gas first fills an expansion chamber, in order to provide a more even pressure curve. In the BTC rifle this was achieved by making the central part of the chamber much wider than the cartridge, and perforating the cartridge case to enable the gas to escape into it. The other novelty was the use of a differential recoil system, in which the barrel and the bolt group were free to recoil in the stock, with the gun firing as they moved forwards, thereby evening out the recoil pulse. This was not conducive to accuracy, and, in the event, the project was unsuccessful since aspects of the firing cycle required precise timing, which was not achieved.

More recent exotic experiments have proceeded in different directions, with different aims in mind. Multiple bullet loadings in a conventional case have already been mentioned. A "salvo-squeezebore" (firing several stacked conical projectiles which were squeezed down to a smaller calibre by a muzzle attachment) was developed for the .50 calibre M2 HMG as a result of Vietnam experience in order to repel short-range ambushes, but was not adopted. A version of this appeared in 7.62 mm NATO, with three steel segments which were squeezed down to .15 inch (3.8 mm) calibre but the evaluation proved unsatisfactory.

There were also several attempts at a multiple-flechette cartridge, particularly in the context of the American 'Future Rifle Program' of the late 1960s. Winchester developed a 7.62 × 51 loading with three 10.2gr. (0.66g) flechettes held within a puller sabot, while another effort used purpose-designed 9.53/10mm straight, belted cases containing between three and five flechettes. By late 1970 a 9.53mm alloy-cased cartridge had been developed; this fired four flechettes at 1,290m/s (4,240ft/s). Amron Aerojet also produced a .330in round which contained three flechettes within its 8.38 × 69 light-alloy case.

Slightly less exotic than the flechettes was the Belgian Schirnecker series, featuring straight, steel cases firing saboted, spin-stabilized bullets in several calibres. Other experiments have looked at different cartridge types to suit novel gun designs. Perhaps the most bizarre was the 'folded' ammunition, stemming from a desire to make the cartridge as short as possible to speed up the firing cycle. These were made in many calibres, including 5.56mm. Another try was the Hughes Lockless (made in calibres from 5.56 to 30mm) which concealed the bullet within a flat, rectangular, plastic case. This was designed to slot sideways into a simple gun action.

The closest to adoption of all of the exotics was the caseless cartridge, in the form of the Heckler & Koch G11 rifle. It was originally designed in 4.3mm calibre, but it was found that its efficiency was reduced by turbulence effects in the bore, and thus it was increased to 4.7mm. The bullet is almost entirely buried in a block of solid propellant, with the primer attached. It was about to be adopted by the German Army to replace the 7.62mm G3 when the Cold War ended, the Berlin Wall came down and military re-equipment spending promptly halted. HK were financially ruined by the cancellation of the G11 and fell into the hands of Royal Ordnance, where they earned their keep by solving the long-running problems of the British Army's SA80 rifle, before being returned to German ownership.

Caseless ammunition has obvious benefits. It is much lighter and more compact (no metal case) and it is unnecessary to arrange for the extraction and ejection of the fired case (perhaps the principal source of weapon jams), which also means that it is easier to seal against dirt getting into the mechanism. The disadvantages are that the ammunition is much more vulnerable to damage (which HK got around by supplying it in sealed, plastic, see-through packs which

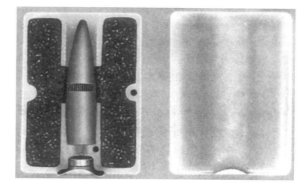

Above *Hughes Lockless cartridge opened out to show the interior layout. The primer kicks the bullet forwards out of the case, which simultaneously allows the compressed charge on either side to be ignited.*

Below *Exotic ammunition (from left to right): .330 Amron Aerojet triple flechette (8.38 × 69); 5.56 × 45 APDS; 4.5 × 46 Schirnecker subcalibre; 5.56 × 35 Schirnecker subcalibre; 5.56mm Hughes Lockless (5.56 × 30); 5.56mm Folded (5.56 × 25); 9/4mm Kaltmann subcalibre (9 × 62); 4.7mm G11 caseless (4.7 × 21).*

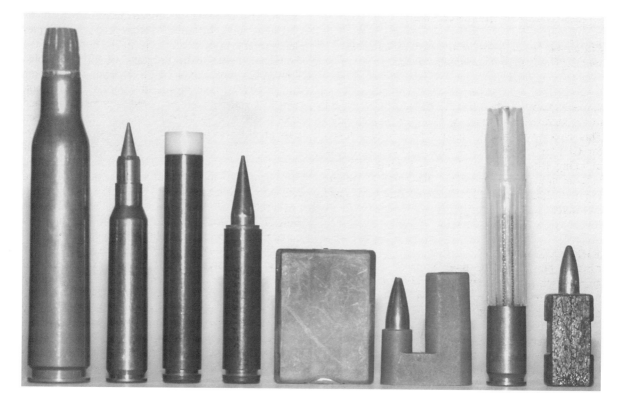

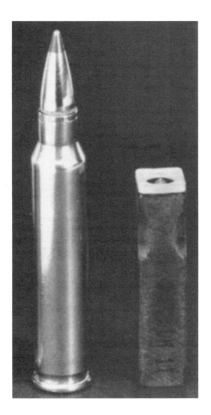

clipped directly to the gun) and the propellant is more likely to 'cook-off' in a hot chamber, a problem exacerbated by the fact that a brass cartridge case makes an efficient job of transporting heat from the gun. Despite this, Dynamit Nobel greatly reduced this problem for the G11 by developing a new, heat-resistant propellant, and the result was a battle-worthy weapon.

Incidentally, German caseless cartridge development had taken place in the Second World War, including tests with a possibly Hungarian-developed 8 mm round which consisted of a case made from solid propellant, containing loose propellant.

An interesting rival to the HK G11 in the late 1970s was Rheinmetall's *'Treibkäfigpatrone Kaliber 9/4 mm mit unterkalibrigem 4 mm Geschoss'*, generally known as the 9/4 mm Kaltmann after the designer. This appeared to be a plastic 9 mm rifle cartridge; however, the projectile part included a 4 mm subprojectile. On firing, the projectile exited the barrel, separating from its sabot in the approved fashion. Not to be left out of the act, the rest of the cartridge case followed it up the barrel, being ejected from the muzzle a fraction of a second later. All that was left behind was the base and primer, which were intended to be combustible. A muzzle velocity of 1,100 m/s was claimed for the 3.1 g bullet (48 grains at 3,600 fps), but the combustible base was never perfected, a metal one (either a 9×19 pistol case or a cut-down 5.56×45) with a plastic upper body being used in tests.

The single flechette weapons which were abandoned along with the SPIW project of the 1960s were

A different pattern of caseless ammunition for the 4.7mm G11 with the bullet concealed within the propellant, next to a 5.56×45; several types were tried.

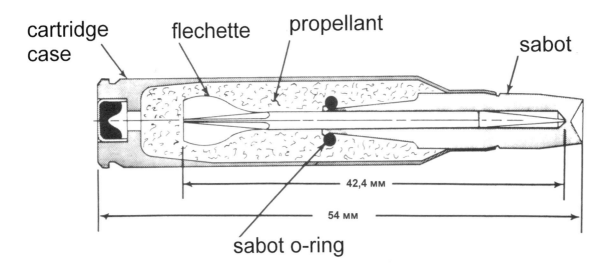

A sectioned view of the AAI flechette round, in a 5.56×45 case.

revived by two of the competitors in the Advanced Combat Rifle (ACR) contest of the late 1980s. This contest was intended to improve the poor hit probability achieved by average soldiers in the stress of battle, which, when using the M16, was only guaranteed (pH = 1.0) at up to 45m, and dropped to a pH of 0.1 (one shot in ten) by 220m. The theory, a revival of the Project Salvo concept, was that firing three slightly dispersed shots in quick succession should enable the pH to be doubled, and several different weapon concepts were prepared.

The Colt ACR contender was simply an improved M16A2 firing a Duplex cartridge as already described, HK submitted the caseless G11, while AAI and Steyr offered weapons firing flechette rounds. The Steyr SCF (synthetic cased flechette) ammunition was plastic-cased, and the 0.76g (11.7gr.) flechette, which started at 1,500m/s (4,920ft/s) at the muzzle, was still travel-

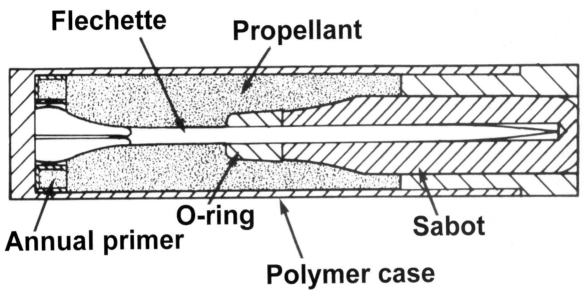

Flechette · **Propellant** · **O-ring** · **Annual primer** · **Sabot** · **Polymer case**

Above *A sectioned view of the Steyr SCF flechette round.*

Below *Disassembled Steyr SCF components.*

Below *The 5.56 × 45 M855 loading, next to the Duplex ACR load.*

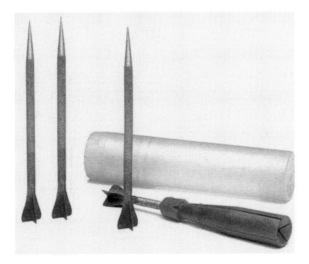

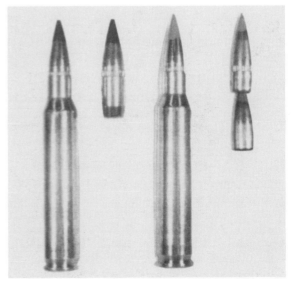

Some sectioned cartridges courtesy of Paul Smith

7.62 x 47: USA Aluminium alloy case with graphite coating. Note the washer within the primer acting as a gas check upon firing.

7.62 x 25: (actually x24) Chinese sub-sonic loading for the Type 64 SMG.

5.56 x 38 FABRL: Note steel and plastic cored bullet of a fine aerodynamic shape.

5.6 x 53 XM110 SPIW flechette round. Note magnesium alloy sabot and two-part piston primer.

4.6 x 36 CETME: the 'spoon tip' loading with lead core.

7.62 x 51 CETME, with lead and plastic core. Note the extremely fine aerodynamic shape.

.22-06 SALVO Note canted base of rear projectile to encourage it to follow a separate path from the front one.

ling at over 1,200m/s at 1,000m (3,940ft/s at 1,090yd), giving an almost 'ray gun' directness. Incidentally, the SCF projectile including sabot weighed 1.36g/21gr., giving an indication of the propulsive efficiency lost in the sabot. Although all of the weapons apparently performed well and did increase the hit probability, none of them managed to meet the stated aim of doubling it.

Despite all these experiments and the growth of interest in different approaches to small arms, focusing on grenade launchers firing air-burst munitions in order to increase the hit probability at long range, there does not appear to be any immediate threat to the dominance of 'intermediate' cartridges of conventional design.

Part II

THE WEAPONS

Above *FARA.*

Left *A female soldier of the Austrian army poses with her Stg.77 rifle.*

ARGENTINA

Argentina's first post-war, self-loading, military rifle was the Belgian FN FAL, which has been produced in several different versions at the ordnance factory in Rosario. The standard rifle is the *Fusil Automatico Liviano Modelo IV*, virtually identical to the FAL Model 50-00. FN's FAL Model 50-64 is also made, with some slight differences in dimensions as the *Fusil Automatico Modelo Para III*; this has the standard length barrel but a side-folding butt. Finally, the heavy barrel FN FAL Model 50-41, fitted with a bipod and again with minor differences, is made as the *Fusil Automatico Pesado Modelo II*.

In the early 1980s Argentina developed its own selective fire rifle in 5.56 × 45; the FARA 83. Production began in 1984 but only about 1,000 were initially made. These were supplemented by other small production batches, but manufacture has now ceased.

FARA 83

Calibre: 5.56 × 45
Action: gas-operated, rotating bolt
Overall length: 1,000mm (745mm butt folded)
Barrel length: 452mm
Weight: 3.95kg
Magazine capacity: 30 rounds
Rate of fire: 750–800 rpm

The FARA is a conventional design made from metal pressings and steel forgings, with GRP used for the foregrip and the side-folding stock. A gas piston system is used, with a two-lug rotating bolt. A bipod is optionally available, along with a modified foregrip to allow it to fold away. The sights are adjustable for 400, 200 or 100m via a three-position drum, the shortest range setting included tritium inserts for poor-light shooting (a tritium foresight is also fitted and can be raised into position when required). The gun was manufactured by *Fabrica Militar Fray Luis Beltran*.

AUSTRIA

Austria always was an advanced industrial country, with significant arms production capabilities. After the end of World War II, Austria looked for a new military rifle and eventually adopted the Belgian FN FAL design, in 7.62 × 51 NATO, as the Stg.58 (Stg = *Sturmgewehr* or assault rifle). The Stg.58 was produced at the most famous Austrian arms factory, at Steyr. From the late 1960s Steyr, along with Austrian army, developed a new, small-calibre (5.56 × 45), modular weapon with a bullpup layout, which was finally adopted by the Austrian military in 1977 as the Stg.77. Since then it has become famous as the Steyr AUG. During the 1980s Steyr gradually improved the AUG and sold manufacturing licences and complete rifles to numerous countries.

The Steyr AUG (*Armee Universal Gewehr* = Universal Army Rifle) was developed by the Austrian Steyr-Daimler-Puch company (now the Steyr-Mannlicher AG & Co.kg) in close co-operation with the Austrian Army. The major design is attributed to the three men – Horst Wesp, Karl Wagner and Karl Möser, who developed most of the rifle's features. From the Austrian Office of Military Technology the project was supervised by Col Walter Stoll. After adoption by the Austrian Army in 1977, production of the Stg.77 (Assault rifle, model of 1977) began in 1978. Since then, the AUG has gained serious popularity, being adopted by the armed forces of Australia, Austria, New Zealand, Oman, Malaysia, Saudi Arabia, Ireland and others. It has also been purchased by several security and law enforcement agencies world-wide, including the US Coast Guard. The Steyr AUG can be considered as the most commercially successful bullpup assault rifle to date. Since 1997, Steyr-Mannlicher has produced an updated version of the AUG, the AUG A2. In general, the AUG is known for its good ergonomics, decent accuracy and good reliability.

Some said that the AUG rifle was revolutionary in many respects when it first appeared, but this is not true. In fact, it is a clever combination of the various previously known ideas, assembled into one sound, reliable and aesthetically attractive package. Let us look at this a little closer; the bullpup configuration: the Steyr AUG is not the first military bullpup ever devised, in fact, the British Enfield EM-2 and the Soviet Korobov TKB-408 bullpup assault rifle preceded the AUG by some twenty-five to thirty years. The French FAMAS bullpup also appeared on the scene at the very same time as the AUG. Plastic firearm housing: another Soviet experimental bullpup design, the Korobov TKB-022, had plastic housing as early as 1962, and the FAMAS rifle, again, had this same feature at the same time as the AUG did. Telescope sight as standard: the British EM-2 bullpup rifle of the late 1940s, as well as the experimental Canadian FN FAL prototypes of early 1950s, also featured low-magnification telescope sights as their prime sighting equipment. A modular design: the first systems, consisting of several firearms based on the same receiver and action (automatic rifle, light machine gun, carbine) were originally developed in the 1920s in France by Rossignol and in the Soviet Russia by

Fedorov, and successfully implemented in the American Stoner 63 system. Considering all of these, the AUG can be described as a logical development of various well known ideas, and a really successful one.

During the same time Steyr also participated in some advanced development projects, such as the American ACR (Advanced Combat Rifle) programme, but, apparently, without any commercial success. The ACR programme was started by the US Army in the late 1980s with the main goal being to improve the hit probability of the average infantry soldier by at least 100 per cent compared with his success with the M16A2. During these trials, held in the early 1990s, some new and existing designs from several companies were tested, with varied success, but no one achieved the 100 per cent improvement over the existing M16A2 rifle, and so the programme was terminated and all participating designs were frozen. One of the most interesting designs was produced by Steyr-Mannlicher, as described below.

STEYR STG.77/AUG

Calibre: 5.56 × 45 NATO
Action: gas-operated, rotating bolt
Overall length: 805mm (with standard 508mm barrel)
Barrel length: 508mm (also 350mm SMG, 407mm Carbine or 621mm LMG heavy barrel)
Weight: 3.8kg unloaded (with standard 508mm barrel)
Magazines: 30 or 42 rounds box magazines
Rate of fire: 650 rpm
Effective range of fire: 450–500m with standard assault rifle barrel

The Steyr AUG is a gas-operated, magazine-fed, selective fire rifle of bullpup layout, built around the aluminium-casting receiver, with steel reinforcement inserts. One such insert is used to provide the locking to the removable barrels and the rotating bolt, thus relieving the receiver from most of the firing stress. Other inserts are used as bearings for the bolt-carrier guide rods.

The AUG uses a short piston stroke, with the gas piston mounted inside the compact gas block, which is fixed to the barrel. The gas cylinder is offset down and to the right from the barrel. The gas piston has its own return spring, contained inside the gas block. The gas system features a three-positions gas regulator, which allows for two open positions (for normal and fouled conditions) and one closed position (for launching rifle grenades). The gas block also contains a barrel fix/release lock and a front grip hinge. Each barrel has

eight lugs, which lock into the steel insert in the receiver, and there are four basic barrel patterns for the AUG as listed above. Each barrel is fitted with the flash suppressor, and the heavy 621mm LMG barrel also is fitted with a lightweight folding bipod. There is no bayonet lug on Austrian service rifles, but one can be installed if required.

The barrel replacement procedure takes only few seconds (assuming that the shooter has the spare barrel handy). To remove the barrel, one must take off the magazine and clear the rifle by operating the cocking handle. Then, grasping the barrel by the front grip, push the barrel-retaining button at the gas block and rotate the barrel and pull it out of the rifle. To install a new barrel, simply push the barrel down all the way into the front of the receiver and then rotate it until it locks. The rifle now is ready to be loaded and fired.

The bolt system consists of the bolt carrier, which has two large, hollow, guide rods attached to its front part. The left rod also serves as a link to the charging handle and the right rod serves as the action rod, which transmits the impulse from the gas piston to the bolt carrier. The rotating bolt has seven locking lugs, a claw extractor and a plunger-type, spring-loaded ejector. The standard bolt has its extractor on the right side, to facilitate right-side ejection, but left-side bolts (with mirrored positions of extractor and ejector) are available for those who need left-side ejection. The two return springs are located behind the bolt carrier, around the two spring guide rods, that are located inside the bolt-carrier guide rods. The cocking handle is located at the left side of the gun and normally does not reciprocate when the gun is fired, but it can be solidly engaged to the bolt group if required by depressing the small button on the charging handle. On the latest AUG A2 variant, the charging handle folds up and is of a slightly different shape. The AUG action features a bolt stop device, which holds the bolt group open after the last round of ammunition from the magazine is fired. To release the bolt after replacing the magazine, the charging handle must be pulled.

The hammer unit is made as a separate assembly and almost entirely of plastic (including the hammer itself); only the springs and pins are steel. The hammer unit is located in the butt and is linked to the sliding trigger by the dual trigger bars. The safety is of the cross-bolt, push-button type and located above the pistol grip. There is no separate fire-mode selector on the AUG rifles; instead, the trigger itself is used to control the mode of fire. Pulling it half way back will produce single shots, while the full pull will produce automatic

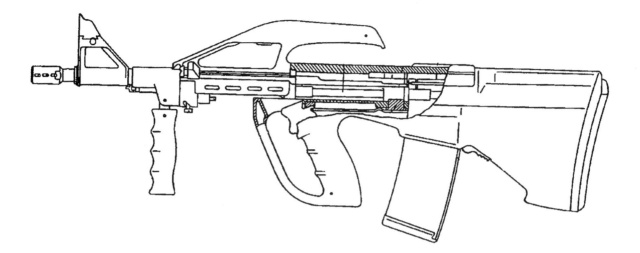

Above *Drawing of a prototype AUG rifle, c.1971.*

The Stg.77/AUG rifle in standard configuration.

Steyr AUG rifle with set of barrels, from to bottom: the SAW barrel with integral bipod; rifle with standard barrel; the carbine barrel; the submachine gun barrel.

fire. The enlarged trigger guard encloses the whole hand and allows the gun to be fired in winter gloves or mittens.

The standard sighting equipment of the Steyr AUG rifle is the 1.5× telescope sight, with the aiming reticle made as a circle. This circle is dimensioned so that its inner diameter is equal to the visible height of a standing man at 300m range. The adjustment knobs on the sight are used only for zeroing. The sight housing, which is integral to the receiver on the AUG A1 models, also features emergency backup iron sights at the top of the telescope sight housing. Some early production AUG rifles of the A1 pattern were fitted with receivers that had an integral scope mounts. On AUG A2 models, the standard scope mount can be quickly removed and replaced by the Picatinny-type mounting rail.

The housing of the AUG rifles, integral with the pistol handle and triggerguard, is made from the high-impact-resistant polymer and is usually green (military) or black (police) in colour. The housing has two symmetrical ejection ports, one of which is always covered by the plastic cover. The rubber-coated buttplate is detachable and, when removed, gives access to the rifle internals, including the hammer unit and the bolt group. The buttplate is held in position by

the cross pin, which also serves as a rear sling swivel attachment point.

The AUG is fed from detachable box magazines, which hold thirty (standard rifle) or forty-two (light machine gun) rounds. The magazines are made from semi-translucent, strong polymer. The magazine release button is located behind the magazine port and is completely ambidextrous – some say that it is equally uncomfortable for use with either hand.

STEYR ACR

Calibre: 5.6mm flechette
Action: gas-operated, rising breech
Overall length: 765mm
Barrel length: 540mm
Weight: 3.23kg, without magazine
Rate of fire: n/a
Magazine capacity: 24 rounds

The Steyr ACR was built as an attempt to revive the flechette ammunition concept, first tried in the 1960s during the US Army's SPIW programme. In the 1960s the flechette concept proved itself a failure; in the 1990s it was much more successful, but not enough so to be worth total rearming with a new infantry weapon system.

The Steyr ACR is built around an especially

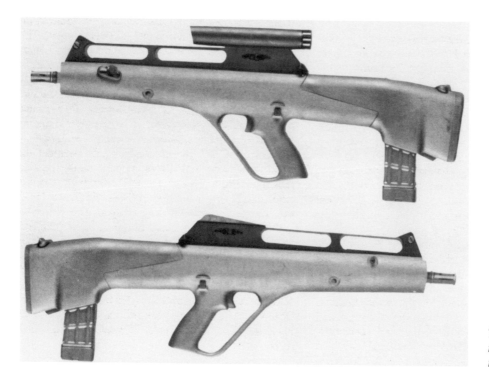

The Steyr ACR rifle; the upper view shows the optical sight.

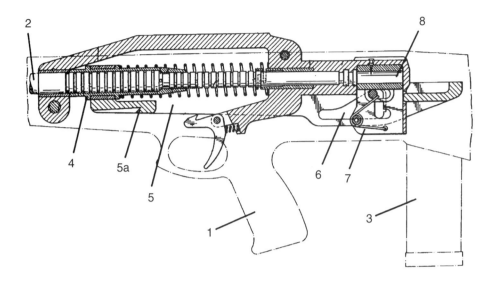

Diagram drawing from original Steyr patent for the ACR operating system; key parts are: 1. frame; 2. barrel; 3. magazine; 4. annular gas piston; 5. operating rod; 5a. sear notch on operating rod; 6. cut in the operating rod that controls the up-and-down movement of the separate breech; 7. breech spring; 8. chamber.

designed cartridge with a nominal calibre of 5.56mm. This cartridge has a simple, cylindrically-shaped, plastic case. The details of this cartridge may be found in Chapter 4.

To fire such an uncommon cartridge, the Steyr ACR has an equally uncommon design. The barrel has a very slow rifling twist to give initial stabilization to the saboted flechette, as well as to help with sabot separation. Instead of the common, linear-moving bolt, the Steyr ACR has a separate chamber (breechblock), which can be moved up or down. The whole action is powered by gas via an annular gas piston surrounding the barrel. A brief explanation of its operation follows: at first, let us suppose that chamber is empty and that the rifle is manually cocked for the first shot. In this position the chamber block is its lowest position, aligned with the topmost round in the magazine. The gas piston with its operating rod is in its rearmost position and under the pressure of the return spring. When the trigger is pressed, the operating rod with the gas piston are released and started forward under the pressure of the return spring, which is located around the barrel. This movement, at first, via a special rammer, feeds the first round forward from the magazine and into the chamber, and then, via shaped cam and breechblock spring, raises the breechblock with the cartridge into the topmost position. In this position the fixed

firing pin passes through the hole in the top of the chamber and penetrates the cartridge wall, igniting the primer and firing the round. When the projectile (flechette with sabot) passes the gas port, some of the gun gases began to move the gas piston back. This movement, via the operating rod and the shaped cam, lowers the breechblock with the empty case out of alignment with the barrel and down to the magazine. When the breech comes to stop in the lowest position, a separate rammer feeds the next cartridge forward and out of magazine, chambering it. At the same time, the fired case is pushed forward, out of the chamber by the next cartridge, and when it has cleared the chamber, the spent case simply falls out of the rifle via the ejection port. The ejection port is located at the bottom of the rifle, ahead of the magazine, and this eliminates one of the biggest problems of any bullpup rifle – a non-ambidextrous (or, in this case, fully ambidextrous) ejection. If the rifle is set to the full automatic mode, the firing cycle is repeated as described above. Otherwise, the empty breech remains in its lowest position, waiting for the next trigger pull. This unusual action is concealed in a sleek and comfortable polymer case with AUG-styled pistol grip and large ventilated upper rib with fixed sights. Optical sights are also fitted.

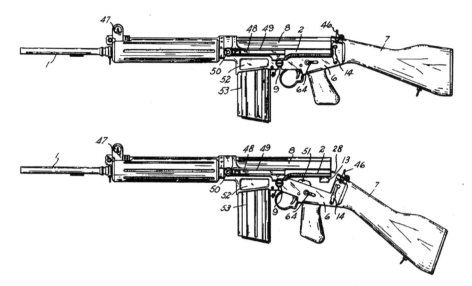

Diagram from the patent, granted to Dieudonne Saive, showing the early configuration of the FN FAL rifle.

BELGIUM

Belgium has been and still is one of the leaders in small arms design since the early 1900s, with most military development conducted at the famous Fabrique Nationale (FN) Company, located at Herstal, near Liège. After the end of the Second World War, FN quickly resumed its operations and development projects. Recognizing the global need for a new, semi-automatic rifle, FN started with a design, which was originally developed before the war and then carried forward in the United Kingdom during the German occupation of Belgium. In 1949 FN produced a semi-automatic military rifle, known as FN-49, SAFN or ABL. This rifle found some military customers, most notably in Belgium itself and Egypt, but, more importantly, it served as a starting point for one of the most successful military rifles of the post-war period, the *Fusil Automatique Léger*, or Light Automatic Rifle, universally known as the FN FAL.

The FN FAL is one of the most famous and widespread military rifle designs of the twentieth century. It has been used by over seventy countries and was manufactured in at least ten. At the present, the service days of most FAL rifles are gone, but it is still used in some parts of the world. The history of the FAL began about 1946, when FN began to develop a new assault rifle, chambered for the German 7.92 × 33 Kurz (short) intermediate cartridge. The design team was lead by Dieudonné Saive, who at the same time worked at a battle rifle, chambered for 'old time', full-power rifle cartridges, which latter became the SAFN-49. It is therefore not surprising that both rifles are mechani-

cally quite similar. In the late 1940s the Belgians selected a British .280 in (7 × 43) intermediate cartridge for further development. In 1950 both the Belgian FAL prototype and the British EM-2 bullpup assault rifles were tested by the US Army. The FAL prototype greatly impressed the Americans, but the idea of an intermediate cartridge was at that time unacceptable to them, and the USA insisted on the adoption of their full-power, T65 cartridge as a NATO standard in 1953–54. Preparing for this adoption, FN redesigned their rifle for the newest T65 (7.62 × 51 NATO) ammunition, and the first 7.62mm FALs were ready by 1953.

Belgium adopted the FAL in 1956, but the first customer was probably Canada, which adopted a slightly modified version of FAL as the C1 in 1955. The Canadians produced the C1 and the heavy barrelled C2 squad automatic rifle at their own Canadian Arsenal factory. Britain followed suit and adopted the FAL in 1957 as an L1A1 SLR (Self-Loading Rifle), often issued with 4X SUIT optical sights. Britain also produced its own rifles at RSAF (Royal Small Arms Factory) Enfield and at BSA (Birmingham Small Arms). Austria adopted the FAL in 1958 as the Stg.58 and manufactured their rifles at the Steyr arms factory. Brazil, Turkey, Australia, Israel, South Africa, West Germany and many other countries also adopted various versions of the FAL. The success of the FAL could have been even greater if the Belgians had agreed to sell the licence to West Germany, which really wanted to produce and issue the FAL as the G1 rifle, but the Belgians rejected the request, therefore Germany purchased the licence for the Spanish

CETME rifle instead, and the resulting H&K G3 rifle became probably the most notable rival to the FAL.

The FAL was built in numerous versions, with different furniture, sights, barrel lengths and so on. There are, however, four basic configurations of the Belgian FAL rifle: FAL 50.00, or simply FAL, with a fixed buttstock and standard barrel; FAL 50.63 or FAL 'Para', with a folding skeleton butt and short barrel; FAL 50.64 with the folding skeleton butt of the 'Para' model and the standard length barrel; and the FAL 50.41, also known as FAL /Hbar or FALO – a heavy barrelled model which was intended primary as a light support weapon. There are also two major patterns of FALs around the globe: the 'metric' and the 'inch' FAL. As the names implied, these were built in countries with the metric or the imperial system of units. These patterns are slightly different in some dimensions, and magazines of metric and inch pattern could sometimes not be interchanged. Most inch pattern FALs were made in British Commonwealth countries (the United Kingdom, Canada and Australia), had folding cocking handles and were mostly limited to semi-automatic fire only (except for Hbar versions such as the C2). Most metric pattern rifles had non-folding cocking handles and may or may not have had selective fire capability, but, as with other light selective fire weapons chambered for the 7.62 × 51 NATO round, the controllability of the full automatic fire was disappointing and the spread of shots in a burst extremely wide. It must be noted that, had it been pursued in its original chamberings, the 7.92mm PP Kurtz (7.92 × 33 German short) or in .280/30 (7 × 43 British/Belgian), it would then have become a true assault rifle. But, regardless of this, the FAL is one of the best so-called 'battle rifles', reliable, comfortable (except for its excessive length) and accurate. It is somewhat sensitive to fine sand and dust but otherwise it is an admirable weapon.

The only countries still producing FAL rifles at present are Brazil, Argentina and, most surprisingly, the USA. Brazil adopted the FAL under the name 7.62mm Fz.961 and manufactured it at the IMBEL facilities. Argentina offers it as the *Fusil Automatico Liviano Modelo IV*. The USA produced a small number of FALs as the T-48 at the Harrington & Richardson factory in the early 1950s for Army trials, but at present a number of private American companies are manufacturing versions of FAL rifles by using either surplus parts kits or newly manufactured parts. Most of these rifles are limited to semi-automatic only and are available for civilian users. Probably the most notable American manufacturer of FAL modifications is the DS Arms Co., which produced its rifles under the name of the DSA-58.

Following the small-calibre trend set by the USA in 1960s, FN developed several small-calibre 'true' assault rifles, starting with the unsuccessful 5.56mm *Carabine Automatique Légère* (light automatic carbine) or FN CAL. Undeterred by the market failure of this design, FN began to develop a new assault rifle for the 5.56 × 45 cartridge in the early 1970s. The final design, called the FNC (Fabrique Nationale Carbine) was completed about 1978 and was subsequently adopted by the Belgian armed forces. It was also adopted by Sweden and Indonesia, and both purchased the licences to build more or less modified FNCs at their own facilities. The Swedish version is known as the Bofors AK-5 and the Indonesian version was designated the Pindad SS1. The FNC also was sold to some police forces around the world and, in limited numbers for civilians, as a 'Sporter' model, limited to the semi-automatic mode only. The FNC was a fine rifle, but it appeared a little too late to catch the first wave of the 5.56mm re-armament. It is still offered for any interested buyer in military or law enforcement.

During the late 1980s and the early 1990s FN began

The unsuccessful 5.56mm FN CAL rifle gave way to the next FN design, the FNC.

the search for its next entry into the assault rifle world. The aim this time was to produce a modern, modular weapon, and this ultimately resulted in the FN F2000 rifle, which was first publicly displayed in 2001. The F2000 offers all the most popular features of the modern assault rifle, such as a compact bullpup layout, completely ambidextrous handling and a modular design with plenty of options and add-ons already available, which allows the rifle to be 'tailored' for any particular mission or tactical situation. For example, for peacekeeping operations the F2000 could be fitted with less lethal M303 underbarrel module, which fires tear gas or marker projectiles by using pre-compressed air. On the other hand, the F2000 could be fitted with one of a variety of 40mm grenade launchers and a proprietary computerized fire-control system, instead of the standard, low-magnification, optical sights. It is yet to be seen whether F2000 will succeed, but it is obviously one of the most promising designs today.

FN FAL

Calibre: 7.62 × 51 NATO
Action: gas-operated, tilting breechblock, select-fire or semi-automatic only
Length: 1,100mm (990/736mm for 'Para' model)
Barrel length: 533mm (431mm for 'Para' model)
Weight: 4.45kg empty (3.77kg empty for 'Para' model)
Magazine capacity: 20 rounds (30 rounds for heavy barrelled SAW versions)
Rate of fire: 650–700 rpm

The FN FAL is a gas-operated, selective fire or semi-automatic only, magazine-fed rifle. It uses a short-stroke gas system, with the piston located above the barrel and having its own return spring. After the shot is fired, the gas piston gives a quick tap to the bolt carrier and then returns, and the rest of the reloading cycle is powered by the inertia of the bolt group and the residual pressure in the chamber. The gas system is

The F2000 rifle is being fired by Belgian soldier; note the spent cases falling out of the ejection port next to the muzzle. (image courtesy FN Herstal)

*The back half of the
FN FAL.*

fitted with a gas regulator so that it can easily be adjusted for a variety of environmental conditions or cut off completely so that rifle grenades can be safely launched from the muzzle. The locking system uses a bolt carrier with a separate bolt that locks the barrel by tipping its rear part into the recess in the receiver floor. The receivers were at first machined from forged steel blocks, but since 1973 FN has manufactured investment-cast receivers to lower production costs. Many makers, however, have stuck to the machined receivers. The trigger housing with pistol grip is hinged to the receiver behind the magazine well and can be swung down to open the action for maintenance and disassembly. The recoil spring is housed in the butt of the rifle in fixed butt configurations or in the receiver cover in folding-butt configurations; thus the folding butt versions require a slightly different bolt carrier, receiver cover and recoil spring. The cocking handle is located at the left side of the receiver and does not move when the gun is fired; it could be folding or non-folding, depending on the country of origin. The safety/fire selector switch is located at the trigger housing, above the trigger guard. It can have two (with semi-automatic) or three (with selective fire) positions. The firing mechanism is hammer-fired and uses a single sear for either semi- or fully automatic fire. The barrel is equipped with a long flash suppressor, which also serves as a rifle grenade launcher; the design of the flash suppressor may differ slightly from country to country. The furniture of the FAL may also differ – it could be made from wood, plastic of various colours or metal (folding buttstocks, metallic handguards on some models). Some models, such as Austrian Stg.58 or the Brazilian LAR, were fitted with light bipods as a standard. Almost all heavy barrel versions were also fitted with bipods of various designs. The sights are usually of hooded front and adjustable aperture rear types, but may differ in details and markings. Almost all FAL rifles are equipped with sling swivels and most of the rifles are fitted with bayonet lugs.

FN FNC

Calibre: 5.56 × 45 NATO
Action: gas-operated, rotating bolt
Overall length: standard model 997mm (776mm with folded butt); 'Para' model 911mm/680mm
Barrel length: 449mm (363mm 'Para' model)
Weight with empty magazine: 4.06kg (3.81kg 'Para' model)
Magazine capacity: 30 rounds (accept all STANAG-compatible magazines)
Rate of fire: about 700 rpm

The FNC is a gas-operated, selective fire, magazine-fed weapon. The gas drive and rotating bolt strongly resemble the AK-47 system, but with some modifications and adapted for more advanced production technologies, such as CNC machining. The long stroke gas piston is located above the barrel and is linked to the bolt carrier. Unlike in the AK-47, the gas piston rod can be separated from the bolt carrier when the gun is disassembled. The gas system features a two-position gas regulator (for normal or adverse conditions) and a separate gas cut-off, combined with folding rifle grenade sights. When the grenade sights are raised into the ready position, the gas cut-off automatically blocks the gas supply to the action, allowing for the safe launching of rifle grenades. Both the gas cut-off and the grenade sight are located on the gas chamber, just behind the front sight. The now common rotating bolt has two massive lugs that lock into the barrel extension.

The receiver comprises two parts (upper and lower), linked by two cross pins. The receiver can be opened for disassembly and maintenance by removing the rear pin, so that the parts can be hinged around the forward pin (which also can be removed to separate the receiv-

FN FNC rifle of late manufacture, with enlarged trigger guard. (image courtesy FN Herstal)

FN FNC rifle with folded buttstock. (image courtesy FN Herstal)

FN FNC rifle partially disassembled. (image courtesy FN Herstal)

er parts). The upper receiver is made from stamped steel, the lower receiver, along with the magazine housing, from aluminium alloy. The barrel of the FNC is equipped with a flash suppressor, which also serves as a rifle grenade launcher in the usual way. The gun is equipped with a hooded post front sight and a flip-up, 'L'-shaped rear aperture sight with two settings, for 250 and 400m range.

The controls of the FNC consist of a four-position, safety/mode selector switch on the left side of the receiver. Available modes are safe, single shot, three-round bursts and full automatic fire. The cocking handle is attached to the bolt carrier at the right side and reciprocates with the bolt group when the gun is fired. The rear part of the cocking handle slot, cut into the upper receiver for the cocking handle, is covered by a spring-loaded cover which is automatically opened by the handle when it goes back and automatically closes the opening when the cocking handle returns forward.

The FNC is equipped with a side-folding buttstock, made of steel and covered by plastic. A solid, non-folding plastic butt is available as an option. The pistol handle and the foregrip are made from plastic. The gun is equipped with sling swivels and can be fitted with a special bayonet or with an adaptor for the US M7 knife-bayonet. The FNC can be fed from any STANAG (NATO standard) compliant magazine, and is issued with a thirty-round magazine. If required, FNC could be fitted with 4× telescope sight or various infra-red/night vision sights.

FN F2000

Calibre: 5.56 × 45 NATO
Action: gas-operated, rotating bolt
Overall length: 694mm
Barrel length: 400mm
Weight: 3.6kg empty, in standard configuration; 4.6kg with 40mm grenade launcher
Magazine capacity: 30 rounds (any NATO/STANAG-type magazine)

The F2000 rifle is a gas-operated, rotating bolt, selective-fire weapon, featuring a polymer stock with a bullpup layout. It utilizes a long-stroke gas piston and a seven-lug rotating bolt which locks into the barrel extension. The unique feature of the F2000 rifle is its patented front ejection system: the spent cases, extracted from the chamber, travel from the rear part of the gun to the ejection port near the muzzle via a special

Right *F2000 rifle: diagram from US Patent 6,389,725, showing the design of the forward ejection system. Key: 1. chamber; 2. fired cartridge case; 3. extractor claw; 4. bolt head; 5. swinging spent case guide; 6. ejection tube.*

Below *F2000 rifle in standard configuration.*

(image courtesy FN Herstal)

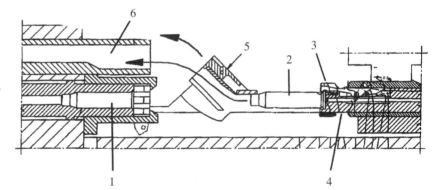

F2000 rifle with 40mm underbarrel grenade launcher.
(image courtesy FN Herstal)

ejection tube and fall out of the gun at a safe distance from the shooter's face. This is achieved by using a special swinging guide, which enters the way of the closing bolt and directs the spent case, which is held on the bolt face, to the ejection tube while, at the same time, lower lugs of the bolt are stripping a fresh cartridge from the magazine. The cocking handle is mounted well forward on the left-hand side, just above the foregrip, and is easily be operated with the right hand when the gun is held in the left hand. The selector switch is mounted at the bottom of the trigger guard. All these features combine to make the F2000 the first genuinely ambidextrous bullpup, able to be used with equal ease by right- and left-handed shooters without requiring any adjustments. In its standard configuration, the F2000 is perfectly balanced around the pistol grip.

The stock has built-in, standard rails on the top of the weapon (for different sights and scopes, for instance) and a mounting point ahead of trigger guard, where additional modules may be installed (such as grenade launchers and non-lethal modules). In the basic configuration, the upper rail mount is fitted with a 1.6× magnification optical sight, and the lower mounting point is covered by a removable handguard. At present, the F2000 rifle may be upgraded, depending on the mission, with FN's 40mm low-velocity grenade launcher (on the lower mount, instead of the handguard), or with the M303 non-lethal module; other options are handguards with built-in laser pointers or flashlights. The standard, low-magnification combat scope, which has back-up open sights on its top cover, may be replaced by any other scope on a WEAVER-style mount or by FN's proprietary computerized fire-control module with laser rangefinder, for both the rifle and the 40mm grenade launcher.

BRAZIL

Brazil is one of the leading arms manufacturers in South America, with several large production facilities. In 1961 the Brazilian Army adopted the Belgian FN FAL as the '7.62mm Fz.961' rifle, and produced it at government-owned factories for both domestic uses and export. During the early 1980s Brazil decided to follow the small-calibre trend and pursued the cheapest way of doing so, by simply re-barrelling the available FAL rifles for the 5.56 × 45 cartridge. This, of course, also required new recoil springs, bolts and magazines to be used, but the receivers and gas systems were taken from old rifles. The first prototype, named the MD-1, was developed by IMBEL (*Industria de Materiel Belico do Brasil*) beginning about 1982 and appeared in 1983. The final designs, known as the '5.56mm Fz. MD2' and the '5.56mm Fz. MD3' (5.56mm rifles, models 2 and 3, respectively) came out about 1985 and were later adopted by the Army. During the late 1990s Brazil developed a new assault rifle, called the MD-97, which, being externally and internally quite similar to the earlier MD-2, featured lightweight aluminium receivers and some other upgrades. This rifle has been tested by the Brazilian military and in late 2003 was apparently scheduled for official adoption, redesignated Model L (rifle) and Model LC (carbine).

There have been other interesting developments, such as the FA-02, developed by Nelmo Suzano at *Laboratorio de Pesquisa de Armamento Automatico* (LAPA). This lightweight bullpup rifle features a plastic housing and an interesting double-action trigger system, but few rifles were made in the mid 1980s, probably no more than 500 in total. Some of the LAPA FA-02 rifles are still used by the special police forces of Brazil. Another bullpup by the same designer is

Above *F2000 rifle partially disassembled* (image courtesy FN Herstal).

Below *The experimental LAPA 03 bullpup rifle.*

IMBEL MD2 rifle.

currently under development in two versions: the FA-1 (rifle) and the CA-1 (carbine). Most unusually, these use a short-recoil operating system.

IMBEL MD-2 AND MD-3
Calibre: 5.56 × 45 NATO
Action: gas-operated, rotating bolt
Overall length: 1,010mm (764mm with folded stock)
Barrel length: 453mm
Weight: 4.4kg
Rate of fire: 700 rpm
Magazine capacity: 20 or 30 rounds

The MD-2 started simply as a rebarrelled FN FAL-type Fz.961 rifle, but during the design process the FAL locking system (tilting block) was replaced by an M16-type rotating bolt. The receiver design is, however, still similar to that of the FAL. The MD-2 is a gas-operated, selective-fire assault rifle, with rotating bolt locking. The trigger group is mounted into the pistol grip unit, which is hinged to the receiver and folds down and forward for disassembly and mainte-

nance. The MD-2 features a side-folding, metal butt-stock; the MD-3 rifle is similar to the MD-2 but has a fixed plastic buttstock. The MD-2 uses any M16-style magazine.

CANADA
Between 1954 and 1984, the general issue rifle of the Canadian Armed forces was the C1 (modified C1A1 since 1960), a licence-built Belgian FN FAL rifle in self-loading (semi-automatic) form with some modifications. Canadian forces also used the heavy-barrelled FAL-type automatic rifle, designated C2 (C2A1), as a squad automatic weapon.

In 1984, Canada adopted a 5.56mm assault rifle. To avoid research and design expenses, the Canadians simply purchased the licence from the USA for a new assault rifle, chambered for the latest 5.56 × 45 NATO ammunition. This was the Colt model 715, also known as the M16A1E1 rifle. Adopted as the C7, this rifle combined features from both earlier M16A1 rifles,

The C7 rifle with accessories.

C7A1 rifle with detachable carrying handle installed on the receiver. (image courtesy Christian Overgaard, Denmark)

such as full automatic fire mode and a two-position, flip-up aperture sight, and from the newest M16A2, such as the heavy barrel, rifled with the faster 1:7 twist, better suited for 5.56mm NATO ammunition. Later on, Diemaco developed a short-barrelled carbine version, fitted with telescoped buttstock, which was designated the C8. While the C7 rifle went to the Canadian Armed Forces, the C8 is in use with Canadian police forces. According to the recent trends in small arms development, Diemaco also produced so called 'flat-top' models of both the C7 and the C8. These models have a Picatinny-style rail instead of the M16A1-style, integral carrying handle with rear sight, and are usually issued with the Elcan optical sights or with the detachable carrying handle with M16A1-type aperture sights. Designated by the manufacturer as the C7FT and the C8FT, in Canadian service these models are issued as the C7A1 and the C8A1, respectively. Other derivatives are the LSW (Light Support Weapon, basically a heavy barrelled C7) and the SFW (Special Forces Weapon, a heavy barrelled C8). The Netherlands adopted the C7 (in both standard and flat-top version) in 1994, and Denmark purchased and adopted the C7FT as the Gevaer M/95 in 1995.

Current plans are to upgrade existing C7 and C7A1 rifles in Canadian service to the proposed C7A2 configuration, which will combine the standard C7-type 50cm barrel with C8-type telescoped buttstock, coloured furniture, C7A1-type Picatinny rail upper receiver and additional, short Picatinny rails on the sides of the front sight block for mounting sighting aids such as laser pointers and tactical lights. The

DIEMACO C7/C8

	Diemaco C7	Diemaco C8
Calibre	5.56 × 45 NATO	
Length	1020mm	840/760mm
Barrel length	510mm	370mm
Weight	3.3kg empty, no magazine 3.9kg loaded with 30 rounds	2.7kg empty, no magazine 3.2kg loaded with 30 rounds
Magazine capacity	30 rounds	
Rate of fire	800 rpm	900 rpm

Close-up of the C8A1 carbine.

C7A2 also most probably will be fitted with improved sights, the Elcan C79A2. Other proposed changes include ambidextrous magazine release and safety/fire selector switch, and some other minor improvements.

Internally, the C7 differs little from the original M16A1 rifle (see below), with the most visible differences being the heavy, M16A2-style barrel and the A2-style handguards. Flat-top models (C7FT/C7A1) are quite similar in appearance to M16A3 rifles and are issued with Elcan optical sight along with back-up iron sights. The C8/C8FT carbines are quite similar to American M4/M4A1 carbines, which are also described below.

PEOPLE'S REPUBLIC OF CHINA

During the early post-war period, the newly established People's Republic of China (PRC) was a close 'friend' to the Soviet Union, and so it was natural for the much less advanced country to adopt the weapons of a more advanced ally. In 1956 the Chinese military adopted two Soviet designs, both carrying the same Type 56 designation and both being chambered for Soviet 7.62 × 39 ammunition. One was the semi-automatic Simonov SKS carbine; the other was the Kalashnikov AK-47 assault rifle. Both were made in large numbers and used by the PLA (People's Liberation Army of China), as well as exported to several countries. The Type 56 assault rifle was an almost exact copy of the Soviet AK-47, with its milled receiver. The only notable differences were the markings in Chinese instead of Russian and the folding, non-detachable, spike-shaped bayonet, which replaced the original, detachable, knife-bayonet of Soviet origin.

Later on, following significant disagreements between the PRC and the USSR during the 1960s, China decided to develop its own small arms, based on the earlier licensed designs. The first domestically designed and mass-produced assault rifle was the Type 63, as its name implies, initially adopted by the PLA in 1963. It is an interesting development because it represents a mix of features taken from other designs, mostly from the AK-47 and the SKS. Several years later, this rifle was improved with the introduction of the lighter and less expensive, stamped receiver instead of the original machined one. This improved version is often referred as the Type 68 rifle. Both Type 63 and 68 rifles were still chambered for 7.62 × 39 ammunition and both featured non-detachable, folding bayonets with spike-shaped blades.

The next indigenous design appeared in the early 1980s, when the PLA adopted the 7.62mm Type 81 assault rifle. This was a further development of the Type 63/Type 68 rifles and is easily distinguished by the separate pistol grip, handguards and buttstock instead of the SKS-style, wooden stock found on earlier types. The Type 81 was more than a single assault rifle – it was a family of infantry firearms, much like the Soviet Kalashnikov AK/RPK family. Type 81 weapons were made as an assault rifle with a fixed butt, an assault rifle with a folding butt for paratroopers (Type 81-1), and a heavy-barrelled Type 81 squad automatic weapon/light machine gun, fitted with a bipod and issued with seventy-five-round drum magazines instead of the typical thirty-round boxes. Despite being externally somewhat similar to the AK-47, it is significantly different from it, with its most easily distinguishable feature being an exposed muzzle part of the barrel, with the foresight moved back. This was done to be able to fire rifle grenades from the barrel. Type 81 rifles replaced some obsolescent Type 56 assault rifles and carbines, as well as Type 63/68 rifles, in most PLA units, and saw some action in border clashes between China and Vietnam during the late 1980s. This rifle was also exported through the NORINCO state company into several neighbouring countries. During the late 1980s and the early 1990s the Type 81 served as a development platform for the next generation of PLA small arms, being used as a test-bed for 5.8 × 42 ammunition.

Chinese armed forces joined the small-calibre world relatively late, but in a novel manner. Instead of adopting the existing and proven 5.45 × 39 Soviet or 5.56 × 45 NATO (both of which were manufactured in China for export), the PLA decided to develop their own cartridge, although whether the decision was based on technical or political considerations is not known. After much testing, they settled on a 5.8mm calibre and then developed a 5.8 × 42 cartridge, apparently designated DBP87, which is claimed to be superior to both the 5.56mm NATO and the 5.54mm Soviet. This cartridge develops a muzzle velocity of 930m/s from a standard barrel, with a bullet weighing 4.26g. This ammunition was first tested in modified Type 81 rifles and light machine guns, apparently designated Type 87. As soon as the ammunition was ready, the PLA began to develop an entirely new and much more modern family of small arms based on the same action. This family, known as QBZ-95 ('*Qing Buqiang Zu*' = light rifles family, 1995), was first displayed outside the PLA in 1997, when China took over Hong Kong; it was observed that the Chinese guards were armed with a new, modern-looking bullpup rifle. In fact, it was one of an entirely new family of weapons, all designed around the same action and bullpup layout, which include the assault rifle, a shorter carbine, a light support weapon (with a bipod, a heavier barrel and large capacity magazine) and a sniper rifle. While being quite similar inside, these guns have different body shapes and cannot be converted from one configuration to another. The QBZ-95 line of weapons is now spreading throughout the PLA, commencing with its elite units.

In the meantime, China has also produced large numbers of various small arms for export, including both civilian, semi-automatic weapons and military, selective-fire ones. These include several Kalashnikov clones, chambered in 7.62 × 39 or 5.56 × 45, with several options and furniture, as well as several AR-15/M16 clones in 5.56mm, such as 'CQ', and even clones of the American M14 in 7.62 × 51. Another export weapon was the 7.62mm Type 86, which was no more than a conversion of the Kalashnikov-type rifle into a bullpup layout. This design apparently (and not surprisingly) failed to find any military sales and was sold mostly in civilian, semi-automatic only versions, known as the Type 86S. China has also developed an export version of the basic QBZ-95 design, designated QBZ-97, chambered for the popular 5.56 × 45 NATO ammunition, although it does not so far appear to have achieved any sales.

TYPE 56 ASSAULT RIFLE
Calibre: 7.62 × 39
Action: gas-operated, rotating bolt
Overall length: 874mm
Barrel length: 414mm
Weight: 3.80kg
Rate of fire: 600 rpm
Magazine capacity: 30 rounds
Type 56 is a gas-operated, selective-fire weapon; the

receiver is machined from steel, the two-lugged bolt locks into receiver walls. Later models, however, were made with stamped-steel, AKM-type receivers, but retained the same Type 56 designation. The Type 56 has AK-47-style controls with a reciprocating charging handle and a massive safety/fire selector lever on the right side of the receiver. The furniture is made from wood, and a compact version with an underfolding, metal buttstock is also available. The only visible difference from the Soviet AK-47 is a permanently attached spike bayonet, which folds under the barrel when not in use. Some sources said that the quality of these guns was worse than that of the Soviet originals. Most notably, at least some Type 56 rifles lacked the chromium plating in the barrel and gas system area, and thus were much less resistant to corrosion. This model has also been made in Albania, where it is reportedly known unofficially as the 'AK-47'.

TYPE 63/TYPE 68
Calibre: 7.62 × 39
Action: gas-operated, rotating bolt
Overall length: 1,029mm
Barrel length: 521mm
Weight: 3.49kg
Rate of fire: 750 rpm
Magazine capacity: 15, 20 or 30-round detachable box magazines
The Type 63/68 rifle is a gas-operated, selective-fire weapon. It shares the stock design and receiver outline with the SKS; but instead of a tilting bolt it has an AK-47-type rotating bolt with dual locking lugs. The gas system is quite original, being not entirely the same as that in the SKS or the AK-47, and has a dual-position gas regulator. This rifle is fed from detachable box magazines of a variety of capacity, which are externally similar to, but not compatible with, AK-47 magazines. The Type 63/68 rifles feature a bolt hold-

Type 56 assault rifle, with integral bayonet extended.

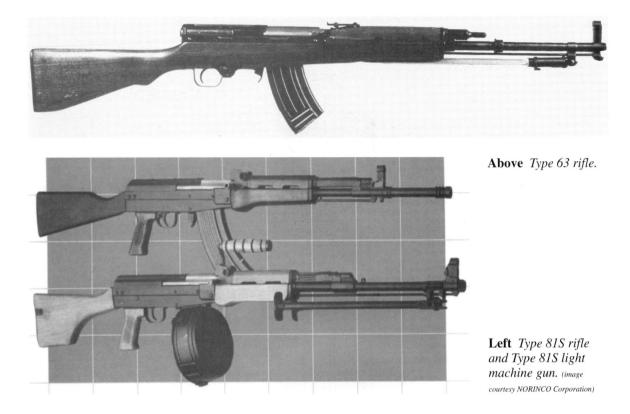

Above *Type 63 rifle.*

Left *Type 81S rifle and Type 81S light machine gun. (image courtesy NORINCO Corporation)*

open device, also borrowed from the Simonov SKS, which holds the bolt open after the last shot has been fired. The bolt carrier also has the charging clip guides machined into its forward part, so that the rifle can be reloaded with the magazine in place, using ten-round SKS stripper clips. Selective-fire capability is controlled by the single safety/fire mode selector lever, located at the front of the trigger guard. All rifles are fitted with a wooden stock and a non-detachable, spike-shaped, down-folding bayonet.

TYPE 81

Calibre: 7.62 × 39
Overall length: 955mm (730mm with butt folded for Type 81-1)
Barrel length: 445mm
Weight: 3.5kg empty, less bayonet
Rate of fire: 650 rpm
Magazine capacity: 30-round detachable box magazines

The Type 81 is a gas-operated, magazine-fed, automatic rifle. It uses a short-stroke gas piston, located above the barrel and a two-position gas regulator, along with a gas cut-off valve for launching rifle grenades.

The gas system, as well as the bolt group with the AK-47-type rotating bolt, is reminiscent of those of Type 63 rifles. Type 81 rifles also retain the bolt hold-open device, which catches the bolt in the open position after the last round has been fired. The fire selector/safety switch is located at the left side of the receiver, just above the pistol grip, and can be easily operated with the right thumb. The late production Type 81S rifles have a separate SKS-type safety switch just behind the trigger. The open sights are marked from 100 to 500m, with the front sight being mounted just ahead of the gas block, leaving the front portion of the barrel free for the rifle grenade launcher. Ammunition is fed from Type 56 (Kalashnikov), thirty-round magazines, or from seventy-five-round drums intended for the Type 81 light machine gun.

At the first glance, the Type 81 assault rifle looks much like the Kalashnikov AKM, but, on closer inspection, there are some significant external differences, most notably in the receiver cover shape and front sight location. There is also a significant gap between the trigger guard and the magazine on Type 81 rifles, while on AK-47 type rifles the magazine is adjacent to the front of the trigger guard. On Type 81 rifles

The QBZ-95 rifle.

the obsolete, spike-shaped, non-detachable bayonet, preferred by the PLA before, is also replaced with the more 'modern', detachable knife-bayonet. Most probably this was required to leave the significant portion of the muzzle area of the barrel unobstructed, which is required for the launching of rifle grenades.

QBZ-95/97
Calibre: 5.8 × 42 DBP87 (5.56 × 45 NATO for export version QBZ-97)
Action: gas-operated, rotating bolt
Overall length: 760mm
Barrel length: 520mm
Weight: 3.4kg unloaded
Rate of fire: about 650 rpm
Magazine capacity: 30 rounds

The QBZ-95 is a gas-operated, magazine-fed, automatic weapon with a bullpup layout. It has a short-stroke gas piston and a rotating bolt. The charging handle is located at the top of the receiver, under the carrying handle. The housing is made from polymer, with an integral carrying handle, which holds the rear sight base, and has mounting points for optical or night-vision scopes. The ejection port is made only at the right side of the weapon so that it cannot be fired from the left shoulder. Standard sights are of the open type, graduated from 100 to 500m. The front part of the barrel in the standard version is left unobstructed, thus the QBZ-95 rifle can be used to launch rifle grenades. It can also be fitted with an underbarrel grenade launcher or with a knife bayonet. A compact carbine

Right, centre and bottom *The QBZ-95 carbine.*

The 5.56mm QBZ-97 rifle.

version, sometimes referred to as the CAR-95, cannot use either a grenade launcher or a bayonet, because of the much shortened barrel.

The export version, the QBZ-97, chambered for popular 5.56 × 45 NATO ammunition, is internally similar to the QBZ-95, but has a different, much deeper magazine housing, which accepts a NATO-standard (M16-type) magazine.

CROATIA

Croatia is one of the youngest European countries, born in 1992 from the remains of socialist Yugoslavia. As a part of its Yugoslav heritage, Croatia received some arms production facilities and manufactured several types of small arms, including quite successful handguns such as the HS-2000, which is now imported into the USA by Springfield Armory as the XD pistol.

Most of the Croatian Army was equipped with ex-Yugoslav M70 Kalashnikov-type assault rifles of various models, but Croatia decided to develop its own rifle. This resulted in the APS-95, developed in the mid 1990s by the Croatian company RH-Alan, and is a licensed copy of the Israeli Galil assault rifle (some

sources said that it is a copy of the South African Vektor R-4 rifle, but it is in essence the same Galil). The APS 95 was adopted in 1995 and was acquired by the Croatian Army in some numbers, seeing some action during the 1995 Yugoslav–Croatian conflict, but due to financial limitations rearming with this weapon is so far incomplete.

APS 95
Calibre: 5.56 × 45 NATO
Action: gas-operated, rotating bolt
Overall length: 980mm (730mm with stock folded)
Barrel length: 450mm
Weight: 3.8kg empty
Rate of fire: 650 rpm
Magazine capacity: 35 rounds

The APS 95 is a gas-operated, long-stroke piston, rotating-bolt locked, selective-fire weapon. The gas system features a gas cut-off, which is activated to fire rifle grenades. The fire-selector/safety switch is of the Galil type; the metallic buttstock folds to the right side of the gun. A 1.5× fixed scope features a ring and dot aiming reticle which allows for effective shooting up to 400m. Back-up iron sights are also provided as a standard. The APS 95 differs from the Galil mostly in external appearance due to its optical sight, which also serves as a carrying handle. The handguards and pistol grip were also redesigned.

CZECHOSLOVAKIA/CZECH REPUBLIC

This country, which existed in several forms during the twentieth century, was and still is one of the leading arms suppliers in Europe. From the end of World War I Czechoslovakia established a significant arms industry which became famous in the inter-war period for its machine guns (such as the ZB-26 and the ZB-53), pistols and submachine guns.

After the end of World War II, Czechoslovaks saw

APS-95 rifle.

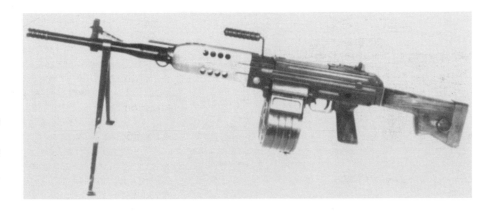

URZ weapon in light machinegun (LM) configuration; this is similar to the rifle configuration except for the added bipod.

the need for an intermediate infantry cartridge and by the early 1950s had produced an indigenous design, the 7.62 × 45, which was used in VZ.52 semi-automatic carbines and VZ.52 light machine guns. A selective-fire assault rifle for this cartridge had also been in development, but due to pressure in the Warsaw Pact from the USSR, the Czechs were forced to adopt the Soviet 7.62 × 39 cartridge. It is unknown why the Czechs decided to develop their own assault rifle instead of simply adopting the Kalashnikov AK-47; possibly it was a matter of national pride. They quickly developed a sound and effective design, with their usual high grade of quality, fit and finishes. The resulting weapon is known as *Samopal vzor 58* or SA Vz.58 (*Samopal* means 'self-firing' or 'automatically fired', and *vzor* for 'type'). It was designed by the Czech arms designer Jiří Čermák, under the project codename KOŠTĚ, or 'Broom'. Development began in January 1956 and the rifle was adopted for service only two years later and issued to the Czech Army from the late 1950s. The state-owned arms factory Česká zbrojovka, located in the town of Uherský Brod (CZ-UB), manufactured the rifle. Production was completed by 1988.

Since the dissolution of Czechoslovakia in 1993 into the Czech and the Slovak Republic, the SA Vz.58 has remained in use with their respective armed forces. It was also sold for export in some quantities. The SA Vz.58 has not seen much real combat and so it is hard to judge how it compares with contemporary rivals such as the Soviet/Russian AK-47 or the US M16A1, but the overall quality, fit and finish of this rifle are excellent.

During the second half of the 1960s, a team lead by Jiří Čermák also developed a modular small arms system intended for export. The URZ (*Univerzální ruční Zbraň* – universal handheld weapon) was developed around the common receiver and barrel and was chambered in 7.62 × 51 NATO ammunition. The URZ used an interesting retarded blowback action, somewhat similar in its basic idea to the Vorgrimler roller delayed system, having a two-part bolt with a couple of rollers on the head. But, instead of being pressed out of recesses in receiver and against the bolt body, in the URZ rollers were used to rotate the bolt head while riding on inclined surfaces on the bolt body, thus slowing down the bolt head movement in the initial stages of opening. The URZ system was available in four basic configurations: automatic rifle (AR), light machinegun (LM), heavy machinegun (HM) and tank weapon (TW). In the AR, LM and HM configurations the URZ fired single shots from a closed bolt and full automatic from an open bolt; in the TW configuration the URZ fired only in full automatic and from an open bolt. In all the configurations except the HM the URZ was fed from special belt-feed 'magazines, with built-in belt feed units and empty link collectors. Each belt magazine contained fifty rounds of linked ammunition. In the heavy machinegun configuration the URZ used standard 250 round belts and a special feed unit instead of the belt 'magazine'.

The AR configuration URZ weighed about 3.9kg, less magazine; in the LM it weighted 5.2kg, and in the HM 11.0kg (on a tripod, less ammunition). In all versions the barrel length was about 490mm, with the total length just under 1m. The rate of fire was about 800 rpm. It is believed that the URZ achieved no sales, and, apparently, never went into mass production.

Another interesting design, also developed by Čermák in the late 1970s was the KRASA (KRÁtký SAmopal – short automatic weapon), a sub-compact assault rifle, originally chambered in 7.62 × 39 and later converted for 5.45 × 39 ammunition. It was a gas-operated weapon with tilting bolt locking. To achieve a compact size in conjunction with a reasonably long

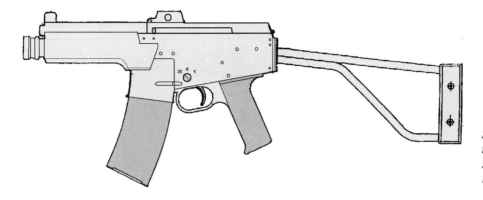

Schematic drawing of the 5.45mm KRASA sub-compact assault rifle.

barrel, the magazine was placed under the barrel; thus the KRASA employed a two-stage feeding system – on the bolt opening stroke, a cartridge was first withdrawn from magazine to the rear and placed against the bolt face, and then pushed forward into the chamber. With the butt folded, KRASA in 5.45mm was only about 350mm long, with a barrel length about 170mm, and weighed about 2.2kg empty. Apparently the KRASA never went past the prototype stage.

Following the trend towards small-calibre, low-impulse military rifle ammunition, the Warsaw Pact, driven by the Soviet Union, began to adopt new small-calibre systems, built around the 5.45 × 39 cartridge of Soviet origin. Czechoslovakia could not avoid that move and this time decided (or was forced) to adopt the Soviet AK-74 rifle, instead of its own design. The Czechs introduced several improvements to the small-bore Kalashnikov rifle and produced two basic versions – one in 5.45mm Soviet, for domestic use, and another in 5.56mm NATO, for export. Both calibres

were to be offered in three versions: standard rifle, shortened carbine and heavy-barrelled, light machine gun with bipod. The development of this system was delayed for some time, so that when the Warsaw Pact dissolved the 5.45mm system, designated 'Lada', was still far from being adopted and issued. During the 1990s the 5.45mm version was abandoned and efforts concentrated on the 5.56mm NATO version, designated CZ-2000. It was completely developed by 2000, if not earlier, but financial restrictions led to limited procurements and issuance of these weapons to the Czech Army. Few if any export sales have been achieved, mostly because the market was already full of 5.45mm Kalashnikov clones.

During the 1990s and the early 2000s, the development of newer systems continued in the Czech Republic, but mostly in the smaller, newly founded, private companies. For example, a company called Czech Weapons S.R.O. produced a 5.56mm assault rifle, with a form of retarded blow-back action, devel-

5.45 × 39 'Lada' assault rifle, based on the Soviet Kalashnikov AK-74.

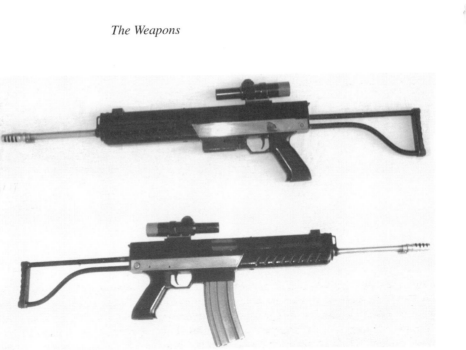

Experimental CZW-556 rifle by CZ Weapons. (image courtesy Ladislav Findorak)

oped by the designer Ladislav Findorak. This rifle is now available in prototype form.

Another Czech company, LCZ Group, attempted to manufacture and market the design of the Russian Baryshev under its own name: LCZ/Baryshev automatic rifles, chambered for 5.56mm and 7.62mm NATO ammunition (LCZ B-10 and B-20, respectively). These weapons were displayed at several defence exhibitions but apparently found no buyers, most probably because of the Baryshev system itself, which also features a form of retarded blow-back and operates from an open bolt.

SA Vz.58

Calibre: 7.62 × 39
Action: gas-operated, tilting breechblock
Overall length: 845mm (635mm with folded stock)
Barrel length: 390mm
Weight: with empty magazine 3.10kg, with loaded magazine 3.60kg
Magazine capacity: 30 rounds
Rate of fire: 800 rpm

The SA Vz.58 strongly resembles externally the famous Kalashnikov AK-47 assault rifle, but internally it is entirely different and of an original and well thought out design. It is a gas-operated, magazine-fed, selective-fire weapon. It uses a more or less conventional short-stroke gas piston, located above the barrel. The gas piston has its own return spring. The locking system features a linearly moving bolt (breechblock) with a separate tilting locking piece. The breechblock

(bolt) is located under the bolt carrier, and the locking piece is hinged to the bolt and located under it. The gun fires from a closed bolt all times. When the gun is fired, the gas piston gives a short tap to the bolt carrier. After a free movement of about 22mm (0.9in), the bolt carrier swings the locking piece up from the locking recesses in the receiver and thus unlocks the bolt. From this moment on, the bolt group moves back at once, extracting and ejecting the spent case and chambering a fresh cartridge. At the end of the return stroke, the bolt stops in the forwardmost position against the breech face, while the bolt carrier continues to move forward, swinging the locking piece down and into the locking recesses, thus locking the bolt to the receiver. The system may be roughly described as a mix between the Walther P-38 pistol and the Czech ZB-26 (or British Bren) machinegun locking. The charging handle is attached to the right side of the bolt carrier.

The trigger/hammer unit also differs from most common designs in that it is a striker-fired design. The massive cylindrical striker is located at the rear, hollowed part of the bolt and has its own spring located under the bolt group return spring. The striker has a lug that interacts with the sear and is used to hold the striker in the cocked position. The design of the trigger unit is relatively simple and has few moving parts. The safety/fire mode selector switch is located at the right side of the receiver and has three positions for safe, single shots and full automatic fire.

The basic variant, SA Vz.58P, has a fixed buttstock and furniture made either from wood (early models) or

Above *SA Vz.58P with fixed buttstock and bayonet.*

Left *SA Vz.58 with folding buttstock.*

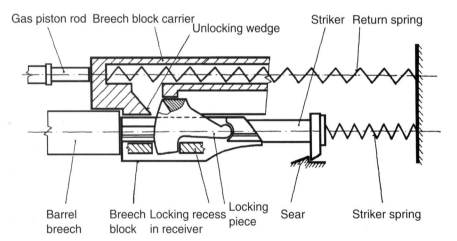

Gas piston rod Breech block carrier
Unlocking wedge
Striker Return spring

Barrel breech Breech block Locking recess in receiver Locking piece Sear Striker spring

Left *Diagram of the Vz.58 locking system.*

from wood-impregnated plastic (late production models). The SA Vz.58V has a side-folding metal buttstock and the SA Vz.58Pi is similar to the SA Vz.58P except that it has a large mounting bracket on the left side of the receiver that allows for IR/night sights to be mounted. The sights are of the open type, with hooded front post and open notch adjustable rear. In recent years some SA Vz.58s have also been fitted with scope rail mountings and red dot sights of Czech origin. These rifles are issued to some Czech Special Forces.

CZ-2000

CZ-2000 assault rifles are gas-operated, magazine-fed weapons, featuring a standard Kalashnikov-type long stroke gas piston, securely attached to the bolt carrier,

CZ-2000

	CZ-2000 rifle	CZ-2000 carbine
Calibre	5.56 × 45 NATO	
Overall length	850mm	675mm
Barrel length	382mm	185mm
Weight	3kg empty	2.6kg empty
Magazine capacity	30 rounds	
Rate of fire	750 rpm	850 rpm

with a two-lug rotating bolt. Receivers are made from stamped steel and the receiver top cover is hinged at the front. A typical AK-style safety/fire-selector lever is coupled with an additional safety/selector lever at the left side of the receiver, above the pistol grip. The barrel is somewhat shorter even than that of an AK-74, not to mention an M16A2, so the effective range with 5.56mm NATO/M855 ammunition is severely limited even for a 'full-size' CZ-2000 rifle. The sights also differ from the AK pattern, with an aperture rear sight being mounted on the receiver cover, with protective fences made from steel wire. Sights are marked up to a fairly optimistic 800m. Both front and rear sights are fitted with luminous inserts for night-time operations. A relatively small muzzle flash suppressor replaces the large AK-74-style muzzle brake. All CZ-2000 rifles are fitted with a side-folding skeleton butt as standard.

FINLAND

Finland fought World War II on the German side in a desperate attempt to regain territories lost to the Soviet Union during the 'Winter War' of 1939–40. When Finland finally saw that there was no chance of winning against the USSR, it eventually abandoned Germany, thus saving itself from being entirely overrun by the USSR. During the war, some Finnish arms designers, most notably Aimo Lahti, experimented with intermediate cartridges and so-called 'heavy submachine guns', which, in the modern sense, were true assault rifles. For example, Lahti developed several cartridges, based on shortened 6.5 × 55 Swedish Mauser cases, in 7.62 and 9mm calibres. He also produced an experimental AL-43 'heavy submachine gun', which looked like enlarged *Suomi* submachine gun and fired 7.62 × 35 intermediate cartridges from a large, fifty-four-round drum magazine. This delayed blow-back weapon was no more than a developmental model, being too expensive for mass production, and during the war the Finns mostly used the Mosin-Nagant bolt action and captured Soviet Tokarev SVT-38 and SVT-40 semi-automatic rifles.

After the end of the war Finland, like most other involved countries, faced the need to re-equip its armed forces. Having no spare resources to develop a domestic design, it wisely decided to adopt a foreign one. At that time, the only really sound and proven design suitable for the harsh conditions of Finland and chambered for a true intermediate cartridge, was the Soviet

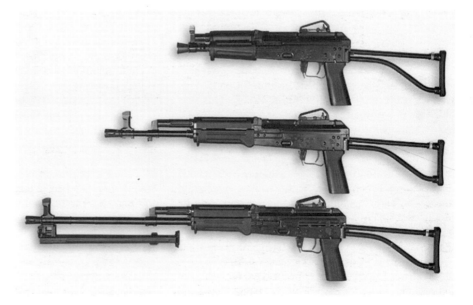

CZ2000 family of firearms, from top to bottom: carbine, standard assault rifle and light machinegun (squad automatic rifle).

Kalashnikov AK-47 rifle. Thus in the late 1950s Finland bought the manufacturing licence and began to develop its own version of the AK-47. The first prototypes of the future Finnish assault rifle, named Rk.60 (*Ryannakkokivaari malli 60* = assault rifle type 60), were submitted for military testing in 1960, resulting in the adoption of the modified RK.62 assault rifle in 1962. This was a refined AK-47 offspring, well suited to extremely cold weather. Finland later continued to develop AK-47-type rifles, but the RK.62, in refurbished form, still forms the core of the small arms in the Finnish armed forces.

In the following years, the state-owned Valmet Company, the manufacturer of the Rk.62, designed some further modifications, some of which were adopted for Finnish military service and acquired by the Army, some being manufactured for export only. The export versions were manufactured in original 7.62 × 39 chambering or in 5.56 × 45, either selective-fire or semi-automatic only. Some semi-automatic variants, named Valmet 78, were manufactured in 7.62 × 51 (.308 Winchester).

Of the military versions, the most interesting are the Rk.76 and the Rk.95TP. The Rk.76 is a modification of the original Rk.62, but with a stamped steel receiver instead of a milled one. This dramatically decreases the weight of the gun. Other changes were to offer four different types of buttstock: the 76W with a wooden, fixed buttstock, the 76P with a plastic, fixed buttstock, the 76T with a tubular, fixed buttstock (like the Rk.62) and the 76TP with a tubular, side-folding buttstock. Another change from the Rk.62 was the handguard, which was more AK-47-style than that of the Rk.62. However, for some reason the Army acquired only limited numbers of Rk.76 rifles, still preferring the older Rk.62s.

The bullpup Valmet M82 was another development, an attempt to create a compact weapon for paratroops without using a clumsy, folding buttstock. This was probably one of the first attempts to convert an existing, 'traditional' rifle into a bullpup layout. Like most such later attempts, it was not successful. The Finnish Army, after some testing, rejected it for unspecified reasons (some unofficial sources said that M82 tended to hit the paratroops in the teeth with its front sight during a hard parachute landing). Later Valmet produced a small batch (about 2,000) of M82 rifles in 5.56mm and sold them on the export market, mostly in the USA.

The Rk.95TP is the latest variation of Finnish military rifles. It features an old-style, milled receiver, but a new, side-folding, skeleton-type buttstock (Galil

type), a new muzzle flash hider and new handguards. The trigger guard is enlarged to allow shooting in gloves during cold winters. It should be noted that the Rk.95TP is referred as Sako Rk.95, not the Valmet Rk.95, because the Sako Company (involved in the production of the Rk.62 and further modifications almost from the start) was merged with the Valmet Company under the common name Sako. The Army has received the Rk.95TP in small quantities (only one batch was manufactured). The semi-automatic version of the Rk.95 is used for civilian training and practical shooting (under IPSC rules), as well as sold for export. The Rk.95 may be equipped with a Finnish-made Reflex sound suppressor. As a result of very limited military sales, the Sako-Valmet Company finally ceased the production of assault rifles in the late 1990s.

To complement domestically made rifles, during the late 1990s Finland also bought stocks of ex-East German and Chinese 7.62mm AK-47 rifles, which were much cheaper than the fine Sako-Valmet weapons. These foreign rifles are mostly issued to reserve and training units. It also must be noted that, while Finland produced many export versions of its own rifles in 5.56mm calibre, their own forces seem to be happy with the old 7.62 × 39 cartridge, which is still general issue in the Finnish Army. Since the late 1990s there have been no reported developments in Finland in the field of assault rifles.

SAKO-VALMET RK. 62/76/95

(data relate to the Rk.62 only)
Calibre: 7.62 × 39 (5.56 × 45 NATO export versions only)
Action: gas-operated, rotating bolt
Overall length: 914mm
Barrel length: 420mm
Weight: 4.3kg without magazine (3.5kg Rk.76 with stamped receiver)
Magazine capacity: 30 rounds

The prototype for these weapons was the Rk.60, internally almost a copy of the AK-47, but showing some external differences. It had a tubular metal buttstock, a plastic handguard that did not cover the gas tube and a plastic pistol grip. The Rk.60 lacked a trigger guard and had a three-prong flash suppressor at the muzzle. The original sights were replaced with a hooded post front sight atop the gas chamber; an aperture sight, mounted at the rear of the receiver cover, replaced the tangent rear sight. Both front and rear sights had folding 'night sights', with white luminous dots. After the testing and following modifications that included new, slightly redesigned handguards and the

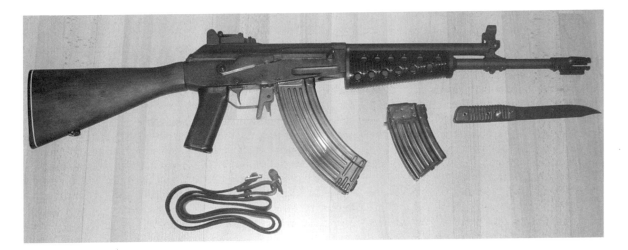

Above *RK.62 assault rifle with fixed wooden stock.*

Right *RK.62 rifle with fixed tubular metallic stock.*

RK.76 assault rifle with side-folding tubular buttstock and forty-rounds RPK magazine.

(image courtesy Dick Venema [Netherlands])

RK.95 assault rifle.

restoration of the trigger guard, the rifle was adopted as the Rk.62.

VALMET M82
Calibre: 5.56x45mm or 7.62x39mm
Action: gas-operated, rotating bolt
Overall length: 710mm
Barrel length: 420mm
Weight: 3.73kg less magazine
Magazine capacity: 30 rounds
Rate of fire: 650 rpm

To save time and money, Finnish engineers decided to keep the well-proven Valmet Rk.76/AKM action, receiver and barrel, and save on total length by putting it into a bullpup housing. Early prototypes featured wooden stocks, while latter models had a polymer housing which enclosed the receiver. The pistol grip with the trigger was moved to the front of the magazine port, and so a long link was introduced between the trigger and the hammer unit in the receiver. The safety/fire mode selector switch was kept in the same place on the receiver, placing it far behind the new

The Valmet 82 bullpup assault rifle, 5.56mm version.

pistol grip and trigger. The sights were mounted on relatively high posts and set to the left from the weapon axis. There were no provisions for right-hand ejection therefore the M82 could not be fired from the left shoulder.

FRANCE

France was one of the first countries to field a semi-automatic infantry rifle in significant quantities, during World War I. However, the majority of the French troops that fought in World War II against Germany were still armed with the 7.5mm or obsolete 8mm, bolt-action rifles. By the end of the war France began to develop several intermediate cartridges and the rifles and carbines to fire them. France also used some ex-German engineers and designers who had worked for Mauser Werke during the war, most notably Ludwig Vorgrimler, the 'father' of the German Mauser Stg.45 assault rifle. Despite this work, the French Army decided to adopt a semi-automatic rifle chambered for the full-power 7.5mm rifle cartridge, and by 1959 it had an excellent rifle, the MAS 49/56. But with the introduction of small-calibre, low-impulse ammunition the French also recognized the need for a new, selective-fire infantry weapon. During the late 1970s the Army acquired significant quantities of the Swiss-designed SIG SG-540 rifles in 5.56 × 45, to familiarize itself with the new cartridge. These weapons were made in France under licence from SIG at the Manurhin arms factory. At the same time France developed its own assault rifle at the famous St. Etienne

arsenal (*Manufacture d'Armes de St-Etienne*), which was adopted by the Army as the FAMAS F1, being the world's second officially issued bullpup rifle (after the Austrian Steyr AUG – Stg.77, and not counting the unlucky British EM-2).

FAMAS stands for *Fusil d'Assaut de la Manufacture d'Armes de St-Etienne* (assault rifle by St-Etienne Arms Factory – a member of the French government-owned GIAT Industries). Development of this rifle began in 1967, under the leadership of the Paul Tellie, a French designer. This new rifle was intended to replace in service the MAS Mle.49/56 semi-automatic rifles, MAT-49 submachine guns and some MAC Mle.1929 light machine guns. The first FAMAS prototype was built in 1971 and the French military began to test it in 1972–73. The FAMAS rifle was adopted by the French in 1978 and since then has become a standard French Army shoulder-fired small arm, known among the French soldiers as 'Le Clairon' (the bugle) due to its ungainly appearance. About 400,000 were built, and the production of the original FAMAS F1 variant is now complete. It is still used by the French Army and was exported in small numbers to some countries such as Senegal and the United Arab Emirates. The FAMAS saw some action during Operation *Desert Storm* in Kuwait in 1991, as well as in some peacekeeping operations in the mid and late 1990s, and has proved itself a reliable and trustworthy weapon, proving popular among French troops.

During the early 1990s GIAT Industries developed an improved version of the F1, known as the G1. This rifle features an enlarged trigger guard, which covers

FAMAS F1 rifle.

the whole hand, and slightly improved plastic hand-guards. The G1 was an intermediate design and was consequently replaced by the latest production model, the FAMAS G2, which appeared in 1994. This rifle has the G1-style enlarged trigger guard but can accept only STANAG type (M16-compatible) magazines. It was adopted and purchased by the French Navy in 1995, with the Army soon following suit, and also offered for export.

GIAT now also offers some variations of the basic FAMAS G2 rifle, such as the 'Submachine gun' with a shortened receiver and a 320mm barrel, 'Commando' with the standard receiver and a 405mm barrel, and 'Sniper', with a longer and heavier 620mm barrel and an integral scope mount instead of the carrying handle.

At the present time the slightly upgraded FAMAS G2 rifle is used as a platform for the future FELIN system (a French counterpart to the US 'Land Warrior' programme), which incorporates various electronic sights and sensors, connected to the soldier-carried equipment, such as helmet-mounted displays and ballistic and tactical computers. It also features in the PAPOP hybrid rifle/grenade launcher system. One interesting aspect of the PAPOP programme is the proposed development of subcalibre 5.56mm ammunition with muzzle velocities as high as 1,500–1,800m/s. This will greatly increase the armour-piercing perfor-

mance of the rifle and simplify sighting due to the extremely flat trajectory and short projectile flight time. GIAT Industries apparently also continues its work on caseless ammunition and the small arms for it, but little information is publicly available about these developments.

FAMAS

	FAMAS F1	FAMAS G2
Calibre	5.56 × 45	
Action	delayed blow-back	
Overall length	757mm	
Barrel length	488mm	
Weight	3.61kg (empty magazine)	3.8kg (empty magazine)
Magazine capacity	25 rounds (proprietary)	30 rounds (STANAG)
Muzzle velocity	960m/s	925m/s
Rate of fire	900–1,000 rpm	1,000–1,100 rpm
Effective range	300m	450m

FAMAS G2 in its standard (top) and 'Commando' (bottom) versions.

FAMAS G2 partially disassembled.

The FAMAS assault rifles have the bullpup layout, with the magazine housing behind the pistol grip and the trigger. The gun is built around the compact receiver, which is enclosed in the plastic housing. FAMAS is one of the relatively rare systems that uses a lever-retarded blow-back action, borrowed from the French AAT-52 machine gun, but originally invented by the Hungarian designer Paul de Kiraly before the Second World War and improved by Paul Tellie for the FAMAS rifle. This system consists of the two-part bolt group, with the delay lever interposed between the light forward part (breechblock, or bolt itself), which has a bolt face and provisions for extractor mountings, and the heavier rear part (the bolt carrier). The lever is pivotally mounted on the front part of the breechblock (bolt), with its lower legs resting against the cross pin in the receiver and the upper legs resting against the face on the bolt carrier (assuming that the bolt group is in its forward position).

The gun is fired from a closed bolt. When the cartridge is ignited and fired, the gas pressure against the cartridge base pushes the cartridge case back in the fluted chamber and against the bolt face. The bolt begins to move back under the pressure, but, in the initial stages of the movement, when the pressure is still high, the delay lever transforms the short movement of the bolt into the longer movement of the heavier bolt carrier, thus retarding the opening of the bolt. As soon as the pressure in the chamber has dropped down to a reasonable level, the lever is

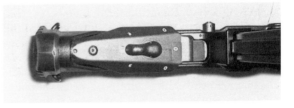

Separate burst mode selector, mounted below the receiver of the FAMAS.

completely withdrawn from contact with the cross pin, and from this moment both the bolt and its carrier begin to move back with the same speed, compressing the return spring and extracting and ejecting the spent case. The bolt face has extractor mounting points on both sides, so that the user can mount the extractor claw on the left or the right side of the bolt, which will result in left- or right-side ejection of spent cartridge cases through the ejection ports on both sides of the gun. The ejection port, which is not in use, is always covered with the detachable cheek piece, which can be installed on either side of the gun, as required. This solves the problem of left-handed use, which is difficult in most bullpup rifles. The charging handle located above the receiver, under the carrying handle, is shaped like a trigger and completely ambidextrous. The charging handle does not reciprocate when the gun is fired.

The firing mechanism unit is contained in the

detachable plastic housing just behind the magazine port. The unit is linked to the trigger by the long trigger rod and the safety/fire selector is located within the trigger guard, just ahead of the trigger. The selector has three positions for safe, single shots, and automatic fire. An additional, three-round-bursts module is built into the firing mechanism housing, with the additional selector under the housing, behind the magazine, that allows for unlimited full automatic fire or three-round-burst modes to be chosen when the main selector is in the full automatic mode.

The sighting system of the FAMAS consists of a blade front and the aperture rear sight, adjustable for range and with two flip-up apertures, for good visibility and low light conditions. Both sights are mounted on the pillars, which are, in turn, mounted on the receiver and concealed by the large plastic carrying handle. The carrying handle has provisions for mounting Weaver- or Picatinny-style sight bases. A special receiver is also available with the integral sights base instead of the carrying handle.

The standard FAMAS barrel is 488mm long and has a NATO-standard 22mm diameter flash suppressor, which is also used to launch rifle grenades from the muzzle. Current FAMAS barrels are rifled with a 1:9 twist (one turn in 228mm, right hand), so both the older M193 and the newer 5.56mm NATO/SS109/M855 ammunition can be fired with good results. Another interesting fact about the FAMAS barrel is that it has only three grooves (most other rifles have from four to six). The 'Commando' variant has the shorter barrel, which cannot be used to launch grenades. Both standard and Commando versions can be fitted with the 40mm M203 underbarrel grenade launcher, if required. Every FAMAS rifle (except for the shortest 'submachine gun' version) can be fitted with a non-adjustable, lightweight bipod, which can be folded along the gun body when not in use. On most rifles these bipods are fitted as standard. Every FAMAS rifle is equipped with a carrying sling and a detachable bayonet.

GERMANY: PRE-1945

Hitler's Germany was the leading country in the development of the assault rifle. Even the very term is no more than a translation of the German *Sturmgewehr*, devised for propaganda reasons by no less a person than Hitler himself. Germany began to develop intermediate cartridges during the mid 1930s. There were some developments in 7 and 7.75mm calibre, but the *Heereswaffenamt* (HWaA, or department of armaments) decided to retain the existing rifle calibre of 7.92mm, to save money on new machinery that would otherwise be required to produce bullets and barrels of a non-standard calibre. The new 7.92mm 'short infantry cartridge' (*Infanteriepatrone Kurz*), developed by Polte Werke in 1938, was officially designated the 7.92mm PP Kurz. It had the metric dimensions of 7.92 × 33, considerably shorter and less powerful than the standard 7.92 × 57 rifle/MG cartridge, and propelled a 8.1g (125gr.) bullet to roughly 680m/s.

In 1939 the HWaA issued a contract to C.G. Haenel Waffen und Fahrradfabrik for the development of a *Maschinenkarabiner*, or machine carbine (MKb for short), chambered for the new Kurz cartridge. Initial development took place under the designation of MKb.42 – *Maschinenkarabiner*, 1942. The new weapon was intended as a replacement for submachine guns, bolt action rifles and, partly, light machineguns for front-line troops and was intended to have an effective range of 600m or so.

The famous designer Hugo Schmeisser led the Haenel development team, which produced the first working prototypes of the new weapon by 1942. In accordance with the specification, the new weapon inherited several features from the MP-40 submachine gun, such as the left-side charging handle with slot safety and magazine housing with button release. Because the new weapon had to be made with the maximum use of stamping and welding, Haenel was joined by Merz Werke, a company with no knowledge of firearms but a great deal of experience in steel stamping and forming. The first weapons were issued to front-line units on the Eastern front by mid 1942 and low-rate mass production began in late 1942. A total of about 10,000 MKb.42(H)s were produced for the Army before production ended in favour of an improved design, the MP-43.

In 1940 another company joined in the development of this new type of small arm: the famous German arms manufacturer Carl Walther, known for its fine and popular pistols. Walther had already been engaged in the development of intermediate-cartridge firearms since 1936, when it produced self-loading carbines for an experimental 7 × 39 cartridge. Later, Walther developed several automatic designs in 'full-size' 7.92 × 57, and one of these experimental prototypes, the 7.92mm A-115, served as a starting point for its 7.92mm Kurz rifle. Walther began to develop its own *Maschinen-karabiner* as a private venture, but in 1941 received official approval from the HWaA for further development in competition with Haenel, the first MKb.42(W) rifles being delivered to the Army in the second half of 1942.

Late in the year, the first small batches of both Haenel and Walther weapons, designated MKb.42(H) and MKb.42(W), respectively, were sent to the Eastern front, for trials against Soviet troops. Initial results were promising, with the Haenel rifles being generally preferred because of their better reliability. The Walther design, which showed better single-shot accuracy, was rejected as unsuitable on the grounds of its questionable annular gas piston system. No further development in this field was apparently undertaken by Walther, which was already busy delivering its P.38 pistols to the Army.

The HWaA asked Haenel for several significant improvements over the original design. Most notably the request to replace the submachine-gun-like open-bolt firing system with a more convenient, closed-bolt system, to improve single-shot accuracy. Schmeisser redesigned the weapon accordingly, and by 1943 submitted the improved version to the HWaA. But by this time Hitler had ordered that only existing types should be developed and manufactured and the *Maschinenkarabiner* was not on this list. To avoid this nuisance, the Germans decided simply to rename the MKb to the MP, or *Machinenpistole* (submachine gun), which was on the 'approved' list. Thus the new and improved weapon received the designation MP-43 and went into limited production and field trials at the front. During the following year, the MP-43 experienced several minor modifications, leading to the MP-43/1 and the MP-43/2 designation, but these differed only in details such as front sight bases and grenade-launcher interfaces.

In April 1944 the designation of all MP-43s was changed to MP-44, with no actual changes made to the design. At this time there were many glowing reports from the troops fighting with MP-43s and MP-44s in the east. Seeing these reports, Hitler finally approved the mass production and issuing of the new 'Wunderwaffe', and in December officially christened it the *Sturmgewehr 1944* (StG.44), or assault rifle, 1944. This was a pure act of propaganda, but the name stuck not only to that gun, but also to the entire new class of automatic weapons designed to fire intermediate cartridges.

The total number of MP-43s, MP-44s and StG.44s produced was about 450,000, and these guns proved very effective, but not without some flaws. After the war the direct development of the Stg.44 was stopped, but the East German police used some remaining guns. Another major post-war user of the Stg.44 was Yugoslavia; their paratroops used it under the designation *Automat, padobranski, 7.9mm M43* (or *M44*),

The 7.92 × 57 Mauser next to the 7.92 × 33 Kurz.

nemacki until the early 1980s, when the Kalashnikov-type M70 rifle finally replaced it. Yugoslavia also produced 7.92 × 33 Kurz ammunition into the 1970s. An amusing side note is that several Stg.44s, captured by the Soviet Army and converted to fire blank cartridges, were used until the late 1980s by several major Soviet film studios to imitate various 'weapons of imperialism', including the American M16. In this case, the crude camouflage consisted of a carrying handle, semi-permanently attached to the top of the receiver.

German development of assault rifles did not stop with the adoption of the Stg.44. This weapon was far too heavy and, while being made mostly of stampings, still required plenty of raw materials. So several German companies continued to produce 7.92mm Kurz rifles of several designs. Most interesting among these was the Mauser design, usually credited to Wilhelm Stähle and Ludwig Vorgrimler. By 1943 Mauser Werke had developed a gas-operated weapon, which featured rigid roller locking, broadly derived

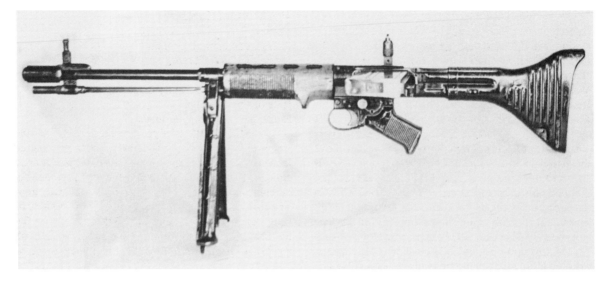

Early model of the FG 42.

from the MG-42 machinegun. This experimental weapon had a factory designation of *Gerät 06* (Device 06). This system (copied several times during the post-war period with equally unspectacular results) proved itself too complicated, but then Vorgrimler devised a version of the retarded (sometimes also called delayed) blow-back system. In this, there was no gas system and piston and no rigid locking. Instead, rollers were used to retard the opening of the breech until the chamber pressure dropped to safe levels. This system was factory designated as *Gerät 06H*, and by early 1945 was officially type-classified as Stg.45. It is believed that no more than thirty specimens of this weapon were made before Allied forces captured Mauser Werke in Oberndorf, and thus it made no impact on the war. But, instead, it made a significant impact on post-war developments, since its chief designer, Ludwig Vorgrimler, went to France, where he continued to develop this design for several years. During the early 1950s he moved to Spain, where he participated in the development of the CETME assault rifles (see below), which led direct to the famous Heckler & Koch family of small arms, including the G3, the HK33 and the G41 assault rifles (all described in the next section).

Another interesting development, which falls slightly outside the scope of this book but has to be mentioned for its historical significance at least, is the FG-42 automatic rifle. Designed at the request of the RLM and dating back to the 1940s, this gas-operated rifle was intended for Luftwaffe paratroops

(*Fallschirmjäger*), and was intended to replace submachine guns, bolt action rifles and even light machine guns in the hands of these elite troops. By 1942 two companies had submitted their designs, Rheinmetall and Krieghoff. The Luftwaffe preferred the former, and the contract was placed with Rheinmetall for the manufacture of these rifles under the designation FG-42 (*Fallschirmjäger Gewehr-42* = paratrooper rifle, model 1942). This rifle featured a gas-operated, rotating bolt design, and fired from a closed bolt in single shots and from an open bolt in automatic fire mode. The gun was fed from a side-mounted, detachable, box magazine, and a muzzle brake and folding bipod were fitted to compensate for the severe recoil of the powerful 7.92×57 cartridge in such a light weapon.

The original design was very expensive to make and virtually uncontrollable when firing full automatic, so the project was handled over to Krieghoff for revision and further mass production. A revised version of the FG-42 (sometimes referred as the FG-42 model 2) had some external differences from the original Rheinmetall model (FG-42 model 1), most notably in the shape of the butt, pistol grip and in the placement of the folding bipod. It also had stamped steel receivers, as opposed to the machined alloy receivers of the early FG-42s. Nevertheless, these upgrades did not help much; the FG-42 was still expensive to make and not properly controllable in fully automatic fire. About 6,000 were delivered to the Luftwaffe before 1945.

HAENEL MKB.42(H)

Calibre: 7.92 × 33 (7.92mm Kurz)
Action: gas-operated, tilting bolt
Overall length: 940mm
Barrel length: 364mm
Weight: 4.9kg with empty magazine
Rate of fire: 500 rpm
Magazine capacity: 30 rounds

The MKb.42(H) is a gas-operated, selective-fire weapon. It uses a long-stroke gas piston, located above the barrel in a long gas tube. The barrel locking is achieved by tipping the rear part of the bolt down into the locking recess, cut in the machined steel insert in the receiver. The gun fires from an open bolt at all times, and the only safety feature is the MP-40-type slot, cut at the rear of the charging handle slot, in which the charging handle can be hooked when the bolt is open. The cross-bolt-type fire mode selector is located above the trigger guard. The MKb.42(H) could be fitted with the standard bayonet, and has a wooden butt.

WALTHER MKB.42(W)

Calibre: 7.92 × 33 (7.92mm Kurz)
Action: gas-operated, rotating bolt
Overall length: 931mm
Barrel length: 406mm
Weight: 4.4kg with empty magazine
Rate of fire: 600 rpm
Magazine capacity: 30 rounds

The MKb.42(W) is a gas-operated, magazine-fed weapon. The gas system has an annular gas piston, located around the barrel and inside the stamped annular handguards. A rotating bolt of somewhat complicated design locks to the barrel via two lugs. The hammer-fired trigger unit allows single shots or fully automatic fire, and the MKb.42(W) is fed by using the same thirty-round magazine as its rival, the MKb.42(H). The MKb.42(W) fires from a closed bolt.

MKb.42(H) automatic carbine, designed by Hugo Schmeisser.

The MKb.42(W).

Haenel MP-43 MP-44 Stg.44

Calibre: 7.92 × 33 (7.92mm Kurz)
Action: gas-operated, tilting bolt
Overall length: 940mm
Barrel length: 419mm
Weight: 5.22kg empty
Rate of fire: 500 rpm
Magazine capacity: 30 rounds

The StG.44 is a gas-operated, selective fire weapon. The receiver and trigger housing with pistol grip are made from steel stampings, with machined steel inserts. The trigger housing with pistol grip is hinged to the receiver and folds down for disassembly. The gas drive utilizes a long-stroke piston, and the bolt is tipped down to lock into the receiver. The gun is fired from a closed bolt. The MP-43 and subsequent versions all were hammer-fired, while the MKb.42(H) was striker-fired. The safety lever is located at the left side of the pistol grip unit and a separate cross-bolt-type of fire mode selector allows for single-shot and full automatic fire. The charging handle is attached to the gas piston rod and the ejection port has a dust cover. The recoil spring is located inside the wooden butt. At the top of the butt there is a container for a cleaning kit, closed by the spring-loaded steel cover. The Stg.44 was provided with open, leaf-type sights and

Stg.44, the first 'assault rifle'. (courtesy Dick Venema)

The same rifle, right-side view. (courtesy Dick Venema)

StG.44 partially disassembled.

could be fitted with telescope sights or a specially developed active infrared sighting unit, called *Vampir* (vampire).

The muzzle of the Stg.44 was threaded to accept a cup-like grenade launcher; a special muzzle nut usually covered the threads. It could also be fitted with a special curved barrel attachment (*Krummlauf*), which allowed the gun to be fired 'around the corner' or from inside a tank, without exposing the shooter to enemy fire. Several types of these attachments were developed, but only one, the 30-degree *Krummlauf Vorsatz J*, was apparently manufactured in any significant numbers. This device had a special mirror sighting adaptor and reduced the bullet velocity down to a mere 300m/s due to the high friction in the curved barrel extension. This apparently did not bother the German Army, since these adaptors were intended for short-range encounters only.

MAUSER STG.45(M)

Calibre: 7.92 × 33 (7.92mm Kurz)
Action: retarded blow-back
Length: 893mm
Barrel length: 400mm
Weight: 3.71kg less magazine
Magazine: 10 or 30 rounds
Rate of fire: 400 rpm

The famous Mauser Werke began to develop its own assault rifle by 1943. It was decided to produce the cheapest possible design, with as much stamping and welding used as possible. The original design, called *Gerät 06*, had a short-stroke gas piston and a locking

Gerät 06 (c. 1943), a gas-operated, roller locked experimental assault rifle from Mauser.

StG.45(M), also known as a Gerät 06H, a retarded-blow-back derivative of the Gerät 06.

system with two rollers, located in the bolt, which was forced out to the barrel extension to lock the bolt. When the gun was fired, the gas piston forced the bolt carrier back and this withdrew the rollers from the cuts in the barrel extension, unlocking the bolt and then pulling it back to eject the spent case and load a fresh round on its way back. This system was later found to be too complicated and experiments proved that the locking system could be done away with since the rollers by themselves were able to retard the initial bolt movement until pressure in the chamber dropped to a safe level. This improved system, usually credited to Vorgrimler, greatly simplified the design. This version was designated *Gerät 06H*. Because there was no primary extraction, a fluted chamber was devised to avoid sticking cases and subsequent torn rims and resulting jams. The receiver, as well as the round handguards, were made from two stamped parts, left and right, connected by simple welding. The gun was built with a straight-line layout to reduce muzzle climb during automatic fire, and so the sights were placed well above the barrel. This also resulted in the development of a shorter magazine with capacity of only ten rounds, requested by the troops. The retarded-blowback Stg.45(M) were easily distinguishable from the original, gas-operated *Gerät 06* rifles by the ribbed handguards of circular cross-section on the former, as opposed to the slab-sided handguards on the latter.

The Stg.45(M) was a good deal lighter than the Stg.44, and required about 50 per cent less raw materials to make. But it appeared too late in the war, and its major impact was on post-war developments, most notably in Spain and West Germany.

GERMANY: FEDERAL REPUBLIC

The *Bundesrepublik Deutschland* (BRD), the Federal Republic of Germany (FRG), more commonly called West Germany, began to develop its own armed forces in 1955. Most of the initial training and weaponry for that new service, called the *Bundeswehr*, was provided by the USA. At about the same time the FRG joined the recently formed NATO. The new army obviously required new armaments, compliant with NATO standards. The most obvious choice for a new rifle was the Belgian FN FAL, which was adopted by the *Bundesgrentzgeshütz* (Border Guard) as the G1 rifle circa 1956. But because of the Belgian refusal to sell the manufacturing licence for the FAL to Germany, the *Bundeswehr* began the search for another design in 7.62 × 51 NATO calibre. After trials held in 1956, the Spanish CETME design (which had been developed with a great deal of input from German engineers) was chosen. Other weapons tested against the CETME (G3) were the FN FAL (G1), the Swiss SIG SG-510 (G2), and the ArmaLite AR-10 (G4). By 1958 the manufacturing licence for the 7.62mm CETME rifles, first granted to the Dutch NVM company, was transferred to the German Heckler und Koch company, located in Oberndorf and founded on the remains of the wartime Mauser factory.

HK slightly modified the CETME design, and in 1959 the *Bundeswehr* finally adopted the CETME/HK rifle as the G3 (*Gewehr 3* = Rifle, [model] 3). From then and until 1995 the G3 in various modifications served as the general issue shoulder weapon not only for German armed forces, but also for a total of more than fifty countries, including Greece, Iran, Mexico, Norway, Pakistan, Portugal, Sweden and Turkey. The G3 was or still is manufactured in several countries including Greece, Pakistan, Iran, Turkey and Portugal. The key reason for its popularity is that it is much simpler and cheaper to manufacture than its major contemporary rivals, the Belgian FN FAL and the US M14. It appears that HK itself continued to produce and offer the G3 until 2000 or 2001, when it finally disappeared from their catalogues. In general, the HK G3 rifle can be described as one of the best of the 7.62mm NATO battle/assault rifles – reliable, versatile, relatively controllable, inexpensive and, finally, very popular. For civilian markets HK produced the semi-automatic-only versions of the G3, initially known as the HK 41 and later as the HK 91. An interesting variation on the theme is the HK-based MC51 short assault rifle in 7.62 × 51, currently offered by the British company FR Ordnance. It is reportedly based not on the G3 but on a lengthened version of the 9mm HK MP5A3 SMG, and has a barrel just 230mm long.

Inevitably, HK had to produce weapons based on the new 5.56 × 45 (.223 Remington) cartridge. Their first attempt was the HK33 assault rifle, developed in the mid to late 1960s as a scaled-down version of the G3, which entered production in 1968. While this was not adopted by the German military, it saw significant use by some West German police and security units and was also widely exported, being used by Malaysia, Chile and Thailand. Turkey has also manufactured HK33 rifles for its army since 1999. The HK33 is still in production in Germany by HK, and also served as a platform for further developments, such as the G41 assault rifle and the HK53 compact assault rifle (known by HK as a submachine gun).

The G41 assault rifle was developed in the early 1980s from the HK33E assault rifle as a companion to the G11 caseless rifle. While the caseless G11 was to be issued to frontline troops, the G41 was intended for second-line troops. The G41 was submitted for the Italian assault rifle trials during the early 1980s in collaboration with Luigi Franchi Spa, but it lost to the Beretta 70/90. However, the Italian Special Forces apparently found the G41 very appealing and purchased undisclosed quantities of it, which is still used by the COL MOSCHIN and SAN MARCO regiments and the COMSUBIN (the Italian equivalents of US Marines and S.E.A.L. forces, respectively). The main drawback of the G41 was its price – it was offered for several times higher, than, for example, the price of the M16A2, and few buyers were able to pay such sums. Consequently, the G41 was dropped from the HK product line in the mid 1990s.

There also were some more HK designs, which, unlike the ones above, came to a dead end. The most famous was the 4.7mm G11 caseless rifle, developed between the late 1960s and the early 1990s, when, due to financial and political considerations, the project was abandoned. The starting point for the design was a decision by the West German government to replace the existing 7.62mm G3 rifle with a lighter weapon

with a much better hit probability. Studies led to the idea of the small-calibre, rapid-fire rifle employing caseless ammunition. To ensure sufficient stopping/killing power for the small-calibre bullets used, as well as an improved hit probability per one trigger pull, the rifle should have a three-round-burst capability and a high-capacity magazine. The new design, called the G11, was created by in conjunction with the Dynamit Nobel Company; HK was responsible for the rifle itself and Dynamit Nobel developed the caseless ammunition.

In the late 1980s the *Bundeswehr* began the field tests of the pre-production G11s. After the early tests, some improvements were devised, such as a removable optical sight, the mounting of two spare magazines on the rifle and the addition of a bayonet/bipod mount under the muzzle. The modified variant, called the G11K2, was tested in 1989, scoring at least 50 per cent better combat accuracy than the G3 rifle. As stated in some sources, the *Bundeswehr* received a first batch of G11K2s about 1990, but the government then canceled the whole programme. The main reason was the end of the Cold War combined with the high cost of the reunion of West and East Germany and sharply reduced funds for military developments; but the general NATO policy for the unification of the ammunition and even magazines for assault rifles probably also played a part.

A slightly modified G11 was also tested in the USA under the ACR (Advanced Combat Rifle) programme, during the late 1980s and the early 1990s, and did quite well. However, like all other ACR programme entrants, it failed to achieve a 100 per cent performance increase over the US standard issue M16A2 rifle.

Another project, briefly developed by Heckler-Koch during the early 1970s, was the HK36 (not to be confused with the later G36). This rifle used the same roller retarded blow-back action of the G3, but fired a micro-calibre, low-impulse ammunition 4.6 × 36, fitted with spoon-tip (*Löffelspitz*) bullets for an increased wounding capability. Other features of the HK36 were the collimating sight, built into the carrying handle, and the unusual feed system, which used prepacked plastic magazines, inserted into the fixed housing via the hinged side 'door'. The HK36 project was terminated in about 1976, with all efforts being concentrated on the more promising G11 caseless rifle.

Recent developments from Heckler & Koch are based on the 5.56mm G36 family of small arms, initiated as the HK-50 project in the early 1990s. The need for this arose because the *Bundeswehr*, following the cancellation of the G11 and G41 projects, was left with

The experimental, micro-calibre 4.6mm HK36 assault rifle; it did not succeed,
but some of its features found their way to the later 5.56mm HK50/G36 rifle.

the outdated 7.62mm G3 rifle and needed a modern one compatible with current NATO standards. The new rifle needed to be flexible, affordable and extremely reliable. The major competitor to this new weapon was the Austrian Steyr AUG, already a popular and proven gun.

It seems that HK has succeeded in every respect with the G36. The *Bundeswehr* adopted the new 5.56mm assault rifle in 1995 after extensive trials, and in 1999 Spain adopted its slightly different export version, the G36E, as its standard infantry rifle. The G36 has also found its way into the hands of several law-enforcement agencies worldwide, including the British police and some American police departments. It also had been or still is being tested by other armed forces, including the Norwegian.

The latest HK developments are being conducted under the leadership of the ATK Corporation in the USA, under the US Objective Force Warrior programme. These include the XM8 lightweight automatic rifle, an entirely modular design based on the HK G36, and the 20 and 25mm grenade launchers, intended for the composite system XM29 (5.56mm XM8 + 20mm semi-automatic grenade launcher) or as stand-alone weapons (25mm XM25), described in the section on American weapons.

During the mid 1990s Heckler & Koch, in serious financial trouble due to the cancellation of the G11, was bought by Royal Ordnance in Britain to fill the gap in the British small arms industry, which had declined since the closure of the famous Royal Small Arms Factory at Enfield Lock. HK was then engaged in the

expensive and apparently successful upgrade programme of the ill-fated, British L85A1 rifle (described in detail in the United Kingdom section). Then in 2002, HK was bought from Royal Ordnance by a group of private German investors, and thus it is now the prime German military and law-enforcement small arms manufacturer.

Heckler & Koch still manufacture a wide variety of firearms based on the G3 design, but of different purposes and calibres, such as the 9mm MP-5 submachine gun, the 5.56mm HK33 assault rifle, the 5.56mm and the 7.62mm HK23 and HK21 machine guns and the PSG1 sniper rifle. HK effectively overshadow all other companies which attempted to achieve any success in small arms in Germany. Military automatic rifles and submachine guns were, and still are, the fields where HK dominates most. But they are not the only company developing small arms in the FRG. Another famous manufacturer, Rheinmetall, reorganized after World War II, developed during the 1960s the 7.62 × 39 RH-4 gas-operated, roller-locked assault rifle, but achieved no sales. This rifle looked much like the HK33, but apparently represented a step back in design to the original Mauser *Gerät 06* of 1943 vintage. Mauser Werke also attempted to enter into the field of caseless weapons during the late 1970s or early 1980s, but lost to HK before the idea was abandoned. Similar results, or a lack of them, were achieved by the lesser-known Vollmer Maschinenfabrik company, which developed a recoil-operated, burst-firing, caseless rifle with multiple chambers in a rotating block during the early 1980s.

HECKLER UND KOCH G3

Calibre: 7.62 × 51 NATO
Action: retarded blow-back
Weight: 4.25kg less magazine; 5kg with magazine loaded with 20 rounds
Overall length: 1,020mm (800mm with butt collapsed in G3A4 version)
Barrel length: 450mm (315mm on G3KA4 model)
Magazine capacity: 20 rounds
Rate of fire: 500–600 rpm

The G3 rifle is a selective-fire, magazine-fed rifle. It uses a retarded (sometimes also called delayed) blow-back action, which had been developed by German engineers at Mauser Werke late in World War II and was subsequently refined in Spain, at the CETME company. The first models of the G3 rifle were quite similar to CETME rifles, and until about 1961 even had 'CETME' markings on the receivers. The roller-delayed, blow-back action is described in detail under the CETME rifles in the section on Spain.

The G3 is built by using as many stamped parts as possible. The receiver is stamped from sheet steel. The trigger unit housing, along with the pistol grip frame, also are stamped from steel and hinged to the receiver by using the cross pin in the front of the trigger unit, just behind the magazine housing. The earliest G3 rifles also featured stamped handguards and CETME-type, flip-up rear aperture sights (*Klappvisier*). The folding cocking handle is located on the special tube above the barrel, at the left side, and

The earliest variant of the G3, with Klappvisier, stamped steel trigger unit and ventilated handguards.

Early production G3A2 rifle, with Drehvisier (drum rear sight), ventilated handguards and stamped steel trigger unit. (courtesy Dick Venema)

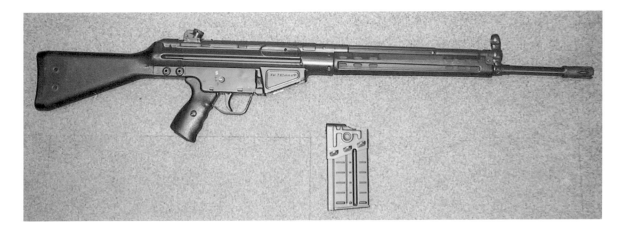

does not reciprocate when the gun is fired. The safety/fire selector is located above the triggerguard on the left side of the trigger group housing and usually is marked 'S – E – F' (Safe – Single shots – Full automatic). The latest models could have selectors marked with coloured icons.

In the mid 1960s the original design was upgraded to the G3A2 and the G3A3 configuration. These rifles had ventilated, plastic handguards and drum-type rear aperture sights (*Drehvisier*), marked from 200 to 400m, with an open notch for the 100m range. The G3A2 was a fixed butt version, with buttstock made from plastic, and the G3A3 was a telescoping butt version, with a retractable metal buttstock with a rubber buttplate. Late German production G3A2 and G3A3 models were built using new trigger units, integral with a restyled pistol grip and trigger guard, made entirely from plastic. The shortest version of the G3 was the G3KA3, similar to the G3A3 but with a shortened barrel. Every G3 rifle can be equipped with a detachable bipod and claw-type, detachable scope mounts. Long-barrelled versions can also be fitted with a bayonet or used to launch rifle grenades from the barrel.

HECKLER UND KOCH HK 33 AND HK 53

The HK33 is a retarded blow-back-operated, selective-fire rifle, which utilizes a two-piece bolt with two rollers to retard the initial bolt opening. The receiver is made from stamped steel and the gun is available with either a polymer fixed buttstock (HK33A2) or a retractable metal buttstock (HK33A3). Carbine versions of the HK33 are also available, featuring shorter barrels and similar fixed or retractable stocks (HK33KA2 and HK33KA3, respectively). All HK33 variants are available with a variety of trigger units, with or without three-round-burst mode. HK's proprietary, claw-type mounts allow telescopic sights to be mounted on any version of HK33. Full-length HK33s can be equipped with a bayonet or an underbarrel, 40mm grenade launcher – the HK79A1, also made by HK. Full-length HK33 rifles also can launch rifle grenades from the combined muzzle compensator/flash suppressor.

Late production G3A2 rifle, with Drehvisier, plain handguards and stamped steel trigger unit.

The HK33.

HECKLER UND KOCH HK 33 AND HK 53

	HK33	HK33K	HK53
Calibre		5.56 × 45	
Length	919mm; 740mm with retracted stock in A3 variant	865mm; 670mm with retracted stock in A3 variant	780mm; 590mm with retracted stock in A3 variant
Barrel length	390mm	322mm	211mm
Weight empty	3.9kg	3.65kg	3.0kg
Magazine capacity		25, 30, 40 rounds	
Rate of fire	750 rpm	750 rpm	750 rpm

The HK53 is an ultra-compact version of the HK33, which is advertised by HK as a 'submachine gun' and, by common sense, falls in the same category as the Soviet AKS-74U or the Colt 'Commando'. All these guns can be classified as 'compact' (or short) assault rifles by the fact that they use the intermediate rifle round. The HK53 was developed in the mid 1970s and is still in production and offered for export. It is internally similar to the HK33 but cannot fire rifle grenades nor mount the underbarrel, 40mm grenade launcher. The HK53 featured a long, four-prong flash suppressor, but cannot be equipped with a bayonet. All HK33 and HK53 guns are equipped with drum-type rear sights, marked from 100 to 400m. They can all use twenty-five-, thirty- and forty-round box magazines, but the last have been out of production by HK for some time.

HECKLER UND KOCH G41
Calibre: 5.56 x45 NATO
Action: retarded blow-back
Overall length: 997mm (fixed butt) or 996/806mm (folding butt)
Barrel length: 450mm
Weight: 4.1kg
Magazine capacity: 20, 30 or 40 rounds

The G-41 is a further development of the early G3 and HK33 rifles, having the same roller-retarded blow-back action, but chambered for 5.56mm NATO ammunition and adapted for NATO standards. The G-41 also features the 0-1-3-30 trigger group, STANAG-compatible magazines and scope mountings, silent bolt closure device (similar to the 'forward assist device' on the M16A1 and the M16A2), an integral dust cover on the ejection port and an integral,

HK G41.

side-folding, carrying handle. The G-41 could be issued with a fixed, plastic butt or with a telescopic (folding) butt.

HECKLER UND KOCH G36

From the technical point of view, the G36 is a radical departure from all previous HK rifles, which were based on the proven Mauser/CETME/G3, roller-retarded system. The G36 is a conventional gas-operated, selective-fire rifle, made from the most modern materials and using advanced technologies.

The receiver and most of the other external parts are made from reinforced polymers, with steel inserts where appropriate. The operating system appears to be a modification of the older American ArmaLite AR-18 rifle, with a similar short-stroke gas piston located above the barrel, a square-shaped bolt carrier and a rotating bolt with seven locking lugs. However, there are many differences between it and the AR-18. The bolt carrier rides on a single guide rod, with the return spring around it. The charging handle is attached to the top of the bolt carrier and can be rotated to the left or the right. When not in use, the charging handle aligns itself with the axis of the weapon under the pressure of its spring and reciprocates with the bolt group at the top of the receiver. The gas block is fitted with a self-adjustable gas valve, which expels all used gases forward, away from the shooter. The ejection window is located at the right side of the receiver and features a spent case deflector to propel ejected cases away from the face of a left-handed shooter. All major parts are assembled on the receiver by using the cross-pins, so that the rifle can be disassembled and reassembled without any tools.

The typical HK trigger unit is assembled in a separate plastic housing, integral with the pistol grip and the

HECKLER UND KOCH G36

	G36	G36K	G36C
Calibre	5.56 × 45 NATO		
Length (buttstock open/folded)	998/758mm	860/615mm	720/500mm
Barrel length	480mm	320mm	228mm
Weight empty	3.6kg (3.3kg G36E)	3.3kg (3.0kg G36KE)	2.8kg
Magazine capacity	30 rounds standard		
Rate of fire	750 rpm		

HK 36 Prototype.

G36K with stock folded.

trigger guard. Thanks to this feature, a wide variety of firing mode combinations can be used on any rifle, simply by installing the appropriate trigger unit. Standard options are single shots, full automatic fire, two- or three-round bursts in any reasonable combinations. The default version is the single shot + two-rounds burst + full automatic. The ambidextrous fire selector lever also serves as a manual safety.

The G36 is fed from proprietary thirty-round box magazines, made from translucent plastic. All magazines have special studs on the sides, so that two or three magazines can be clipped together for faster reloading. The magazine housings of the G36 are made as separate parts, so that any G36 rifle can be easily adjusted to the several magazine interfaces. As standard, the magazine release catch is located just behind the magazine, in the G3- or AK-47 style, rather than on the side of the magazine housing (M16-style). Hundred-round, Beta-C dual drum magazines of American origin may also be used (these magazines are standard for MG36 squad automatic versions of the G36). The side-folding, skeletonized buttstock is standard on all G36 rifles. It folds to the right side and does not interfere with rifle operation when folded.

The standard sighting equipment of the G36 consists of *two* optical sights – one 3.5× telescopic sight, built into the carrying handle, with the second, 1× red-dot sight mounted directly above it. The sights are completely independent, with the former being suitable for long-range, accurate shooting, and the latter for fast target acquisition at short ranges (up to about 200m). Both sights are built into the plastic carrying handle and both are pre-zeroed to 200m. The 3.5× telescopic sight also features a range-finding scale and additional sighting marks for ranges of 400, 600 and 800m. Export versions of the G36 are available with a single 1.5× telescopic sight, with the emergency open sights moulded into the top of the carrying handle. The subcompact G36K Commando version is available with an integral Picatinny-type scope and accessory rail instead of the carrying handle and standard sights. The dual sighting arrangement, with no back-up iron sights, is often noted as a major downside of the G36 system, since, if the optics are affected by snow, rain or mist, there will be no way in which to aim the rifle until the optics are cleared.

The standard G36 rifles can be fitted with the HK AG36 40mm underbarrel grenade launcher. It can also be fitted with a bayonet. Interestingly enough, the G36 uses AK-74-type bayonets, which are left over from the former NVA (the East German Army).

HECKLER UND KOCH G11
Calibre: 4.7mm caseless
Action: gas-operated, rotating breech
Overall length: 750mm
Barrel length: 540mm
Weight: 3.6kg empty
Magazine capacity: 50 or 45 rounds
Rate of fire: dual, 2,000 or 600 rpm

The G11 rifle features a unique cylinder breech/chamber system that rotates 90 degrees. The cartridges in the magazine are located above the barrel, in a single row, bullets pointing down. Before each shot, the first

Prototype G11 rifle (early 1980s).

G11K2, a pre-production version of the G11.

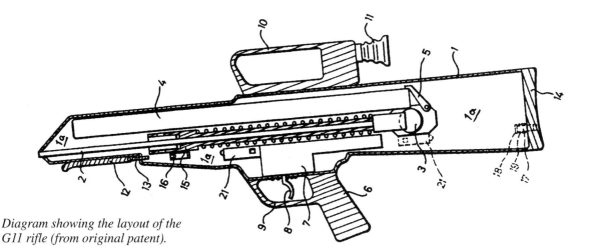

Diagram showing the layout of the G11 rifle (from original patent).

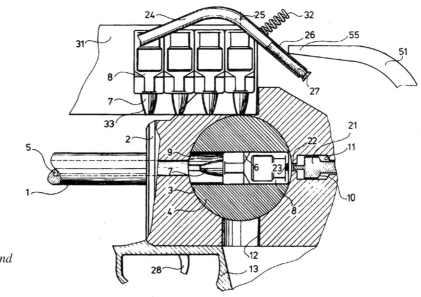

Diagram showing the unique rotating breech/chamber unit and feeding system of the G11 rifle (from original patent).

cartridge is pushed down from the magazine into the chamber. The breech/chamber then rotates 90 degrees to align the cartridge with the barrel. The cartridge is then fired and some propellant gases are used to operate the gas system, which is used to rotate the breech/chamber back, ready for the next cartridge to be chambered. In the case of cartridge ignition failure, the failed cartridge is pushed down from the chamber by the next onee. The breech can be manually 'cocked' by the rotating handle at the left side of the rifle, located beyond the pistol grip. The cocking handle does not move when the gun is fired. Another interesting detail

is that the barrel, rotating breech, feed module and magazine are mounted in a housing which can move back and forth in the rifle under recoil force, against its own return spring and buffer. When firing single shots, the housing moves back and forward after each, damping the perceived recoil. When firing full-automatic, the housing also moves back and forward during each shot, resulting in a moderate rate of fire of about 600 rpm; but when firing three-round bursts, the second and the third cartridge are fed and fired as soon as the chamber is ready, and the third bullet leaves the barrel *before* the moment when the housing reaches its rearward position. This results in a very high rate of fire with three-shot bursts – approximately 2,000 rpm. This also means that the actual recoil affects the rifle and its user *after* the last bullet in the burst is fired, thus all the bullets will strike close together.

The G11 features a built-in 1× optical sight with a simple, circular aiming reticle. Early prototypes featured one fifty-round polymer magazine, while the latest versions have forty-five-round magazines – one in the loaded position within the movable housing and two spare magazines on the top of the rifle, in addition to the loaded one. Details of the caseless ammunition for the G11 rifle, designated as DM11, are to be found in Chapter 4.

INDIA

Most of the small arms used by India in the post-war period were inspired by Britain. In the mid 1980s the most important rifle in the Indian Army was the L1A1, a copy of the British L1A1 SLR, which, in turn, was a licensed copy of the Belgian FN FAL rifle. At that time it was apparent that an FP rifle had to give way to an RCAR weapon. Interestingly enough, India decided to go its own way and develop a domestic system. India began to develop the INSAS (Indian National Small Arms System), which incorporated features from several popular, foreign designs. The INSAS system was originally planned to have three components – a standard rifle, a carbine and a squad automatic rifle (LMG), all chambered for 5.56 × 45 NATO ammunition. In 1997 the rifle and the LMG were ready for mass production, and in 1998 the first units were observed on an Independence Day parade armed with INSAS rifles. The mass introduction of the INSAS rifle was delayed by the lack of domestically made 5.56mm

ammunition and India accordingly bought significant stocks from the Israeli IMI company. By the time of the writing of this book, according to some sources, at least 300,000 INSAS rifles were in service with the Indian Army. The Ishapore Rifle Factory is manufacturing it for the Indian military and for export.

INSAS

Calibre: 5.56 × 45
Length: 945mm (960/750mm in the folding butt version)
Barrel length: 464mm
Weight: 3.2kg less magazine, 4.1kg with loaded magazine and 30 rounds of ammunition
Magazine: 20 rounds standard (also 30 rounds from INSAS LMG)
Rate of fire: 650 rpm

The INSAS rifle is broadly based on the famous Kalashnikov AK-47 action, but with many modifications. The basic, gas-operated action with long stroke gas piston and a rotating bolt, as well as the stamped steel receiver, are generally the same as in modern Kalashnikov rifles. However, the gas system is fitted with a manual regulator, similar in design to that found on FN FAL rifles, as well as a gas cut-off. The charging handle has been moved from the bolt carrier to the left side of the forearm; it is similar in position and design to German G3 rifle. The selector/safety switch is located at the left side of the receiver, above the pistol grip, and allows for single shots and three-round bursts. The rifle is fitted with a side-folding carrying handle, and either a solid or a side-folding metal buttstock. The furniture may be made from wood or polymer. Standard magazines are made from semi-translucent polymer and contain twenty rounds. Longer thirty-round magazines of similar design are available for the

The INSAS rifle.

INSAS LMG but can also be used with the rifle. The sights consist of a hooded front, mounted on top of the gas block and an aperture rear, mounted on the receiver cover. The flash hider is shaped to accept NATO-standard rifle grenades. INSAS rifles can be fitted with AKM-style, multipurpose knife-bayonets.

ISRAEL

The state of Israel was founded in 1948 and almost immediately began to fight for its survival against its neighbouring Arab countries. The Israeli Defense Forces (IDF) initially adopted the bolt-action 7.92mm Mauser K98K as its standard rifle but soon replaced this with licence-built FAL rifles of Belgian origin. In the hands of IDF troops the FAL proved itself a decent rifle but experience gained in the Six Day War of 1967 showed that, in some respects, the FAL was inferior to the 7.62mm Kalashnikov assault rifles used by the Arabs. FAL rifles were heavier, longer and more cumbersome to carry (especially for motorized troops); they also were more sensitive to fine sand and dust, so typical of desert warfare. During the late 1960s Israel also received a supply of American M16A1 and CAR-15 rifles and the 5.56mm ammunition gave quite good results. So the IDF set requirements for a new assault rifle in 5.56 × 45.

After initial tests which included the M16A1, the Stoner 63, the AK-47 and the HK33, as well as a design from Uziel Gal (the author of the famous UZI submachine gun), a design by Israel Galili was selected in 1973, but its actual adoption was delayed by the next Yom Kippur War in that year. The Galili design was based on the Finnish Valmet RK.62 rifle, which, in turn, was a licence-built, Kalashnikov AK-47. The machinery and documentation package was bought from Valmet and transferred to the state-owned Israel Military Industries (IMI). There were some rumours that the first production Galil rifles were built on unmarked Valmet-made receivers. The basic Galil rifle later evolved into several configurations, including the full-size, 5.56mm AR and ARM assault rifles, the compact 5.56mm SAR rifle for tank and vehicle crews, the 7.62mm NATO AR selective-fire and the 7.62mm NATO semi-automatic Galatz sniper rifle, the 5.56mm MAR subcompact assault rifle (also known as the Micro-Galil) and some other variations such as the .30 Carbine (7.62 × 33) Magal police rifle.

While being a successful weapon, the Galil was not widely issued to the IDF during its lifetime, because, during the late 1960s and the early 1970s, Israel received large shipments of the US M16 and CAR-15 assault rifles at very low prices. M16 rifles became the major armament of the IDF, with the Galils mostly issued to the armoured corps, the artillery corps and some units of the Israeli Air Force. In practice the Galil was more of back-up weapon for the IDF, with its production kept at a minimal level to ensure that there would be no shortage of small arms should the USA, for some reason, stop supplying the M16; furthermore, IDF troops generally preferred the M16A1 and the CAR-15 rifle to the Galil because the last was much heavier. Galil rifles were also exported to several South American, African and Asian countries, and Estonia has received some since 2000. The South African Vektor Company, a division of the DENEL, manufactures slightly modified Galil rifles; these models have included the R-4 (Galil AR), the R-5 (Galil SAR) and the R-6 (Galil MAR) assault rifles, and are used by the South African Military. Another offspring of the Galil is the Croatian APS-95 assault rifle. Galil rifles were also tested in Italy, Sweden and the Netherlands, but lost to other designs. In general, Galil rifles are fine weapons, but somewhat heavy and expensive to manufacture; the semi-automatic-only versions of the both the 5.56mm and the 7.62mm Galil AR rifle were widely sold to domestic and foreign civilian and law enforcement markets.

During the early 1990s the IDF decided to acquire a new rifle of domestic origin to replace both the over-expensive Galil and the ageing M16 rifle. IMI (now TAAS), in close co-operation with the IDF, developed the new rifle which received the name 'Tavor' and the designation TAR-21 (Tavor Assault Rifle for the 21st Century). The new rifle first appeared in public in 1998 and was tested by the IDF in 1999–2002. For some time the fate of the Tavor was uncertain due to a lack of funding but by 2003 the IDF had decided to purchase a significant number of the rifles and some units had already been armed with it. In general, the TAR-21 represents the mainstream of present assault rifle developments. It shares all the 'modern' features already tried and proved successful by previous designs, such as the bullpup layout, polymer housing, optical sights as prime sighting equipment, modular design with several different configurations– from a very short submachine gun up to a standard assault rifle plus a para-sniper accurized rifle with a heavy barrel. So far it has not seen much real action and only time will show whether it is successful. India has bought an undisclosed number of Tavor rifles for its special forces to complement the 5.56mm INSAS rifles of Indian origin. At the present IMI continues to develop the model and is producing the Tavor-2 compact rifle.

GALIL

	Galil AR/ARM	Galil AR/ARM	Galil SAR	Galil MAR
Calibre	7.62 × 51 NATO	5.56 × 45 NATO	5.56 × 45	5.56 × 45
Overall length (stock open/folded)	1,050/810mm	979/742mm	840/614mm	690/445mm
Barrel length	535mm	460mm	332mm	195mm
Weight, empty	3.95kg (4.35kg ARM)	3.95kg (4.35kg ARM)	3.75kg	2.95kg
Magazine capacity	25 rounds	35 or 50 rounds		35 rounds
Rate of fire	650 rpm	650 rpm	650 rpm	600–750 rpm

Basically, the Galil assault rifle may be described as a modified Kalashnikov AK-47 design, and a detailed description of its functioning can be found in the section below on the USSR and the successor states. The key differences between the Galil and the AK-47 are that the Galil features machined steel receivers of the original AK-47 pattern, but of a slightly different shape; these were apparently preferred over the pressed steel type because the 5.56 × 45 operates at much higher pressures than the 7.62 × 39. For the same reason, the gas port to operate the action is much smaller. The bolt lugs lock into recesses milled into the receiver body, rather than into the barrel extension unit. The operating parts are not interchangeable with those of the AK-47. The AK-47-style safety/selector switch at the right side of the gun is complemented by the additional, smaller switch at the left side of the receiver, above the pistol handle. The cocking handle is bent upward, so that it can be operated with either hand. The sights of the Galil feature a front hooded post, mounted on the gas block, with a rear aperture sight mounted on the receiver top cover. The rear sight is of the flip-up type, with settings for 300 and 500m. Additional folding night sights with luminous inserts can be raised into position, which permit the aiming of the gun in low light conditions at ranges up to 100m. The barrel and the flash suppressor can be used to launch rifle grenades using blank or live cartridges (depending on

Galil ARM 5.56mm rifle standing on its integral bipod. (courtesy Dick Venema)

Galil ARM 5.56mm rifle, left side view; clearly seen is the second fire selector/safety switch above the pistol grip with Hebrew markings.
(courtesy Dick Venema)

Galil SAR 5.56mm, shortened version of the basic rifle.

Galil ARM 7.62mm.

the rifle grenade type). The Galil ARM also features a folding, detachable bipod and a carrying handle; the bipod base incorporates a wire cutter. The standard folding buttstock is patterned after the FN FAL 'Para' and folds to the right to save space. Some of the late production Micro-Galil (MAR) rifles are also fitted with a Picatinny-type rail, which allows for the mounting of a variety of sighting devices. Standard AR and ARM rifles can be fitted with a scope mounting rail on the left side of the receiver. All 5.56mm Galil rifles are fed from proprietary thirty-five- or fifty-round, curved box magazines with AK-47 style locking. M16-type magazines may be used via a special adaptor; 7.62mm Galil rifles are fed from proprietary twenty-five-round box magazines.

Above *Tavor TAR-21.*

Above *Tavor CTAR-21.*

Below *Tavor MTAR-21.*

Below *Tavor-2 compact rifle.*

Tavor TAR-21

Calibre: 5.56 × 45 NATO
Action: gas-operated, rotating bolt
Overall length: 720mm
Barrel length: 460mm
Weight: 2.8kg empty, 3.63kg with loaded 30-round magazine and sling
Magazine capacity: 20 or 30 rounds standard
Rate of fire: 750–900 rpm

The Tavor TAR-21 is a gas-operated, selective-fire, magazine-fed assault rifle of bullpup configuration. It is available in several configurations, which differ in barrel length, handguard shape and accessories. The basic configuration is the TAR-21 assault rifle with the 460mm (18.1in) barrel. Next are the compact assault rifle, called CTAR-21, with a 380mm (15in) barrel and the MTAR-21 micro assault rifle with a barrel of only 250mm (10in). The last model also features a redesigned front part of the housing for a more comfortable grasp of the short weapon.

The TAR-21 utilizes the now-common, long-stroke piston with the gas piston rigidly attached to the bolt carrier. The gas cylinder is located above the barrel and is completely enclosed by the gun housing. The rotating bolt is similar to that found on the M16 and has seven lugs. Ejection ports are provided on both sides of the weapon and right- or left-side ejection can be selected by installing the bolt with the ejector mounted on the right or on the left, as appropriate (this change requires the gun to be partially disassembled). The bolt carrier rides on the single guide rod, with the return spring unit located above it, behind and inside the hollow gas piston rod. The charging handle is located at the front left side of the gun and does not reciprocate when the gun is fired. The charging handle slots are cut on both sides of the gun housing so that the handle can be installed on either side of the weapon as required. The trigger unit is more or less conventional, with an ambidextrous fire mode selector/safety switch located above the pistol grip.

The TAR-21 has no separate receiver; instead, all parts are mounted within the high-impact-resistant plastic housing, reinforced with steel inserts where appropriate. Access to all the internal parts is controlled by the hinged buttplate, which can be swung down for internal inspection and disassembly. The gun utilizes STANAG-compliant, M16-type magazines, with the standard capacity of thirty rounds. The TAR-21 has no open sights. It is fitted with the standard Picatinny-type accessory rail on the top of the gun. At the present, the standard sighting equipment for all the TAR-21 series rifles (except for the STAR-21 sniper rifle) is the Israeli-made, ITL MARS, a complicated and expensive, reflex-type red dot sight with a built-in laser pointer. For night-time operations the MARS could be complemented with the ITL Mini N/SEAS compact night-vision device. The TAR-21 in its basic configuration can also be fitted with the 40mm M203 underbarrel grenade launcher.

ITALY

Italy finished World War II having no satisfactory semi-automatic rifle available. In the post-war period Italy was heavily oriented to the USA and during the late 1940s and the early 1950s bought significant numbers of US M1 Garand rifles, as well as a manufacturing licence and some equipment and machinery to produce these rifles in the country. With the advent of NATO, Italy, like many other countries, faced the need for the rearming of its forces with the new infantry rifle, chambered for 7.62mm NATO ammunition. Italy selected the simplest way to achieve this by redesigning the M1 Garand for the new ammunition and by fitting these rifles with detachable box magazines instead of the integral ones. The resulting rifles, which accumulated several other modifications such as NATO-standard muzzle grenade launchers and gas cut-off valves, were adopted in 1959 and used by the Italian military until well into the 1980s.

The famous Italian arms company Pietro Beretta Spa began to develop a new assault rifle chambered for the American 5.56 × 45 cartridge in 1968. The prototype rifles appeared at about 1972 and, after trials, were adopted by Italian Special Forces, as well as by some foreign armies such as those of Jordan and Malaysia. The rifle was designated AR-70/223 and was available in three basic versions: the standard assault rifle AR-70/223, the carbine SC-70/223 with the same barrel and a folding butt, and a short carbine SCS-70/223 with a shortened barrel and a folding butt. A squad automatic (light machine gun) variation of the basic 70/223 design, with a heavy, quickly-detachable barrel, was also developed but never produced in quantity.

Some forces within the Italian military and law enforcement agencies began to use various 5.56mm rifles during the 1970s; but the 7.62mm BM-59 rifles were generally replaced in service with 5.56mm assault rifles only in 1990 after extensive trials. During these, several designs were tested, including the Bernardelli VB-SR, a licensed copy of the Israeli 5.56mm Galil ARM; the Heckler & Koch 5.56mm G41 rifle (had this design won the contract, it would have been made by Franchi under licence from HK); and the SOCIMI 5.56mm AR-871 assault rifle. The last company also submitted the 7.62mm NATO AR832-FS automatic rifle, but this was ultimately rejected because of its calibre. The last design was the updated 5.56mm Beretta rifle, based on the earlier AR-70 design and designated AR-70/90. This upgraded version appeared in 1985 and eventually won the trials. In 1990 it was adopted as the basic AR-70/90 assault rifle, together with the SC-70/90 (the same rifle but with a folding buttstock for special forces) and the SCP-70/90 (an airborne troops carbine with a shortened barrel and folding butt). A squad automatic version with a heavy, non-detachable barrel and detachable bipod is available as the AS-70/90. The Beretta AR-70/90 is a general issue, shoulder weapon with the Italian Army and also is offered for export. Both the 70/223 and the 70/90 rifle are available in semi-automatic-only versions, for police or civilian markets.

However, some elite military and law enforcement units retain their own inventory of 5.56mm rifles. For example, the elite law enforcement NOCS unit (*Nucleo Operativo Centrale Di Sicurezza, Special Security Operational Group*) has Bernardelli VB-SR (Galil) rifles, while elite military units such as the COL MOSCHIN and SAN MARCO regiments and the COMSUBIN group, have some HK G41s.

BERETTA BM 59

Calibre: 7.62 × 51 NATO
Action: gas-operated, rotating bolt
Overall length: 1095mm
Barrel length: 491mm
Weight: 4.4kg empty
Rate of fire: 750 rpm
Magazine capacity: 20 rounds

The Beretta BM59 may be described as a rechambered M1 Garand, with the addition of a removable, twenty-round magazine and a selective-fire trigger. Another addition was a flash-suppressor of NATO-standard diameter, which also served as a rifle grenade launcher. To launch grenades, one must turn on the gas

Beretta BM59 with bayonet.

cut-off valve by raising the grenade front sight, mounted on the gas block. If this is not done the excessive gas pressure will damage the rifle. The BM59 is a gas-operated rifle, with the gas chamber and gas piston located under the barrel. The chamber locks via a rotating bolt with two massive lugs. The fire mode selector/safety switch is located at the front of the trigger guard, while the charging handle is attached to the gas rod and reciprocates during the fire cycle.

The BM59 was available in four basic modifications:

1. BM59 Mark I had a wooden stock with a semi-pistol grip.
2. BM59 Mark II had a wooden stock with pistol grip to achieve better control during full-automatic fire;
3. BM59 Mark III, or Ital TA, was a gun with a pistol grip and a folding metal buttstock and intended for mountain troops; the BM59 'Para' was similar to the BM59 Ital TA but had a shorter barrel and shorter flash-hider, and was intended for paratroops;
4. BM59 Mark IV had a heavier barrel and a plastic stock, and was used as a light squad automatic weapon.

BERETTA AR-70/223 AND AR-70/90

The AR-70/223 and AR-70/90 rifles are very similar in their basic design, albeit with some differences. The description below is for the AR-70/90, with its differences from the 70/223 noted where appropriate.

The AR-70/90 is a gas-operated, magazine-fed, selective-fire weapon. The receiver is made from stamped sheet steel and consists of two parts, upper and lover, connected by two cross-pins, at the rear and at the front. For maintenance and field stripping the rear pin is pushed out and the receiver is hinged around the front pin. If required, the front pin may be removed too, so that the receiver halves will be separated completely. On the AR-70/223 the upper receiver is of square cross-section, with stamped bolt guides. This design proved to be not strong enough, and so the AR-70/90 features a trapezoid-shaped upper receiver cross-section, with separate bolt guides welded in place.

The gas-operated action of the AR-70/90 is fairly conventional with the long-stroke gas piston located above the barrel. The gas piston rod is linked to the bolt carrier by using the cocking handle as a lock, and the return spring is located around the gas piston, above the

BERETTA AR-70/223 AND AR-70/90

	AR-70/223	AR-70/90, SC-70/90	SCP-70/90
Calibre	5.56 × 45 M193	5.56 × 45 NATO (SS109/M855)	
Length	995mm	998mm; 756mm SC-70/90, with folded butt	908mm; 663mm, with folded butt
Barrel length	450mm	450mm	360mm
Weight empty	3.8kg	4.07kg	3.80kg
Magazine capacity	30 rounds		
Rate of fire	650 rpm	670 rpm	

AR-70/223 rifle (top) and carbine.

SCS-70/223 short carbine (top) and SC-70/223 carbine (bottom).

AR-70/90 rifle.

barrel. The gas block features a two-position gas regulator (for normal and adverse conditions) and the gas cut-off, integral with the elevating grenade sight. When the grenade sight is raised into the firing position it automatically closes the gas port. The rotating bolt is somewhat similar to the one found in the Kalashnikov AK-47 rifle and has two massive lugs which are locked into the barrel sleeve, which is welded into the receiver. The charging handle is attached to the bolt carrier.

The barrel is fixed to the receiver by using the threaded barrel nut, allowing for quick barrel replacement (for repair purposes only, not in the field), without extensive headspace adjustments. The barrel chamber and bore are chromium-plated. The conventional trigger/hammer mechanism allows for single shots and full automatic on the AR-70/223 rifle and for single shots, three-round bursts (optional) and full automatic on the AR-70/90 series. The safety/selector switch is ambidextrous on the AR-70/90 series and is located on the right side of the receiver on the AR-70/223 series.

The feeding of the AR-70/90 series weapons is achieved by using STANAG (M16-type)-compliant magazines, with the ambidextrous magazine release button located on both sides of the magazine housing in the lower receiver. On AR-70/223 rifles, feeding is from the proprietary, thirty-round magazine, with the magazine release lever located between the magazine and the trigger guard. Both the AR-70/90 and the AR-70/223 series of rifles feature a bolt stop device which holds the bolt open when the last round from the magazine is fired. The bolt release button is located at the left side of the receiver, above the magazine housing.

The sights of the AR-70/90 rifles consist of the hooded front sight, mounted on the top of the gas block, and the flip-up aperture rear marked for 250 and 400m range. The top surface of the receiver is fitted with the NATO-standard scope/accessory rail. A detachable carrying handle with a see-through base is available for all AR-70/90 series rifles. The AR-70/90 can also be equipped with a Zeiss 'Orion' night-vision sight or the Aimpoint 4× telescope sight (any other sights with compatible mountings may also be easily installed, if required).

The furniture on all the rifles is made from plastic, with the standard rifles having fixed plastic buttstocks. The SC-70/223 and SC-70/90 Special Forces carbines are different from the AR rifles only by having side-folding, skeleton-type metal buttstocks, covered with plastic. The SCP-70/90 carbine is similar to the SC-70/90, except that it has a shortened barrel which

cannot be used to launch rifle grenades direct. However, a special detachable rifle grenade launcher is available for the short-barrelled carbines which can easily be clamped on to the muzzle of the gun. The hollow pistol grip of all AR-70/90 series rifles is used to store a cleaning kit. A wide variety of accessories are available for AR-70/90 rifles, including knife-type bayonets, lightweight, foldable and detachable bipods and blank firing adaptors.

JAPAN

Following World War II, Japan restricted its military forces to pure self-defence operations and also imposed severe restrictions on military exports. During the early post-war period, the Japanese Self-Defense Forces (JSDF) were armed mostly with American weaponry such as the .30 calibre M1 Garand self-loading rifles. By 1957 these rifles were obsolescent and the JSDF began the search for a new automatic infantry rifle. Being seriously biased toward the US in its military trends, Japan probably had no option in ammunition other than to adopt the newest US creation, the 7.62 × 51 NATO cartridge. However, the JSDF felt that it was too powerful, especially for the smaller and lighter Japanese soldiers. Japanese experts accordingly developed a reduced loading, similar in all dimensions to the standard 7.62mm NATO, but with a lighter bullet and a smaller powder charge that generated muzzle velocities of about 715m/s instead of the 'NATO original' 810m/s. The Howa Machinery Co developed the rifle for the new cartridge, working closely with the JSDF. In 1964 the 7.62mm prototype rifle R6E was adopted for service as the Type 64 rifle. Howa produced it exclusively for the JSDF until about 1988. Since 1990 the Type 64 rifle has been gradually phased out of service in favour of the 5.56mm Type 89 rifle; this was never exported.

During the late 1960s the Howa Co. acquired the manufacturing rights for the American 5.56mm ArmaLite AR-18 rifle, but severe limitations imposed by the Japanese government on the exporting of military *matériel* to the USA (then engaged in the Vietnam War) effectively killed the AR-18 in Japan after only a few thousand had been made. However, the experience gained by Howa during the short production run was not lost. About twenty years later the company incorporated several design features of the AR-18 into the new JSDF service rifle, the 5.56mm Type 89, which replaced the 7.62mm Type 64 in service from 1990 onwards. As with the Type 64 rifle, the Type 89 is exclusive to the JSDF and is not exported.

Type 64

Calibre: 7.62 × 51 (reduced load)
Action: gas-operated, tilting bolt
Overall length: 990mm
Barrel length: 450mm
Weight: 4.31kg less magazine
Magazine capacity: 20 rounds
Rate of fire: 450–500 rpm

The Type 64 rifle is a gas-operated, selective-fire weapon. The gas and bolt system were most probably inspired either by the Belgian FN FAL or by the Soviet Tokarev SVT-40 rifle. The Type 64 has a short-stroke gas piston located above the barrel and fitted with a manual gas regulator. The barrel has a massive muzzle brake, which also serves as a rifle grenade launcher. The bolt is locked by tipping its rear end down into recess in the receiver floor. The charging handle is located above the bolt carrier and is readily accessible by either hand. The safety switch/fire mode selector is located on the right side of the receiver, above the trigger guard.

The striker-fired trigger unit is of an original design and features a patented fire-rate reducer, which produces a controllable rate of fire of about 450–500 rpm. Type 64 rifles are fitted with solid wooden buttstocks and hinged steel buttplates and lightweight, folding bipods. The open sights are mounted on folding posts, and the rear sight has two range settings, for 200 and 400m. The reduced load cartridges and the reduced

rate of fire arguably make these and the original Spanish CETME guns the only true assault rifles in 7.62 × 51 calibre since they are the only ones which stand any chance of being controllable in fully-automatic fire.

Type 89

Calibre: 5.56 × 45 NATO
Action: gas-operated, rotating bolt
Overall length: 864mm
Barrel length: 420mm
Weight: 3.5kg unloaded
Magazine capacity: 30 rounds
Rate of fire: 750 rpm

The Type 89 rifle is a gas-operated, magazine fed, selective-fire weapon. It features a typical AR-18-style bolt carrier with a rotating, multi-lug bolt. The gas system has a relatively large expansion chamber ahead of the piston head, to smooth the otherwise violent operation of the gas group. The receiver is made from steel stampings. The trigger unit features a separate, three-round-burst mechanism so, should it fail, the rifle will continue to fire in single shots or fully automatic mode. The mode of fire selector and safety are incorporated into one four-position rotating lever, located at the right side of the receiver. Type 89 rifles are fitted with polymer furniture and a solid polymer or skeleton, side-folding buttstock. A lightweight folding bipod is standard. All rifles are fitted with two positions, flip-up

Type 64.

Type 89.

aperture sights and hooded front sights, mounted on the gas block. This leaves the front part of the barrel unobstructed and so it is possible to fire rifle grenades from the barrel.

SINGAPORE

Singapore, one of the so-called 'Asian tigers', began its domestic small arms development during the 1970s in the company then known as Chartered Industries of Singapore (CIS), with the intention of replacing the licence-built M16A1-type rifles (Colt Model 614S with no forward assist). To save time and effort, CIS decided to exploit the experience of several Western small arms designers. Work on the first Singaporean assault rifle was started in 1976 when CIS teamed with the British company Sterling Armament, using the experimental Sterling Assault Rifle as a starting point. The Sterling rifle was based on the 5.56mm ArmaLite AR18, which was manufactured by Sterling under licence from ArmaLite Inc. (USA). Thus it was no surprise that the first CIS rifle, designated SAR-80 (Singapore Assault Rifle, 1980), was also quite similar to the AR-18. During the 1980s CIS slightly improved the design and by the end of the 1980s began to offer a new 5.56mm rifle, the SR-88. Most of these rifles went for export, because the Army still had plenty of American M16A1 rifles.

During the mid 1990s CIS, now Singapore Technologies Kinetics (STK), began the development of a more modern assault rifle. This rifle, first shown at the DSEi-99 exhibition in 1999 and designated SAR-21, represents most of the trends in current small arms development. Made with as many plastic parts as possible, in bullpup layout, and fitted with an integral telescope sight and laser designator as standard, the SAR-21 is also offered in a variety of versions, including ones with, for instance, various utility rail systems and a 40mm grenade launcher. The SAR-21 is scheduled to replace all M16A1, SAR-80 and SR-88 rifles in Singaporean service and is offered for export.

At the present it is hard to judge this rifle, but the available reports are quite favourable, stating that the gun is comfortable to carry and fire, accurate, reliable and has a low recoil. While the SAR-21 is much shorter than the M16 rifle with the same barrel length, the SAR-21 has the disadvantage of right-side-only extraction, with no provision to change it to the left (unlike most other modern bullpup rifles, such as the Steyr AUG, the GIAT FAMAS or the IMI Tavor).

SAR-80
Calibre: 5.56 × 45
Action: gas-operated, rotating bolt
Overall length: 970mm (738mm with butt folded)
Barrel length: 459mm
Weight: 3.7kg empty
Rate of fire: 600 rpm
Magazine capacity: 20 or 30 rounds

SAR-80 is a gas-operated, selective-fire weapon of simple construction. It uses a short-stroke gas piston that pushes a massive bolt carrier with an AR-18-type rotating bolt. The bolt carrier rides on two guide rods. Each rod has a recoil spring around it; the gas piston rod has its own return spring. The gas system features a regulator and a cut-off for launching rifle grenades. The receiver is made from steel stampings. The pistol grip, handguards and buttstock are made from plastic. The SAR-80 uses M16-style magazines.

SR-88

Calibre: 5.56×45
Action: gas-operated, rotating bolt
Overall length: 960mm (810mm when butt folded)
Barrel length: 460mm
Weight: 3.68kg with empty magazine
Rate of fire: 700–900 rpm
Magazine capacity: 30 rounds

The SR-88 is a conventional, selective-fire, gas-operated rifle. It uses short-stroke piston action with a rotating bolt, and both the gas piston and the gas cylinder are chromium-plated for improved durability. The gas system features a three-position gas regulator: two open positions, for normal and harsh conditions, and one closed, for launching rifle grenades. The barrel is equipped with a flash suppressor, which also serves as a rifle grenade launcher. The lower receiver is machined from an aluminium forging and the upper receiver is made from steel stampings. The furniture (butt, pistol grip, handguards) is made from plastic. The standard butt is fixed but the SR-88 is also available with side-folding buttstock. The side-folding carrying handle is mounted at the forward end of the receiver.

SAR-80.

SR-88.

SAR-21

Calibre: 5.56 × 45 NATO
Action: gas-operated, rotating bolt
Overall length: 805mm
Barrel length: 508mm
Weight: 3.82kg without magazine and accessories,
4.44kg loaded with magazine and 30 rounds of
ammunition
Magazine capacity: 30 rounds
Rate of fire: 450–650 rpm

The gas system of the SAR-21 is located above the barrel. The long-stroke piston is rigidly attached to the bolt carrier. The M16-style rotating bolt has seven lugs and locks into the barrel extension. The return spring is partly housed inside and behind the hollow gas piston rod. The charging handle is located above the gun housing, under the scope/carrying handle unit, and folds forward when not in use. The charging handle does not reciprocate when the gun is fired. On the SAR-21 P (Picatinny rail) and the SAR-21 RIS (Rail Interface System) versions of the basic design the charging handle is moved to the left side of the gun, leaving the place at the top for the sights/accessory rail.

The housing of the SAR-21 is made from tough, high-impact-resistant polymer, and consists of the barrel section with the barrel/gas system, forearm and sights, the upper receiver with the pistol grip and magazine housing and the lower receiver with the buttplate

SAR-21 rifle in basic configuration. (courtesy VT Systems Co., USA)

Variants of the SAR-21 rifle. (courtesy VT Systems Co., USA)

SAR21 P-rail   SAR21 M203   SAR21 Modular
                                          Mounting System (MMS)

and the hammer unit inside. All the major parts are held together by push-pins and can be separated for disassembly without any special tools. The upper receiver also incorporates a special safety system which protects the shooter's face in the event of the cartridge case's rupture or explosion. The safety switch is located at the front of the enlarged triggerguard and is of the cross-bolt, push-button type. The SAR-21 can provide two modes of fire – single shot and full automatic. The SAR-21 is fed from proprietary thirty-rounds box magazines, made from translucent plastic.

The standard sighting equipment includes an integral 1.5× magnification telescope sight, with the emergency back-up open sights formed at the top of the telescope housing. The SAR-21 P and the SAR-21 RIS have no integral sights, instead these feature a NATO-standard Picatinny-type scope rail at the top of the gun, which can be fitted with a wide variety of day and night sighting devices. Another interesting feature of the SAR-21 is that it incorporates a laser-aiming module (LAM, also sometimes referred as a laser pointer) as a standard feature. The LAM is mounted below the barrel, inside the forearm, and can emit either visible or infra-red beams. The LAM switch is built into the forearm of the rifle. The standard SAR-21 can be fitted with the 40mm underbarrel grenade launcher, either the US-made M203 or the Singapore-made CIS 40GL. The SAR-21 RIS can sport a wide variety of add-on tactical accessories, including a vertical 'assault' foregrip and tactical lights.

SOUTH AFRICA

The South African National Defence Forces (SANDF) adopted the Belgian FN FAL rifle as the R1 in 1960. A shortened version of the basic design appeared a little later as the R2. Both rifles were made at the Lyttelton Division of DENEL Corp. With the advent of the 5.56mm assault rifles, the SANDF selected the Israeli-made Galil as their next infantry rifle because of the relatively close military co-operation with Israel during that period. IMI, the original manufacturer of Galil rifles, licensed its design to Vektor, a division of the state-owned DENEL military industrial corporation. Vektor produced slightly modified versions of the Galil ARM, SAR and MAR (micro-Galil) as the Vektor R4, R5 and R6, respectively. The changes were mostly cosmetic, in the shape and the colour of furniture, as well as in size – South African rifles were manufactured with slightly longer buttstocks.

During the second half of the 1990s, Vektor developed an interesting conversion to the proven and familiar R4 rifles. This conversion, designated CR-21 (Compact Rifle for the 21st Century), looked like an extremely futuristic and original bullpup design, but inside it was the same venerable 5.56mm Galil, less its furniture but with minor modifications to suit the bullpup layout. This decision saved much time and money that would otherwise be required to develop and produce a new action, and also allowed for the remanufacture of existing stocks of the 'old' R4 rifles into the 'new' CR-21 bullpup. Another advantage of the CR-21 was that it inherits all the reliability and strengths of the original AK-47/Galil design, combined with improved balance, ergonomics and advanced sighting equipment. It is also interesting to note that the CR-21 is relatively light, despite the fact that it has a complete and relatively large receiver, milled from a steel block. On the other hand, the use of an existing action of 'traditional' origin imposed some design limitations. For example, the CR-21 has no provision for left-hand spent case ejection, since this would require a serious redesign of the original R4 receiver and bolt group. The fire mode selector also remained in its 'original' place and is not comfortable to operate when the gun is shouldered. But this is not a unique decision; for example, Russia developed some Kalashnikov-based bullpup rifles which likewise have no left-side ejection, and, furthermore, some bullpup rifles, designed from scratch, are also limited to right-hand use only; for example, the British L85A1 and the Singaporean SAR-21.

The CR-21 was first displayed in public in 1997, with the hope that it would replace the R4 and R5 assault rifles in SANDF service. It represents probably the most interesting or, at least, the best-looking conversion of any conventional rifle into a bullpup layout. However, it failed to achieve any sales and by 2003 was no longer being marketed.

VEKTOR CR-21
Calibre: 5.56 × 45
Overall length: 760mm
Barrel length: 460mm
Weight: 3.8kg loaded
Magazine capacity: 20 or 35 rounds
Rate of fire: 650–700 rpm

The CR-21 is a gas-operated, selective-fire, magazine-fed rifle of bullpup layout. The receiver, with a long-stroke piston gas drive and rotating bolt, is taken from the R4/Galil ARM rifle, and thus for a general description of its operation see the account of the AK-47 in the section below on the USSR and its successor states.

Vektor CR-21.

The firearm housing is made from strong plastic and consists of a lower part with an integral pistol grip and magazine housing and an upper part with an integral buttpad. The fire controls of the CR-21 consist of a separate safety switch (a cross-bolt type button) at the front of the trigger guard and the ambidextrous fire mode selector, located at the rear part of the housing near the buttpad. The trigger is linked to the trigger mechanism by a long link. The cocking handle is located at the left side of the gun, above the forend, and does not reciprocate when the gun is fired, being linked to the bolt carrier by the long push-rod.

The sights of the CR-21 are mounted on a rail at the top of the receiver and are of the reflex type, with 1× magnification and illuminated reticle. The reticle consists of two horizontal marks and an inverted V-shaped centre mark, which allows for faster target acquisition. Illumination is achieved by using a light-gathering, fibre-optic device at the top of the sight and requires no batteries to operate. The sight can be quickly dismounted and remounted on the rifle, with no re-zeroing required. The CR-21 can be equipped with a 40mm underbarrel grenade launcher of South African manufacture.

SOUTH KOREA (REPUBLIC OF KOREA)

The armed forces of South Korea were originally equipped mainly with American armaments, including licence-built M16A1 rifles, which were used by the Army during the 1970s. Thanks to the economic and industrial development of the country, the large industrial concern Daewoo Precision Industries Ltd (a division of the industrial corporation DAEWOO International Corporation) began to develop domestic arms, including small arms, during the 1980s. Starting with the already familiar M16A1 design, Daewoo integrated several features from other designs, such as the ArmaLite AR-18 and later the Kalashnikov AK, to create the 5.56mm K1 short rifle (or carbine) to replace obsolete 9mm M3A1 submachine guns and 5.56mm XM177 carbines, used by tank crews and special forces, and supplied from the USA. Several years later Daewoo improved the basic design by getting rid of the troublesome Stoner direct gas system and replacing it with a much more reliable, long-stroke gas piston system, also converting the short carbine into a full-size rifle. The new rifle uses an AR-18-style bolt carrier, which rides on dual guide rods. The return springs are located around the guide rods, inside the receiver, and this allows for an entirely retractable buttstock to be used. There were several other improvements, such as a side-folding buttstock, and the improved version, the Daewoo K2, appeared about 1987.

At the present the K2 assault rifle and K1A carbine are the general issue shoulder arms of the South Korean Army. Semi-automatic export versions of the K2 rifle, known as the Daewoo DR-100 (pre-1994), DR-200 (post-1994, both chambered for the .223 Remington cartridge) and DR-300 (post-1994, chambered for the Russian 7.62 × 39 cartridge), are intended for both the civilian and police market. The earlier semi-automatic versions of the K1 and the K2 were exported as the Daewoo MAX-1 and MAX-2 rifles (both in .223 calibre).

During the DSEi-2003 exhibition in London, South Korea demonstrated its newest assault rifle, the Daewoo DAR-21. The DAR-21 represents the current mainstream in assault rifles design, being quite similar to most other assault rifles with the '21' index in the designation. It is a bullpup, with a polymer housing, telescope sight as standard (with back-up iron sights) and a conventional gas-operated action with rotating bolt, inherited from the Daewoo K2. In fact, the DAR21 is no more than a K2 receiver enclosed within a polymer bullpup housing. The DAR-21 can be fired in single shots, three-round bursts and full automatic, and accepts NATO-standard (M16-type) magazines. It is fitted with Picatinny-type top and bottom rails, with the standard sight being a 3× telescopic one. At present (November 2003) it is still to be seen if and when the DAR-21 will enter service with ROK Armed Forces.

There are also some rumours that the ROK Army, in conjunction with Daewoo Precision and probably other companies too, now is developing a combination infantry weapon along the lines of the American OICW system, which combines a 5.56mm rifle component, a small calibre (probably 20mm) grenade-launching component and an advanced rangefinding and sighting system.

DAEWOO K1 AND K2

	Daewoo K2 rifle	Daewoo K1A carbine
Calibre	5.56 × 45 NATO	
Overall length (butt open/ folded)	980/730mm	838/653mm
Barrel length	465mm	263mm
Weight	3.26kg less magazine	2.87kg less magazine
Magazine capacity	30 rounds	
Rate of fire	750 rpm	800 rpm

The Daewoo K2 is a gas-operated, selective-fire, magazine-fed weapon. The K1A carbine differs from the K2 rifle by its different gas system, a shorter barrel with a different muzzle compensator/flash suppressor and a different type of buttstock. The K2 gas system features a long-stroke gas piston, located above the barrel. The bolt group is more or less similar in design to that of the ArmaLite AR-18, with a rotating bolt with

DAR-21 rifle on display at the DSEi-2003 exhibition. (courtesy PLATOON magazine, South Korea)

seven lugs and a bolt carrier, which rides on guide rods. The cocking handle is attached to the right side of the bolt carrier and reciprocates when the gun is fired.

The receiver is generally similar in design to that of the M16 rifle and is made from two components, upper and lower, machined from aluminium alloy forgings and linked by two cross-pins. It must be noted, however, that Daewoo receivers are not interchangeable with any AR-15/M16-type receivers.

The trigger unit is fitted with a four-position safety/fire selector switch, located at the left side of the receiver, above the pistol grip. The switch has positions for safe, single shots, three-round bursts and full automatic fire. It must be noted that the three-round-burst counter does not reset itself if the trigger is released before all three rounds are fired.

Feeding is achieved from M16-type magazines. Both the K2 and the K1A rifle incorporates a bolt stop device, which holds the bolt open after the last shot from the magazine has been fired. The sighting system consists of a hooded front sight, mounted on the gas block, and an L-shaped, dual-aperture rear sight, with one small aperture for daylight conditions and another larger one for low-light conditions. A rotating knob at the right side of the rear sight block provides a range adjustment, with a maximum setting of 600m. The K2 can also be fitted with a see-through scope

rail just ahead of the rear sight block. The rifle is fitted with a side-folding, plastic buttstock and plastic furniture. The K1A carbine has a retractable, steel wire buttstock.

SPAIN

In 1949, Spain, facing the need to rearm its forces, established a special government-owned organization, known as CETME (*Centro de Estudios Tecnicos de Materiales Especiales* = Special Materials Technical Studies Centre, now known as *Empresa National Santa Barbara*). Spain also used the experience of many ex-German engineers and designers, most notably Dr Voss, the renowned ballistician, and Ludwig Vorgrimler, the former small arms designer from Mauser Werke. Voss was responsible for the development of a new intermediate cartridge, the 7.92 × 40 CETME, notable for its long, sleek bullet with a lightweight aluminium core. Vorgrimler adapted the original Mauser Stg.45 assault rifle design, which he brought from Germany via France, for the ammunition, and the new 7.92mm CETME assault rifle was submitted for Spanish Army trials around 1952.

The general design was found to be adequate, but the cartridge was rejected in favour of the 7.62 × 51 NATO round with a lighter bullet and a reduced

K2 rifle (above) and K1A carbine (below). (courtesy PLATOON *magazine, South Korea*)

Folding-stock version of the experimental CETME 7.92mm assault rifle.

powder charge; thus in 1955 CETME produced a 7.62mm version of the new rifle, based on the Vorgrimler roller-retarded blow-back action. The new rifle entered serial production in 1956 and was adopted by the Spanish Army in 1957. In 1958 CETME introduced a slightly improved design, known as the Modelo B or Model 58. This rifle was intended to fire 7.62 × 51 reduced loads, but it could also fire the standard 7.62mm NATO, if the bolt group and the return spring were replaced by the appropriate set of parts. The Modelo 58, unlike its predecessors, was designed to fire both single shots and full automatic from a closed bolt.

In 1964, CETME introduced the Modelo C, which also was adopted by the armed forces. This rifle was intended to fire only standard, full power 7.62 × 51 NATO ammunition. Its key improvements were four-position aperture sights (instead of the earlier leaf-type open sights), wooden handguards instead of the earlier steel ones, the bipod was made as a separate part and, most important, the chamber was fluted to improve extraction and avoid torn rims and cartridge case failures in harsh environmental conditions. Production of the Modelo C ceased in 1976.

During the 1970s a 5.56mm version of the design was developed. Production of the resulting assault rifle Mod. L and carbine Mod. LC began in 1984, and gradually replaced the 7.62mm rifles. The CETME Mod. L had a relatively short service life because in 1999 the wheel of history turned back and Spain adopted the 5.56mm G36E rifle, developed by Heckler & Koch. The irony is that HK became most famous for its weapons based on a CETME design, but the G36 has abandoned the roller-retarded blow-back system since this is apparently less suitable for the high-pressure

5.56mm ammunition than the gas-operated system used in the G36.

CETME Mod. A, B, 58 and C

[Data for Mod. B (Mod. 58)]
Calibre: 7.62 × 51 reduced power load; also 7.62 × 51 NATO
Action: retarded blow-back
Overall length: 1,015mm
Barrel length: 450mm
Weight: 4.4kg
Rate of fire: 550–600 rpm
Magazine capacity: 20 or 30 rounds

All 7.62mm CETME rifles are built around Vorgrimler's roller delayed blow-back system. This employs a two-part bolt with two rollers. The front bolt part (the bolt head) is relatively light and has a bolt face with an extractor on it. It also has a hollow cavity at the rear in which the inclined, forward end of the rear part of the bolt (the bolt body) is inserted. The system features two rollers, inserted from the sides into the bolt head and resting on the inclined, forward end of the bolt body. When the gun is fired, the pressure began to move the cartridge back against the bolt face. The rollers, which are extended into the recesses in the barrel extension, began to move inward into the bolt head, due to the inclined shape of the recesses. This movement translates into the faster rearward movement of the heavier bolt body, thus, at the initial instant of firing when pressure in the chamber is still high, the bolt face moves relatively slowly. As the pressure drops, the rollers gradually leave the recesses in the barrel extension; as soon as the rollers are completely pushed into the bolt, the bolt head and the bolt body begin to move backwards at the same speed, extracting

Above *CETME Modelo B, also known as Modelo 58.*

Below *CETME Modelo C.*

Below *5.56mm CETME Modelo L.*

and ejecting the spent case and chambering a fresh cartridge on the way back.

Early 7.62mm CETME rifles fire from the closed bolt in single shots and from the open bolt in full automatic mode. The trigger mechanism is hammer-fired, and in military versions is capable of semi-automatic and fully automatic modes of fire. On early models the safety/fire mode selector switch was located above the trigger at the right side of the gun. From the Modelo C the safety/selector switch was relocated to the left side of the gun. The receiver is made from sheet steel stampings, as well as the trigger group housing, which is hinged to the receiver just behind the magazine housing. Early models (before Modelo C) were issued with integral, folding, metal bipods and open leaf-type rear sights. Modelo C rifles were issued with wooden handguards and separate, detachable bipods. The rear sights were replaced by four-position aperture sights, marked for a 100–400m range. All rifles feature a wooden buttstock and a folding carrying handle above the receiver. The flash suppressor of the Modelo C rifles is shaped to accept and launch NATO-standard rifle grenades. Most rifles were issued with magazines of twenty-rounds capacity, made of steel, but thirty-round magazines were also available.

CETME Mod. L and Mod. LC

	Modelo L	Modelo LC
Calibre	5.56 × 45 NATO	
Action	retarded blow-back	
Overall length	925mm	860mm 665mm with collapsed buttstock
Barrel length	400mm	320mm
Weight	3.4kg empty	3.22kg empty
Magazine capacity	30 rounds	
Rate of fire	600–750 rpm	600–750 rpm

Like the previous models, the CETME Mod. L is a retarded blow-back, selective-fire assault rifle. It has a two-piece bolt with two rollers. The chamber walls are fluted to help the initial extraction. The overall design is somewhat similar to that of HK 33 rifles, but Mod. L is easily distinguished from the HK designs by a larger triggerguard and different plastic pistol grip and handguards. The sights on the Mod. L also are different from the HK pattern, with the rear sight being a simple flip-up L-shaped type with two apertures, for 200 and 400m. The magazine port is also different from the HK pattern and is designed to accept M16-type magazines. The carbine Mod. LC differs from the Mod. L by having a shorter barrel and telescoping metallic butt-stock.

SWEDEN

Sweden adopted its first 7.62mm assault rifle in 1963, as the AK-4. It was a licence-built version of the Heckler & Koch G3 rifle, which served well until the adoption of the 5.56mm ammunition in 1984. After extensive trials, which included designs such as the Israeli Galil (made under licence by FFV of Sweden), the German HK33, the American M16A1, the Swiss SIG SG-540 among others, the Swedish Army finally selected the Belgian FN FNC as its next weapon. The basic FNC rifle was modified to suit Swedish requirements, the most notable changes being the omission of the three-round-burst mode of fire, an enlarged trigger guard, a thicker forend and improved, corrosion-resistant finish on all metallic parts. First deliveries were made from FN in about 1986, and domestic rifles began to enter service a year later, made at Bofors's Karl Gustaf factories. The modified FNC rifle, adopted as the AK-5, is now in service with the Swedish armed forces.

In the meantime, a private Sweden company, Interdynamic, attempted to enter the assault rifle market with two interesting designs. First was the MKS, a conventional, 5.56mm gas-operated design, packed in a somewhat unconventional layout with the magazine serving as a pistol grip, which appeared in late 1970s. Since the magazine was swept forward and had significant depth front-to-back, the distance from the rear of the 'grip' to the trigger was about 2–3cm longer than, for example, on the M16 rifle, resulting in poor and uncomfortable handling. The receiver of the MKS was made from steel stampings, and the rifle featured a side-folding, skeleton buttstock. It did not succeed, as well as the later and more 'advanced' design, the 4.5mm MKR bullpup. The MKR was designed to fire a proprietary micro-calibre round with a pointed 4.5mm bullet, launched from a rimfire case, based on the .22WMR commercial hunting round. Since the cartridge was relatively low-powered, the MKR featured a simple blow-back design, with a large capacity, semicircular magazine housed behind the pistol grip. The manufacturers claimed that the MKR was on a par with M16 rifle at ranges up to 300m, but the MKR. unsurprisingly, soon disappeared from the

Above *AK-4 with grenade launcher.*

Left *The special rimfire cartridge for the MKR.*

Above *Prototype 5.56mm Interdynamic MKS rifle.*

Below *Prototype 4.5mm Interdynamic MKR rifle.*

AK5B rifle with optical sight, used as a marksman's rifle.

scene. It is interesting to note that the MKR cartridge was somewhat similar ballistically to the modern PDW cartridge, especially the German 4.6 × 30 HK.

BOFORS AK5

Calibre: 5.56 × 45 NATO
Action: gas-operated, rotating bolt
Length: 1,008mm (buttstock extended)/753mm (buttstock folded)
Barrel length: 450mm
Weight: 3.90kg
Magazine: 30-rounds box
Rate of fire: 650 rpm

The AK5 assault rifle is essentially similar to the Belgian FN FNC rifle, described in detail above, but with several modifications. First, the AK5 has no provision for the three-round-burst mode, and will fire only single shots or full automatic. Secondly, the butt-stock and handguards are made longer and more suitable for winter conditions and the charging handle is enlarged for a better grip when using Arctic mittens. Special surface treatment is used for better protection against the elements. The AK5 is manufactured in

several modifications, including the basic AK5; the AK5B with a 4× telescopic sight (British SUSAT L9A1) and a cheek-pad on the buttstock, which is issued as a squad-level marksmen rifle; the AK5C with a Picatinny rail and no open sights; the AK5D with the shortened barrel, and integral carrying handle with built-in telescope sight, intended for commando units and paratroops; and a grenade-launching version, fitted with the American M203 40mm grenade launcher, which is used mostly by rangers and amphibious forces.

SWITZERLAND

Switzerland began to experiment with intermediate cartridges before the Second World War and, being neutral, closely watched the developments made during and after the war. Being entirely satisfied with the power and accuracy of its 7.5mm GP11 cartridge, the Swiss Army tried to achieve a full power, selective-fire rifle. After a couple of false starts, first with the gas-operated Sk-46 self-loading rifle and then with the most unusual AK-53 blow-forward design, the famous

The experimental 7.5mm AK-53 rifle, designed by Rudolf Amsler, featured a highly unusual system of operation with blow-forward barrel and stationary breechblock.

SIG company finally produced a weapon which satisfied the Army in 1955.

This was the 7.5mm AM-55, a retarded blow-back design, developed under the leadership of Rudolf Amsler. The basic principles of the action were borrowed from German wartime Mauser *Gerät 06H* and Stg.45(M) assault rifles, but with much altering involved. In 1957 the Swiss Army adopted the AM-55 as the *Sturmgewehr-57*, or Stgw.57. Made between 1957 and 1983, the Stgw.57 represented one of the finest and most expensive automatic rifles ever issued to any army in the world. Chambered for full power 7.5 × 55 GP11 ammunition, the Stgw.57 provides long-range, accurate shooting in semi-automatic mode, necessary for typical Swiss mountain country, in combination with significant full automatic firepower, thanks to its relatively heavy weight, integral bipod and shrouded barrel. In the modified form, known as the SIG-510, this design was relatively successful, being sold to several South American countries, most notably Chile, chambered for 7.62mm NATO ammunition.

During the late 1960s and the early 1970s, SIG began to work on a 5.56mm rifle, first attempting to revive the original Mauser roller-locked, gas-operated action, since the roller-retarded blow-back apparently worked unsatisfactorily with the higher-pressure, 5.56mm cartridges. The resulting design, known as the SIG SG-530, did not succeed, and was soon replaced by the SG-540, built around a modified Kalashnikov-type action, with a long-stroke gas piston and rotating bolt. This was developed in both the 5.56mm (SG-540 rifle and SG-543 carbine) and 7.62mm (SG-542 rifle) calibres, although the latter had no significant sales. The SG-540 itself was not adopted by the Swiss military, but it became the platform for further improvements and led to the SIG-550/Stgw.90 assault rifle. The SG-540 series were made under licence by Manurhin of France and FAMAE of Chile, and served with both countries, as well as several others, mostly in South America and Africa. Chile still makes modified, SG-540-type weapons.

In the late 1970s the Swiss Army began the search for a new, smaller calibre rifle. Tests were done with the 5.6 × 48 Eiger and the 6.5 × 48 GP80 ammunition. Prototype rifles were developed by SIG (based on their SG-540 design) and by the state-owned Waffenfabrik Bern (W+F). However, the Army selected a slightly improved version of the 5.56 × 45 NATO cartridge as the 5.6mm GP90, and further testing proved the superiority of the SIG SG-541 rifle over its W+F rival. In 1983 the Army officially adopted the SIG SG-541 as the *Sturmgewehr-90*, or Stgw.90 although for financial

reasons production began only in 1986. Currently, the Stgw.90 is a standard Swiss service rifle.

The Swiss Army took its last deliveries of the Stgw.90 in the mid 1990s, but these rifles are still offered for export by the international SIGARMS organization, as well as sold for the civilian market in semi-automatic-only versions. In its export form this rifle is known as the SIG SG-550. 'Carbine' and subcompact 'Commando' assault rifle versions are available in the form of the SIG-551 and the SIG-552, respectively. Civilian versions of the SIG-550 and the 551 are known as the Stgw.90 PE in Switzerland or the SIG 550-SP and 551-SP when sold for export. The SIG-550 is often referred as the finest 5.56mm rifle ever made. It is also, not surprisingly, quite expensive.

Stgw. 57/SIG 510

	Stgw.57	SIG 510-4
Calibre	7.5 × 55 GP11	7.62 × 51 NATO
Action	retarded blow-back	
Overall length	1,105mm	1,016mm
Barrel length	583mm	505mm
Weight	5.56kg empty	4.25kg empty
Magazine capacity	24 rounds	20 rounds
Rate of fire	500 rpm	600 rpm

The action of the Stgw.57 was derived from the roller-retarded, blow-back system devised by Mauser engineers in Nazi Germany. However, the Swiss designers replaced the rollers with roller-shaped pivoting flaps, interposed between the bolt head and the bolt body. The receiver is made from stamped steel, with a separate trigger unit housing made integral with the pistol grip frame and triggerguard. The fixed barrel has a perforated steel jacket with two mounting points for an integral bipod – one near the muzzle and another near the receiver. The front part of the barrel is exposed to act as a rifle grenade launcher. To smooth out the excessive recoil generated in full automatic fire, and especially by rifle grenades, the fixed buttstock is fitted with a recoil buffer. The safety/fire mode selector is located at the left side of the trigger unit. Stgw.57 is fitted with large, T-shaped charging handle and with the folding 'winter trigger', which, when unfolded, extends down below the trigger guard, enabling the rifle to be used in Arctic mittens. Since the Stgw.57 was designed with the so-called straightline layout, the

Above *Swiss Stgw.57 7.5mm rifle.*

Below *SIG 510-4 7.62mm NATO rifle.*

raised sights are mounted on high, folding bases, with the rear sight being micrometer-adjustable from 100 to 650m. The Stgw.57 could also be fitted with the special Kern 4× telescope sight. Stgw.57 is fed from curved box magazines, made from steel and containing twenty-four rounds. The small forend is made from plastic and the gun is fitted with a side-folding, carrying handle. Other accessories include the sling, the bayonet and a special, small-capacity magazine for blank grenade-launching cartridges.

Export military versions of the Stgw.57, known as the SIG SG-510, were constructed in four modifications, of which only one was made in any significant quantities, the SG-510-4. This was chambered in 7.62 × 51 NATO, had a shorter barrel and non-folding aperture sights. The forend and buttstock were made from wood. Other versions included the SG-510-1 (exactly the same rifle as the Stgw.57), the SG-510-2 (a lightweight modification of the Stgw.57, also in 7.5mm), and the more compact SG-510-3, chambered for the Soviet 7.62 × 39 cartridge. Civilian semi-automatic-only versions of the Stgw.57 were designated PE-57 (in

7.5mm GP11) and SIG AMT (a semi-automatic version of SG-510-4 in 7.62mm NATO).

SIG SG-540, SG-542 AND SG-543

To make the rifle as inexpensive and reliable as possible, SIG designers selected the AK-47-style, gas-operated action, with a long-stroke gas piston attached to the bolt carrier and a rotating bolt with two massive lugs. The recoil spring is located around the gas piston rod and the bolt carrier is attached to this rod by the removable charging handle. The gas port has a regulator with two open (for standard and adverse conditions) and one closed position (for firing rifle grenades). The receiver is made from stamped steel and has two major parts, upper and lower, connected by pushpins. The barrel is screwed into the upper receiver. The trigger unit has a safety/fire selector switch on the left side of the receiver, with three settings: safe, semi-automatic and full-automatic. If desired, an additional module can be installed in the trigger mechanism to allow a three-round-burst mode. The rear sights are drum-type (like those found on HK rifles). The SG-540 has a

SIG SG-540, SG-542 AND SG-543

	SIG-540	SIG-542	SIG-543
Calibre	5.56 × 45	7.62 × 51	5.56 × 45
Length	950mm	1,000mm	805mm/569mm
Barrel length	460mm	465mm	300mm
Weight empty	3.26kg	3.55kg	3.0kg
Magazine capacity	20 or 30 rounds	20 or 30 rounds	20 or 30 rounds
Rate of fire	650–800 rpm	650–800 rpm	650–800 rpm

Above *5.56mm SIG SG-540 rifle.*

Left *5.56mm SIG SG-543 carbine.*

Below *7.62mm SIG SG-542 rifle.*

muzzle compensator/flash suppressor of NATO-standard diameter, thus it is possible to launch rifle grenades from the muzzle. The SG-540 has an integral folding bipod under the handguard and can be issued with a fixed plastic buttstock or with a side-folding, tubular metal buttstock.

The carbine version of the SG-540 is the SG-543 and has a shorter barrel. The SG-543 cannot fire rifle grenades. The 7.62 × 51 version of the SG-540 is known as the SG-542 and visually differs from it most conspicuously by a rectangular magazine of greater depth. The civilian version of the SG-540 can fire only in semi-automatic and can also be chambered for .222 Remington cartridges. Other chamberings such as the 7.62 × 39 Russian and the .243 Winchester are possible but extremely rare.

STGW.90/SIG SG-550, SG-551 AND SG-552

In essence, the SIG-550 is a somewhat lightened and refined SIG-540/541 rifle with a very similar mecha-nism and therefore only the differences will be discussed. The trigger unit has an ambidextrous safety/fire selector switch, with four settings: safe, semi-automatic, three-round-burst, full-automatic. The SIG-550 is issued with a side-folding, skeletonized, polymer buttstock. Every rifle of the SIG-550 family can be fitted with proprietary, quickly detachable scope mount. The Swiss Stgw.90 is often seen with a 4× fixed-power scope; export versions can be equipped with commercial telescope or 'red dot' sights for customer preference. The SIG-550 also can be fitted with a bayonet. Most recent accessories for the SG-550, the SG-551 and the SG-552 also included Picatinny-rail adaptors for receivers, as well as fore-arms with multiple Picatinny rails for equipment such as tactical lights and laser pointers.

The carbine version of the SIG-550 is the SG-551, which has a shorter barrel but cannot fire rifle grenades. An even more compact rifle, the SIG-552, is similar to the SIG-551 except that it has an even shorter

STGW.90/SIG SG-550, SG-551 AND SG-552

	Stgw.90/SIG 550	SIG 551	SIG 552
Calibre	5.56 × 45	5.56 × 45	5.56 × 45
Length (stock open/folded)	998mm/772mm	833mm/607mm	730mm/504mm
Barrel length	528mm	363mm	226mm
Weight empty	4.05kg without magazine	3.3kg without magazine	c.3.0kg without magazine
Magazine capacity		20 or 30 rounds	
Rate of fire	700 rpm	700 rpm	780 rpm

SIG SG-550, or Stgw.90 (Swiss designation). (image courtesy Dick Venema)

SIG SG-551 SWAT. *(image courtesy SIGARMS)*

SIG SG-552 Commando. *(image courtesy Dick Venema)*

handguard and barrel. The shorter gas piston rod also requires the return spring to be moved to the rear part of the receiver (as in the Kalashnikov AK), so that the bolt carrier of the SG-552 is different from that of the SG-550 or the SG-551. A version of the 551, called the SIG 551 SWAT, is intended for law enforcement. It is equipped with accessory rails on the forend and comes with a Trijicon ACOG optical sight and a cheek-pad on the buttstock. All SIG-550/551/552 rifles are equipped

with semi-translucent plastic magazines that may be clamped together by using special, integral studs for faster reloading.

TAIWAN

Taiwan, formally known as the Republic of China (as distinct from the People's Republic of China) occupies the island of Taiwan (formerly Formosa) off the coast of China. It was the last refuge of the pre-Communist Chinese regime and is still claimed by the PRC. As a result, a strong emphasis has always been given to defence against potential invasion, in which the country has traditionally been supported by the USA and has principally used American weapons.

Taiwan has developed two indigenous 5.56mm assault rifles based on American designs but with some interesting variations. The first was the Type 65 or T65, which resembles the M16 but was designed with a gas-piston system from the AR-18. This is now being replaced by the T86, which features a shorter barrel and a telescoping stock.

TYPE 65 (T65)
Calibre: 5.56 × 45
Action: gas-operated, rotating bolt
Overall length: 991mm
Barrel length: 508mm
Weight: 3.32kg
Magazine capacity: 20 or 30 rounds (M16)
Rate of fire: 700–800 rpm

The T65 closely resembles the M16A1 and uses its lower receiver, fixed plastic butt (including the recoil spring), foresight and magazines. The barrel is also of the same length. However, the piston-type gas operating system comes from the AR-18, and the plastic foregrip is longer than the M16A1's (a bipod may be fitted). The M16A1's characteristic carrying handle is also absent so that the rearsight has to be mounted on a large bracket, and the cocking handle is from the original M16 rather than the M16A1. The T65 experienced several problems and numerous modifications were made, leading to the T65K1 and the T65K2, the latter having a shorter barrel with rifling modified to use the SS109 bullet. There is also a T65K3 with a longer barrel, increasing the total length from 815 (K2) to 880mm.

TYPE 86 (T86)
Calibre: 5.56 × 45
Action: gas-operated, rotating bolt
Overall length: 880mm (800mm with stock retracted)
Barrel length: 375mm
Weight: 3.17kg (without magazine)
Magazine capacity: 30 rounds (M16)
Rate of fire: 600–900 rpm

The T86 is based on the T65 but its appearance is quite different: the barrel is much shorter, the stock telescopes and the foregrips are of an entirely different shape. However, a carrying handle resembling the M16's is fitted and used as the base for a telescopic sight; iron sights are also fitted and reflex and night sights are optional. A quick-release bipod and a sling may be fitted, as may the indigenous T85 40mm grenade launcher. As well as the usual M16 magazines, a hundred-round drum may be used. A short-barrelled carbine version has also been produced, but details are not available.

UNITED KINGDOM
British infantry fought throughout the Second World War armed with the bolt-action, .303in calibre Lee-Enfield of various marks, as well as with the crude but effective 9mm Sten submachine gun and the .303in calibre Bren light machinegun. Experience gained during the war showed that both submachine guns and bolt-action rifles could, and actually should, be replaced with a single, more effective automatic weapon. Wartime experience also showed that infantry ammunition had to be effective only about to 1,000yd

Taiwan T65.

(about 900m), with a rifle needing to be capable of only 600m – considerably less than full-power rifle/MG ammunition could achieve. British military experts felt that there could be a single intermediate round, to be used either in an automatic rifle or in a light machine gun. As described in Chapter 4, a new round designated the .280 (7 × 43) was chosen. This was carefully calculated to combine long-range effectiveness with a recoil low enough to permit accurate automatic fire in a shoulder-fired weapon, propelling a pointed, 9m bullet to about 750m/s at the muzzle.

With the 'ideal' infantry cartridge being developed, several British arms manufacturers started in 1947 to develop weapons for it. The Royal Small Arms Factory (RSAF) at Enfield Lock produced two designs of an assault rifle, universally known as the EM-1 and the EM-2 (Experimental Model 1 and 2). A third entrant, developed by the Birmingham Small Arms Co. (BSA), was a conventional, gas-operated rifle, with a traditional rifle layout and a semi-pistol grip stock.

Although the EM-1 was originally conceived with a traditional layout, this was changed and both Enfield rifles were made as bullpups in order to achieve the compactness required to replace the submachine gun. It must be noted that these rifles were not the first ever built with this layout – at least one bolt-action bullpup rifle is known, dating back to the beginning of the twentieth century. An experimental 7.62mm assault rifle in bullpup layout was also developed by 1946 in Tula, in the USSR. However, the British designers had been toying with the idea of a bullpup service rifle since 1944, being influenced by three experimental designs: an Enfield sniper rifle in 7.92 × 57, the EM-1 Korsac LMG (which achieved prototype status) and a concept known as the Harris rifle. In addition to the

assault rifles, Enfield produced a general-purpose machine gun, called the TADEN, to use the same ammunition. It was based on the Bren LMG, only with belt feed and would have replaced the Bren and probably the Vickers Medium MG as well.

The EM-1 was apparently heavily influenced by German late-war designs, since it used as many stamped and welded parts as possible, as well as a gas-operated, roller-locked action, somewhat similar to the Mauser wartime *Gerät 06*. The EM-2 looked quite similar in outline, but was very different in its design and method of manufacture. The EM-2 design team, led by Edward Kent-Lemon and the engineer Stefan Janson, chose more traditional machined parts and used a gas-operated action with flap locking, similar to another German wartime design, the 7.92mm, self-loading Gew.43(W)/Kar.43.

The traditional construction of the EM-2 was better suited to existing British industrial techniques and, after extensive trials, it was nominally adopted for British service in 1951 as the 'Rifle, Automatic, calibre .280, Number 9 Mark 1'. As already described, Britain, joined by Belgium and Canada, which had also seen the potential of the 7mm intermediate round, had attempted to sell this sound idea to the USA, but failed. In 1954 the USA forced the newly founded NATO to adopt its new 7.62 × 51 round as NATO's standard infantry cartridge. The EM-2 was a well balanced and well laid out rifle, with comfortable controls, accurate and reliable, and with ease of control in full-automatic fire. In addition to its unorthodox layout, it was probably the first service rifle intended to rely on optical sights as standard. The 1× sight (which could be replaced with a 3.5× model for sniping) was fixed to the carrying handle. Had it been put into service,

British L1A1 SLR (FN FAL) with SUIT optical sight.

4.85mm SA80 Individual Weapon prototype.

British troops could probably have had a first-class assault rifle before 1960. British designers converted the EM-2 to the significantly bigger and more powerful 7.62mm NATO cartridge, at first in selective fire but later, more realistically, as semi-automatic only, but it was too late; the political decision to adopt another weapon had been taken. As a result, Britain adopted its first post-war rifle only in 1957 and this was the already famous Belgian made FN FAL, restricted to semi-automatic only fire and designated L1A1. It was popularly known as the SLR, for self-loading rifle.

When the NATO trials were announced in 1977 to select a new cartridge, the British state-owned Enfield Small Arms Factory had already developed its own small-calibre, high-velocity round, which was basically the American .223/5.56mm case necked down to 4.85mm calibre (it was originally known as the 5mm after the bullet calibre) but with a longer neck, giving a case length of 49mm. Alongside this cartridge, Enfield developed a new weapon, originally designated the XL65. This, although somewhat similar in outline to the much earlier Enfield EM-2 assault rifle, was internally quite different, and more or less the US-made ArmaLite AR-18 rifle, put into a bullpup stock and rechambered for the 4.85mm cartridge. After the NATO trials, which to no one's surprise resulted in the adoption of the American 5.56mm cartridge – albeit in the improved Belgian SS-109 loading, the Enfield engineers rechambered the XL65 for this cartridge and continued its development under the designation XL70. This resulted in a family of weapons, collectively known as SA80 (Small Arms for the 1980s), principally an assault rifle, referred to as the Individual Weapon (IW) and a light machine gun with a longer barrel and a bipod, the Light Support Weapon (LSW). These were officially designated the L85 and the L86, respectively, with the initial production being designated L85A1 and L86A1.

Owing to the Falklands War (1981) the new system was actually adopted only in 1984. The original SA80 weapons (both the L85 and the L86) were plagued with many problems, some being very serious. In general, the weapons proved unreliable and troublesome to handle and maintain and were subject to severe criticism as a result of their performance in the harsh conditions of the 1991 Gulf War. Even regardless of these, the L85A1 is somewhat heavy and clumsy by modern standards, with most of the weight being located toward the butt. The principal advantages are its considerable accuracy (much aided by the standard telescopic sight) and the compactness common to all bullpups. After many attempts to achieve simple fixes, it was finally decided in 1997 to carry out a major overhaul of the design and to upgrade the weapons in service. The upgrading programme, carried out in 2000–02, was undertaken by Heckler & Koch, then owned by the British Royal Ordnance. It included internal machining to clear feed and ejection paths, a new breechblock and bolt, a new extractor and ejector (with spring), new recoil springs, a new firing pin, a new cocking handle, an entirely new pressed-steel magazine, a new gas plug and cylinder, a new hammer, a new barrel extension and (for the LSW only) a new barrel. About 200,000 rifles were upgraded into the L85A2 configuration, of the total of 320,000 or so original L85A1 rifles produced.

Above *The unsuccessful EM-2 rifle.*

Left *Diagram from the original patent, showing the layout and bolt locking system of the EM-2.*

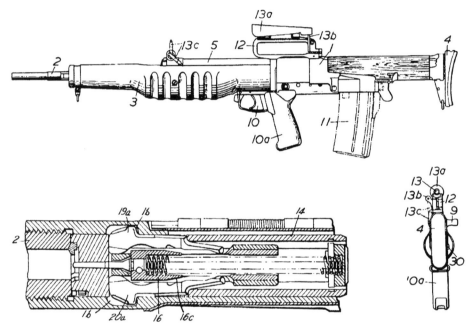

Similar improvements were made to the L86. The extensive (and expensive) HK modifications at last produced a reliable weapon, which performed well in the 2003 invasion of Iraq. The upgraded L85A2 rifles can be fitted with 40mm AG-36 underbarrel grenade launchers, designed and made by HK. Other than the basic L85A1 variant, the SA80 IW also appeared in the shortened carbine version, which never had an official 'L' designation, and in the manually-operated L98A1 rifle, which had its gas system removed and a larger cocking handle attached. The L98A1 is used to train Army cadets in basic rifle handling and shooting skills, and the rifle is fired as a manually operated, straight pull magazine repeater rifle.

ENFIELD EM-2/RIFLE, AUTOMATIC, CALIBRE .280, NUMBER 9 MARK 1

Calibre: 7 × 43 (.280 British)
Action: gas-operated
Overall length: 889mm
Barrel length: 623mm
Weight: 3.41kg with empty magazine
Magazine capacity: 20 rounds
Rate of fire: 450–600 rpm

The EM-2 rifle is a gas-operated, magazine-fed, selective-fire rifle. It uses a gas system with a long piston stroke, located above the barrel. The locking system is generally similar to the one found in the German wartime Gew.43 or in the Soviet Degtyarov

DP-27 machine gun (but turned back to front). The bolt locks into the receiver by two flaps, which are pivoted at their rear to extend out of the bolt and into the locking recesses in the receiver walls. The firing pin sleeve, coaxially located inside the hollow bolt, controls the flaps, and the sleeve is in turn connected to the gas piston rod by the projection on the rod. The recoil spring is located at the rear part of the gas piston, above the bolt. When the gun is fired, the hot powder gases cause the gas piston to go to the rear. This movement first makes the firing pin sleeve retract within the still stationary bolt, causing the locking flaps to be withdrawn from the locking recesses and into the bolt. As soon as the bolt is unlocked, it begins to move back against the pressure of the return spring, ejecting the spent case and feeding a fresh round into the chamber on its return into battery. The EM-2 fires from a closed bolt all the time. The firing mechanism is striker-fired, with the main spring and the sear located in the bolt. The sear is located at the bottom of the bolt and is operated by the long trigger lever, connected to the trigger. In general, this is a somewhat complicated but dust-proof, reliable, neat design.

The cocking handle is located at the right side of the weapon, on the front part of the gas piston rod, and can be removed when gun is disassembled. The safety switch is located at the front of the trigger guard and is similar in operation to one found in M1 Garand or M14 rifles, and the fire selector is of cross-bolt, push-button type and is located above the pistol handle. All controls are easily reachable with the firing hand. The furniture (pistol handle and forend) is made from wood; the buttplate is attached to the receiver directly and can be easily removed for field stripping. The EM-2 was fitted with optical sights as standard, mounted on the integral carrying handle. These sights were non-adjustable, and the range adjustment capability was built into the aiming reticle picture. Emergency (back-up) iron sights were also fitted – a rear folding aperture sight was attached to the left side of the carrying handle, and the folding front post sight was mounted on the left side of the gas block.

ENFIELD SA-80 IW: L85A1 AND L85A2
Calibre: 5.56 × 45 NATO
Action: gas-operated, rotating bolt
Overall length: 780mm (709mm in carbine variant)
Barrel length: 518mm (442mm in carbine variant)
Weight: 4.13kg (with SUSAT optical sight and no magazine); 5kg with SUSAT and loaded with magazine of 30 rounds
Magazine capacity: 30 rounds
Rate of fire: 650 rpm

The L85A1 is a gas-operated, magazine-fed, selective-fire rifle of bullpup layout. The receiver of the L85A1 is made from stamped sheet steel, reinforced with welded and riveted machined steel inserts. The steel of the receiver is somewhat thin and can be dented when the rifle is handled roughly, possibly resulting in serious malfunctioning. The gas-operated action has a short stroke gas piston, located above the barrel. The gas piston has its own return spring. The gas system has a

SA80 IW – L85A1 rifle.

three-position gas regulator: one for normal firing, the second for firing in adverse conditions and the third for launching rifle grenades (the gas port is shut off). The machined bolt carrier rides inside the receiver on the two parallel, steel guide rods, with the single return spring placed above and between the guide rods. The rotating bolt has seven lugs which lock into the steel insert in the receiver, just behind the breech. The charging handle is rigidly attached to the right side of the bolt carrier and, before the A2 upgrade, caused some problems by deflecting the ejected cases back into the action, thus causing stoppages. In the L85A2 configuration the charging handle was redesigned to avoid such problems and folds up when not in use. The charging handle slot is covered by a spring-loaded dust cover. The bolt and its extractor claw also were upgraded in the L85A2, to achieve a more reliable extraction of spent cases.

The trigger/hammer assembly of the L85A1 is also typical for a modern bullpup rifle, with the long link from the trigger to the hammer unit, located in the butt-stock. The hammer assembly of the L85A2 was redesigned to introduce a slight delay before the hammer release when the gun is fired in full automatic mode. This did not affect the cyclic rate of fire but improved the reliability and stability of the weapon during automatic fire. The fire mode selector is located at the left side of the receiver, behind the magazine housing and allows for single shot or full automatic mode of fire. The cross-bolt safety button is located above the trigger. The barrel is rifled for NATO-standard 5.56mm ammunition, with a 1:7 twist and is fitted with a NATO-standard flash suppressor, which allows the launching of rifle grenades from the barrel. The L85A1 is fed by using NATO-standard magazines, similar to M16-type magazines, with the standard capacity of thirty rounds. Early L85A1 steel magazines caused much trouble; furthermore the magazine housing itself had thin walls that could be easily dented, thus blocking the magazine way. Both the magazines and their housings were upgraded in the L85A2 configuration.

The standard sighting equipment is the 4× SUSAT (Sight Unit, Small Arms, Trilux) telescope, with illuminated post reticle. The SUSAT is mounted on a

SA-80 carbine.

L85A2, as modified by Heckler & Koch.

The 6.5mm Fedorov 'Avtomat'.

quickly-detachable mount at the top of the receiver, and features emergency back-up open sights at its top. The SUSAT is probably the best feature of the ill-fated SA80 package, since it allows for accurate fire (mostly in single shots) out to 400m or so. For second-line troops an alternative sighting system is available, which consists of the removable front post sight with high base and protective 'ears' and a detachable carrying handle with built-in aperture rear sight. The L85 can be fitted with the proprietary, knife-type, multipurpose bayonet.

USSR, RUSSIA AND OTHER FORMER SOVIET REPUBLICS

The development of the automatic infantry rifle began in Imperial Russia as early as 1913, when Col Fedorov of the Artillery Committee began to develop such weapon of his own design. He also proposed a 6.5mm rimless cartridge of lesser power and better shape than the standard rimmed 7.62 × 54R round then used in Russian firearms. The Fedorov automatic rifle impressed the Russian Army, and it ordered small quantities for troop trials on the German front. Since the start of the First World War had effectively blocked the development of a new cartridge, Fedorov redesigned his rifle for the Japanese 6.5 × 50R Arisaka ammunition, which was close to Fedorov's own cartridge, and readily available. Despite a somewhat complicated and dirt-sensitive recoil-operated design, the Fedorov rifle proved itself quite well. It had been produced in relatively small numbers, but after the Revolution of 1917 the newly founded Red Army adopted these rifles and used some during the subsequent Civil War. Fedorov's role, however, was as more of a teacher, theoretician and historian in the field of small arms. During the mid to late 1920s, working closely with his 'student' and protégé Fedor Tokarev, he proved that it was possible to build a family of small arms, ranging from a semi-automatic carbine and automatic rifle up to a general purpose machine gun, based on the same receiver and action, thus greatly simplifying logistics and manufacturing, as well as training. He also strongly promoted throughout his entire life small-calibre (6–6.5mm) intermediate cartridges as being ideal for an infantry rifle.

By the start of the Great Patriotic War in 1941 most of Fedorov's work on automatic rifles was all but forgotten. The first two years, however, proved the value of mobile automatic fire to Soviet tactics and so the 7.62mm submachine guns began to appear in the hands of the Soviet troops in ever-increasing numbers. But submachine guns, despite their advantages, lacked two essential properties: effective range (which was barely up to 250m) and accuracy. During the winter of 1942, the Red Army captured the first specimen of the newest German weapon, the machine carbine Mkb.42 (H) (see above) and its 7.92mm Kurz ammunition. These trophies were carefully examined and proved to Soviet experts that it was entirely possible to improve both the range and the accuracy of shoulder-fired automatic weapons, while retaining the weight and the size close to those of the typical PPSh-41 submachine gun. The Army immediately requested development of an intermediate cartridge in 7.62mm calibre and the designers Semin and Elizarov developed such ammunition by the end of 1943. It had a bottlenecked case 41mm long and fired a pointed, jacketed bullet.

With the new cartridge to hand, Soviet designers began to work on automatic (assault) rifles. First was

Sudaev AS-44 7.62mm assault rifle.

Sudaev, who developed his first assault rifle by early 1944. His first weapon was too cumbersome and somewhat unreliable and so he quickly developed another design, known as the AS-44. This was a gas-operated, locked-breech design with tilting bolt locking, submitted for trials by mid 1944. The Army then ordered a small batch of AS-44s with an appropriate amount of ammunition for extended field trials and received it in 1945. Unfortunately, Sudaev's severe illness and untimely death in mid 1946 (he was just 33) terminated the development of the AS-44.

By 1946 it was entirely clear that such an automatic rifle was necessary for the Army and the first competitive trials were ordered. Meanwhile, the already famous designer Simonov had developed a semi-automatic carbine for the new cartridge, based on his earlier 7.62 × 54R experimental semi-automatic rifle. This was tested against the Germans during the last months of the war with great success and consequently recommended for acceptance. In 1947 this carbine was adopted as the famous Simonov SKS, along with the new 7.62mm cartridge with a slightly improved case, now 39mm long.

The first official trials for a new 'Avtomat' (automatic [rifle], a designation first used in the early 1920s; see Chapter 1) were conducted in 1946. Several designers submitted their ideas, such as Degtyarov, Tokarev, Bulkin, Dementiev, Shpagin, Kalashnikov and Korobov. Sudaev's illness and death precluded his participation. One of designs, the TKB-408 by Korobov, was among the most interesting ones, since it was a bullpup, gas-operated and locked by using a tilting bolt. None of the tested designs were found to be

entirely satisfactory and further development and trials were ordered.

Mikhail Kalashnikov, then an Army sergeant and working with his small team, thoroughly changed his first design, originally known as the AK-46. He changed the receiver design, replaced the short stroke, separate gas piston with the now familiar long stroke piston integral with the bolt carrier; he also replaced the separate safety and fire selector with the also now familiar single lever. It must be noted that some of these features were borrowed from competing designs, most notably the Bulkin, or were suggested by others. After trials held in 1947, the modified Kalashnikov design, the AK-47, was officially recommended for adoption. The Soviet Army ordered significant numbers of AK-47 rifles for final troop trials, which were conducted in extreme secrecy. During the following two years the *Avtomat Kalashnikova* incorporated more than a hundred modifications and changes. Finally, in 1949 the improved rifle was officially adopted as the *7.62mm Avtomat Kalashnikova*, or simply the 'AK' (with fixed buttstock) and AKS (with underfolding buttstock). It must be noted that the designation AK-47 was officially used only for the prototype rifles submitted for trials in 1947 and never appeared in any Soviet official documents regarding Army issue rifles. There were some attempts in the post-Soviet Russian gun press to debunk the 'myth of the Kalashnikov', but so far it has been hard to obtain access to the real reports of the trials, as well as the documents which first suggested features later incorporated into AK rifles. The one thing that is clear, however, at least for one of the authors of this book, is

Kalashnikov AK-46

Simonov

Dementiev

Bulkin

Korobov TKB-408

Some of the assault rifles submitted to the 1946 trials.

Above *Korobov TKB-571, 7.62mm, retarded blow-back assault rifle, a major rival to the Kalashnikov AKM during the trials of 1957–59.*

Above *Korobov TKB-022, a 7.62mm, experimental bullpup rifle (1962). Note several novel features, such as polymer housing.*

Below *Another experimental bullpup rifle from Tula, the 7.62mm Afanasiev TKB-011M (1964). Note the forward-pointing ejection port just behind the pistol grip and polymer housing.*

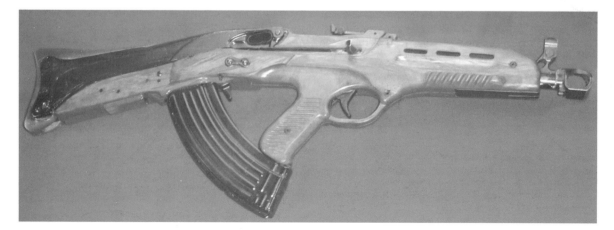

that the true history of the Soviet assault rifle is much deeper and much more controversial than it appears from most readily available Russian and Western sources.

The year 1947 marked the start of an era of the 'Kalashnikov'. Made in millions (most sources state that more than 70 million AK-pattern rifles have been made in the world to date), this became one of the most famous and widely used small arms in history. Most of its descendants, made in the USSR and Russia during the following fifty years as well as in many other countries, actually introduced very few changes. The technology was improved with the introduction of the stamped receiver *AKM* rifles in 1959, and the calibre was reduced from 7.62 to 5.45mm in 1974. But internally the AK-74M, manufactured since the early 1990s, is mostly still the same AK of 1949 vintage. Some experts dare to say that the domination of Kalashnikov and his rifle were not good for the Russian arms industry. Indeed, there were many interesting designs submitted for trials against the Kalashnikov in 1957–59 and 1971–74, but each time the Army preferred the already familiar and proven AK derivatives over the more effective and less expensive but entirely new designs. The AK was designed with the high probability of a Third World War in mind. It was extremely simple to learn and to maintain and can survive tremendous amounts of abuse, which can be expected in a large-scale war fought by large masses of poorly educated and trained conscripts. Fortunately this never happened, but these properties of the AK have made it extremely popular among all revolutionary movements, freedom fighters and all other non-professional warriors who needed crude, simple yet effective weapons.

One of the basic problems with small arms (and with all arms in general) in the USSR and Russia was, and still is, the conscript army. If you have eighteen-year-olds, some of whom hardly can read and speak Russian,[1] you cannot easily and quickly teach them to use any advanced weaponry effectively. And even if you can, and spend a huge amount of money and effort to train these conscripts, within two years all of them will have retired and you have to start all over again afresh. This experience had been clearly demonstrated

during World War II, when only technically advanced troops, such as the Marine Infantry, were able to use the relatively sophisticated, semi-automatic, Tokarev SVT-40 rifles with any degree of success. Most infantry units did not like this rifle, which required much more care and maintenance than a bolt-action Mosin-Nagant rifle, which was almost as foolproof as a wooden club. This was, and still is, a real problem. Even a relatively simple device such as a gas regulator was unacceptable for Army experts, since they could not believe that any conscript would set it properly each time (as had happened with the SVT-40 before). The rifle must be as simple to maintain and fire as possible. Thus it had to have an overpowered gas drive to work in all conditions, despite fouling and dirt, and it had to have loose tolerances and a super strong construction, to withstand rough handling. But there is a price: increased recoil, poor ergonomics and moderate accuracy were and still are typical properties of all Kalashnikov rifles.

The trials in 1957–59, which included the modified AK, the Simonov assault rifle (loosely based on his famous SKS carbine), the Korobov TKB-517 and several others, resulted in the adoption of the slightly modified Kalashnikov AKM. It is almost unknown to the general public that the AKM prototype was outperformed by the TKB-517, which also was lighter, about 30 per cent less expensive and more stable in full automatic fire, thanks to its Kiraly-type, retarded blow-back system. The exact reasons for the rejection of the Korobov system were not published, but it is believed that the Army decided that 'the best is the enemy of the good', and stuck to the familiar.

The switch to a smaller calibre, which occurred in the Soviet Army in 1974, did not help much. This change was caused by the American M16 rifles, captured in Vietnam during the early 1960s and supplied to the USSR in exchange for military support. The small-calibre M16 greatly impressed the Soviet experts and in the mid 1960s work was started on such cartridges. The smaller and lighter 5.45mm cartridge generates much less recoil and has a flatter trajectory and so it is easier to control the rifle in full automatic fire or to fire single shots accurately in rapid fire. There is also a huge logistical gain because even a typical, one-man combat load of eight magazines (240 cartridges) resulted in a weight saving of about 1.4kg. Given the size of the Soviet Army, this provided an impressive total saving in weight as well as in the amount of raw materials needed to produce the new ammunition.

After the trials conducted in 1970–71, the Army

---

1 Russia is a large, multinational and multilingual country. Though the Russian language is official (and was so in the USSR), many people of other than Russian nationality prefer to speak their native languages. In the USSR the spectrum of languages was much wider, which, of course, did not help the Army.

Above *Tkachev AO-46 compact assault rifle.*

Left *Stechkin TKB-0116 compact assault rifle.*

again selected the famous and familiar AKM, rebarrelled for the smaller-calibre round and designated A-3, over the more effective, SA-006 Konstantionov assault rifle, developed in Kovrov. Designated in service as the AK-74, it was essentially the same old AKM of 1959, with the same properties, handling, extreme simplicity and reliability (after some teething problems with insufficient receiver strength and barrel bulging). Interestingly, Mikhail Kalashnikov resisted this changeover himself, feeling that the existing 7.62mm rifles were entirely satisfactory, and he was literally forced to produce a smaller-calibre version of the AKM.

During the mid 1970s several designers developed and offered the Army new compact assault rifles,

intended as personal defence weapons for tank and helicopter crews and other non-infantry personnel. This resulted in a research programme and subsequent trials, codenamed 'Modern'. Several designs were tested, including the short-recoil operated TKB-0116, developed in Tula by Stechkin, as well as the gas-operated AG-043 by Simonov (of the famous SKS carbine) and the AO-46 by Tkachev (this was a most unusual design, with a proprietary box magazine serving as a pistol grip), developed in Klimovsk. Not surprisingly, the Army preferred the slightly modified but still familiar Kalashnikov design from Izhevsk, adopted as the AKS-74U in 1979.

But it was soon discovered that even the newest AK-74 left much to be desired and thus in 1979 the Army ordered a new research programme, codenamed 'Abakan' (after a small city in Russia). This was intended to develop a new 5.45mm rifle, which had to be at least 150 per cent as effective[2] as the AK-74. The initial requirements of the Abakan programme were based on the experimental results, obtained during the late 1960s and the early 1970s from several prototype assault rifles, developed in Tula by Gennadij Korobov and in Klimovsk by Pavel Tkachev. These rifles introduced the experts to such concepts as a dual high/low rate of fire, with the low rate intended for long bursts and the high rate for limited length bursts of two or three rounds, as well as balanced and soft-recoil systems. The three-round bursts with high rate significantly increased accuracy and effectiveness; this was one of the fundamental requirements included in the programme from the start.

The first trials were held, again in deep secrecy, in 1984. Several designers (more properly, design teams) submitted their prototypes to be tested against the AK-74. All were gas-operated, 5.45mm rifles and all featured both full automatic and two- or three-round-burst capabilities. There were three basic approaches for increased combat effectiveness. The first was a more or less traditional design, with burst limiter, high rate of fire and a rate reducer which was activated in full automatic fire. Korobov had taken this approach in his TKB-0111 rifle, as well as Afanasiev in his TKB-0136 model, both made in Tula. The second approach is known as a 'balanced action'; first developed during the late 1960s by the designers Alexandrov and Paranin in Izhevsk and by Tkachev in Klimovsk, this system used a counter-mass to compensate for the recoil impulse, generated by a massive bolt group slamming against the receiver in its rearmost and foremost position during the reloading cycle. The counter-mass is linked with a second gas piston and moves in the opposite direction to the bolt group. Synchronization is achieved by using a simple rack and pinion system. In this, only the impulse of the fired cartridge is transferred to the receiver, and through the buttstock to the shoulder of the shooter. The impulses of the heavy and fast-moving bolt group are offset by the counter-mass and do not affect the shooting, unlike the AK's operation, where the moving bolt group produces much additional recoil and vibration. The 'balanced system' was used in the AKB rifle, developed by V.M. Kalashnikov (son of the famous Mikhail) in Izhevsk,

and in the AEK-971 rifle developed in Kovrov by Koksharov.

The last approach, usually known as 'lafetted system, 'soft-recoil system' or shifted recoil system', is no more than an adaptation of the old artillery principle of reducing the peak recoil by allowing the gun to recoil in its mount. In this system the barrel and the receiver with the gas system and bolt group are allowed to recoil inside the outer weapon housing, against the special recoil buffer springs. In single shots or full automatic mode, the full recoil cycle begins for each shot, simply reducing the felt recoil. In burst mode, several shots (two or three) are made at a high rate (of about 1,800 rpm or more) within one recoil cycle, and so the recoil of the whole burst is 'accumulated' in the buffer springs and released to the housing and to the shooter only when the last bullet of the burst has already left the barrel. The recoil is the major factor which disturbs the aim of the rifle and so the rifle remains almost steady on the target during the quick burst. First tested during the late 1960s in the AO-62 experimental assault rifle, developed at TSNI-ITOCHMASH (Central Institute of Precision Equipment) by P. Tkachev, this system was later incorporated into several 'Abakan' prototypes. This is the most complicated system, since it requires the loading of cartridges into the moving (recoiling) receiver. One of contestants, the Nikonov 'AS' rifle from Izhevsk, which was built around this system, solved this problem simply by having a magazine which recoiled along with the receiver/barrel group; this, obviously, was unacceptable because of reliability and safety issues. Two other 'soft-recoil' prototypes featured a type of complicated, two-stage feeding system to load cartridges from the stationary magazine into the recoiling barrel/receiver unit. Stechkin developed one such prototype in Tula, the TKB-0146, and it was the only bullpup submitted for the trials. It also featured an ambidextrous handling, with spent cases being ejected forward from the aperture above the pistol grip, at the right side of the receiver. The second experimental design was another rifle by the Nikonov team from Izhevsk, and this was the ASM.

The 'Abakan' trials continued until the summer of 1986, when they were suddenly stopped before recommencing late in the year. At that point the Army announced the Nikonov ASM as the favourite; it had achieved a 130 per cent increase in effectiveness over the AK-74. The second was the Kalashnikov AKB with a 70 per cent increase, and the third – the Korobov TKB-0111 with a 50 per cent increase. The trials were completed in 1987 and the Nikonov ASM was recom-

---

2 The exact requirements as well as the criteria of effectiveness used in the 'Abakan' trials are still classified and so far not disclosed to the general public.

TKB-0111
G.A.Korobov

TKB-0146
I. Ya. Stechkin

TKB-0136
N.M. Afanasiev

AEK-971
S.I. Koksharov

AS
G.N. Nikonov

AKB
V.M. Kalashnikov

ASM
G.N.Nikonov

5.45mm assault rifles, submitted to the 'Abakan' trials in 1984.

mended for adoption. But it was not until 1994, when the modified Nikonov design had been officially adopted by the government as the *5.45mm Avtomat Nikonova obraztsa 1994*, or simply the *AN-94*. This rifle is described in detail below. According to sources at IZHMASH, the development of the AN-94 still continues, attempting to improve some technological and ergonomic issues. Another development which is under way is the AN-94-type weapon in 7.62 × 39, because of the constant popularity of the older 7.62 × 39 cartridge among Russian troops.

It must be noted that, while 5.45mm rifles were standardized in the Soviet Army in 1974, the earlier 7.62mm AKM rifles were not declared obsolete and may still be encountered among some non-infantry units, such as the air forces and air defence. The special Police and Internal Affairs Ministry troops, especially those operating against the separatists in Chechnya, also sometimes prefer the 'hard-hitting' 7.62mm rifles to the more modern 5.45mm weapons. This steady popularity of 7.62 × 39 ammunition, as well as export prospects, resulted in the appearance in the early 1990s of the so-called 'hundred series' Kalashnikov rifles, chambered for 7.62mm as well as 5.56 × 45 NATO ammunition.

During the last decade of the twentieth century several design bureaux and small arms manufacturers continued their developments, despite the preferences of the Army, with the intention of selling their designs to the MVD (Internal Affairs Ministry) troops or for export. Such developments are the AEK-971 from Kovrov (rejected during the 'Abakan' trials but still considered to be the rival of the AN-94), the A-91 bullpup from the KBP (Instrument Design Bureau from Tula, particularly known for its confusing small arms designation system, as well as for outstanding aircraft, antiaircraft and antitank weapon systems), and the Groza OTs-14 from the TSKIB SOO (also from Tula; *Tsentralnoe Konstruktorskoe Buro Sportivnogo i Okhotnichiego Orujija* = Central Design Bureau for Sporting and Hunting Arms). All these weapons were bought in relatively small numbers either by the MVD or other law enforcement agencies in Russia.

But this is not the end of the story. There also were several other lines of development. In the early 1960s, following the successful development of the APFSDS rounds for the 100mm, towed antitank gun, a group of designers from the NII-61 (State Scientific and Research Institute No.61 of the Defence Industry Ministry, now the famous TSNIITOCHMASH), began to develop APFSDS ammunition for small arms. Known in West as the 'flechette' (little arrow), such ammunition has the benefits of an extremely high velocity, low recoil and deep penetration. A new experimental cartridge, developed by Gryazev, Shipunow, Shiryaev and Fadeev, launched a 2.4g, finned, arrow-like projectile at a muzzle velocity of about 1,060m/s. In 1961 Dimitry Shiryaev developed an experimental, gas-operated assault rifle for this ammunition, designated AO-27. Trials demonstrated a significant increase in hit probability over the Kalashnikov AKM in full automatic mode, especially when being fired from unsupported positions (from the shoulder or the hip). However, the single-shot accuracy was disappointing, the ammunition was expensive and the lethality was questionable. The development of the assault rifle was consequently abandoned, and later efforts concentrated on flechette cartridges of 10mm

9 × 39 OTs-11 'Tiss' compact assault rifle, based on the AKS-74U.

Shiryaev AO-27 experimental flechette-firing assault rifle (1961). (courtesy Soldier of Fortune magazine, Russian edition)

nominal calibre and a machine gun to fire them. It must be noted that, at about the same time, the Americans wasted huge amounts of money and time working on the equally unsuccessful SPIW and later the ACR programme, which also included the development of the flechette-firing weapons (see Chapter 4).

The next line of development was the caseless cartridge and the gun for it. The only available information about such developments was that there were several prototype caseless rifles. We have so far been unable to obtain any reliable information on the precise developments in this field in the USSR and Russia, other than some brief information about the Simonov AO-31-7 assault rifle of 1965. This featured a fairly typical, long stroke gas piston action and a rotating bolt, but had neither extractor nor ejector and fired experimental, 7.62mm caseless ammunition with a pressed powder charge. The AO-31-7 was a full-automatic-only weapon. Tests proved that the ammunition was far from being satisfactory and the project was dropped.

The Special Forces, generally known as 'SpetsNaz' (after the Russian *Voiska Spetsialnogo Naznacheniya* – Special Purpose Troops), always played a key role in Soviet military doctrine. One aspect of every Special Force is that it prefers to operate stealthily, with as little sound and flash as possible from their weapons. The first generation SpetsNaz weapons were no more than AK and AKM rifles, fitted with quickly-detachable sound suppressors, and loaded with special subsonic ammunition with heavy bullets. Apparently this was not enough, since in the mid 1980s the development of

new, more effective silenced weapons was begun. At first, designers from TSNIITOCHMASH in Klimovsk developed a special-purpose, 9mm, subsonic cartridge, based on the necked-out 7.62 × 39 case. These cartridges were fitted with heavy (about 16–17g) standard 'ball' or armour-piercing bullets, with muzzle velocities of about 280–300m/s. Having the ammunition, the team at TSNIITOCHMASH, led by P. Serdyukov, developed a family of integrally-silenced, 9mm weapons, which included the *VSS 'Vintorez'* sniper rifle and the *AS 'Val'* assault rifle. Both are based on the same action and integrally-silenced barrel, which are described in detail in the section on the *AS 'Val'* below. During the 1990s the 9 × 39 ammunition found some favour in the ranks of law enforcement and state security agencies, thanks to its good hitting power, relatively short dangerous zone and good armour penetration. Starting in the early 1990s, several new designs appeared in 9 × 39 chambering, including compact assault rifles such as the *SR-3 'Vikhr'* (based on the *AS 'Val'*), the original 9A91, made in Tula, and experimental designs such as the *OTs-11 'Tiss'* (basically, an AKS-74U rebarrelled for 9 × 39 ammunition) and the *OTs-14 'Groza'*, an odd-looking bullpup with a modular grenade launcher. The *OTs-11* never made it past the prototype stage, but the *OTs-14* was produced in small numbers around 1995 and saw limited use in the hands of MVD troops during the first counter-terror campaign in Chechnya in 1999.

The last, but not the least line of development included unique underwater assault rifles. The research in this field was started in the late 1960s to provide the combat divers of the Soviet Navy with effective underwater weapons. By the early 1970s designers at TSNIITOCHMASH had developed a hydrodynamically stabilized, needle-shaped, underwater projectile, which used a cavitation effect to retain its trajectory in the water. Such projectiles could be fired from smoothbore firearms, and the first such weapon to be produced and issued to divers was the SPP-1 four-barrelled underwater pistol. Following the initial success of the concept, a group of engineers and designers at TSNIITOCHMASH, led by V. Simonov, created a unique design, a selective-fire, underwater assault 'rifle'. In fact, this was a smoothbore weapon to launch long, 5.66mm, cavitation-stabilized, non-rotating projectiles. Several special naval warfare units of the Soviet and the Russian Navy have used this weapon since the late 1970s as the '*5.66mm Avtomat Podvodnyj Spetsialnyj*' (special underwater automatic [weapon]) or '*APS*'. The major drawback of this indigenous system is that it is almost ineffective above water, in the atmosphere. The non-rotating projectile tumbles in its trajectory when fired in the air and the effective range is no more than several tens of metres. Furthermore, the service life of the APS severely degrades when it is fired in the air, from a claimed 2,000 rounds under water down to a miserable 180–200 rounds in air. Recognizing that, a group of designers from Tula, lead by Dr Daniloff, during the late 1990s developed an even more unusual 'dual-medium', amphibious assault rifle, the *ASM-DT 'Morskoj Lev'* (sea lion), which is still in experimental form. This rifle is designed to take deep APS magazines and fire special 5.45mm cavitation-stabilized projectiles, and, with only a change of magazine, take standard 5.45 × 39mm ammunition from any AK-74-type magazine to be used above

water. Both the APS and the ASM-DT also are described below.

After the demise of Soviet Union in 1991, most Soviet military industrial facilities, including all small arms factories, remained in Russia. Additionally, the poor financial state of most of the post-Soviet independent states has not helped development in the field of small arms. Many countries have continued to manufacture variants of the AK series, apart from those already described: the Arsenal Company Bulgaria offers several models in 7.62 × 39, 5.56 × 45 and 5.45 × 39; the Maadi Company of Egypt makes the MISR 7.62 × 39 and several civilian semi-automatic models; the Hungarian state factories make the AKM-63 and the AMD-65 (Para) – both in 7.62 × 39, Iraqi state factories have made the Tabuk 7.62mm; North Korea's state factories make the Type 68 in 7.62mm, Poland's state factories produce the AK, the AKM and the AKMS in 7.62mm, and the Zaklady Metalowe LUCZNIK SA produces the Tantal and Onyx 5.45mm, and the Beryl and Mini-beryl 5.56mm; Romania's ROMARM makes the 7.62mm AKM, the 5.45mm Model 86/AK-74 and the 5.56mm Model 97, and finally, the former Yugoslavia used to make AKMs which enjoyed a good reputation for rigidity since their receivers were pressed from 1.5mm rather than 1.0mm thick steel. These were designated M70B1 (fixed wood stock) and M70B2 (folding skeleton stock). Yugoslavia also made a stretched version of the gun, the M77B1 selective-fire rifle in 7.62 × 51 NATO.

The only two known recent developments are the Armenian 5.45mm K-3 and the Ukrainian 5.45mm '*Vepr*' assault rifles. The weapons are surprisingly similar and represent no more than moderately successful attempts to convert a standard Kalashnikov

The latest Ukrainian 'Vepr' assault rifle, first presented in 2003; it is actually no more than a Soviet-era 5.45mm AK-74 fitted into a rough bullpup stock with a red dot sight of domestic origin.

AK-74 rifle into a bullpup layout. In both cases this was achieved simply by stripping the furniture and the buttstock, fitting a buttplate and a type of cheek rest directly over the receiver and the placing of a new pistol grip ahead of the magazine, plus a side-mount for a type of collimating sight. The magazine release, as well as the safety/fire mode selector, remained in their original places, now well behind the pistol grip and the trigger. No provisions were made to avoid damage to the shooter by ejected cases, when firing from the left shoulder. Despite all claims, these weapons represent no significant advantages over the conventional AK-74M, except for their total length, and even less over the modern bullpups, such as the IMI Tavor or the FN F2000. The K-3 reached preproduction status in 1996, but does not appear to have progressed further.

KALASHNIKOV AK AND AKM

Calibre 7.62 × 39
Action: gas-operated, rotating bolt with two lugs
Overall length: 870mm
Barrel length: 415mm
Weight: AK 4.3kg empty; AKM 3.14kg empty
Magazine capacity: 30 rounds
Rate of fire: 600 rpm

The Kalashnikov AK and AKM are gas-operated, selective fire assault rifles. The gas-operated action has a massive bolt carrier with a permanently attached, long stroke gas piston. The gas chamber is located above the barrel. The bolt carrier rides on the two rails, machined in the receiver, with significant clearances between moving and stationary parts, which allow the gun to operate even when its interior is severely fouled with sand or mud. The rotating bolt has two massive lugs that lock into the receiver. The bolt is so designed

that on the unlocking rotation it also makes a primary extraction movement to the fired case. This results in positive and reliable extraction even with a dirty chamber and cases. The rotation of the bolt is ensured by the curved cam track, machined in the bolt carrier, and by the appropriate stud on the bolt itself. The return spring and a spring guide are located behind the gas piston and are partly hidden in its hollow rear part when the bolt is in battery. The return spring base also serves as a receiver cover lock. The cocking handle is permanently attached to the bolt carrier (it forms a single machined steel unit with the carrier) and reciprocates when the gun is fired.

The receiver of the AKM is made from stamped sheet steel, with a machined steel insert at the front. The earliest AK-47 receivers were also made from stamped and machined parts, riveted together, but this soon proved to be unsatisfactory and most of the AK rifles made between 1951 and 1959 were made with completely machined receivers. The receiver cover is a stamped sheet metal part, with stamped strengthening ribs found on the AKM covers. The easiest way to distinguish the machined and the stamped receiver is to look at the receiver wall above the magazine housing: on the milled (machined) receivers there are relatively large, rectangular, lightening cuts on both sides; on stamped receivers there are relatively small, oval-shaped indents, also on both sides of the receiver.

All AK rifles feature a threaded muzzle, covered with a special, screw-on thread protector on AK rifles, or with a spoon-shaped, muzzle-climb compensator on AKM rifles. These threads were originally intended for the mounting of a blank fire attachment. The same thread could also be used for mounting a quickly detachable silencer, to be used with special subsonic

Cross-sectional diagram of AKM rifle.

Above *Kalashnikov AK rifle (post-1951 manufacture), with machined receiver.*

Above
*Kalashnikov
AKM rifle
(1959 pattern),
with stamped
receiver.*

Right
*Kalashnikov
AKMS rifle
(1959 pattern),
with folding
buttstock.*

ammunition. A special, spring-loaded plunger is built into the front sight base to keep these attachments from self-unscrewing.

The relatively simple trigger/hammer mechanism is loosely based on 1900s-period Browning designs (much like most other modern assault rifles) and features a hammer with two sears – one main, mounted on the trigger extension, and one for semi-automatic fire, that intercepts the hammer in the cocking position after a shot is fired and until the trigger is released. An additional automatic sear is used to release the hammer in full automatic mode. The AKM trigger unit also features a hammer -release delay device, mounted on the primary sear, which serves to delay hammer release in full automatic fire by a few microseconds. This does not affect the cyclic rate of fire but allows the bolt group to settle in the foremost position after returning into battery. The combined safety/fire selector lever of distinctive shape is located on the right side of the receiver. In the 'safe' position (topmost) it locks the bolt group and the trigger, and also serves as a dust cover. The middle position is for automatic fire, and the bottom one is for single shots. The safety/fire selector switch is considered by many as the main drawback of the AK design, not cured in most derivatives until now. It is slow, uncomfortable and sometimes stiff to operate (especially when the user is wearing gloves or mittens), and, when actuated, produces a loud and distinctive click. There is no bolt-stop device and the bolt always goes forward when the last shot from the magazine is fired.

The AKM is fed from the thirty-round, stamped steel magazines of heavy but robust design. Early AK magazines were of a slab-sided design, but the more common AKM magazines feature additional stamped ribs on the sides. Late production magazines were made from a brick-red plastic and the current production 7.62mm magazines are made from black plastic. A positive magazine catch is located just ahead of the trigger guard and solidly locks the magazine into place. Insertion and removal of the magazine require a slight rotation of the magazine around its front lip, which has a solid locking lug. If they are available and required, forty-round box magazines of similar design or the seventy-five-round drums (both from the RPK light machine gun) may be used.

AKM rifles were issued with wooden stocks and pistol grips. Late production AKM rifles have a plastic pistol grip. The wooden buttstock has a steel buttplate with a mousetrap cover over the accessory container in the butt. AK buttstocks are more angled downwards than AKM ones. The folding-stock version was devel-

oped for airborne troops and has an underfolding steel shoulder stock. These modifications of the AK and the AKM were designated AKS and AKMS, respectively. AK rifles were issued with detachable knife-bayonets and the AKM introduced a new pattern of shorter, multipurpose knife-bayonet, which can be used in conjunction with its sheath to form a wire-cutter. All AK and AKM rifles were issued with canvas carrying slings. The sights of the AKM consist of the hooded front post and a U-notch open rear. The sights are graduated from 100 to a rather optimistic 1,000m (800m on the AK), with an additional, 'fixed' battle setting that can be used for all ranges up to 300m. AKM rifles can also be fitted with the 40mm GP-25 grenade launcher, which is mounted under the forend and the barrel. This has its own sights on the left side of the unit.

KALASHNIKOV AK-74, AKS-74 AND AK-74M

Calibre: 5.45 × 39
Action: gas-operated, rotating bolt with two lugs
Weight: 3.3kg (with empty magazine and without bayonet); 3.6kg (with loaded magazine)
Length: 943mm (AKS-74 with folded butt : 690mm)
Barrel length: 415mm
Magazine capacity: 30 rounds standard
Rate of fire: 600–650 rpm

The AK-74 is little more than a 7.62mm AKM rifle adapted for 5.45mm ammunition. Being internally similar to the AKM in every respect, it differs externally by its large, effective muzzle brake, which is known for its ability to deflect the sound of firing to the sides. The early production, wooden buttstocks were made with longitinual grooves on both sides for easier visual recognition and as a minor weight-saving measure. The magazines are made from brick-red plastic and hold thirty rounds. The paratroops model, the AKS-74, is fitted with a sturdy, side-folding buttstock made from steel stampings. Early production AK-74 rifles were equipped with wooden furniture, and later production rifles were fitted with polymer furniture and buttstocks. Special versions of the AK-74 originally included the AK-74N, with a night scope rail on the left side of the receiver. During the late 1980s Izhevsky Zavod, the main manufacturer of Kalashnikov rifles in the world, introduced the AK-74M, which replaced the AK-74, the AKS-74 and the AK-74N in production. The AK-74M features a strengthened receiver cover, a side-folding, solid, polymer buttstock, and a scope rail on the left side of the receiver as standard. Like the earlier AK-74 and AKS-74, the AK-74M can be fitted with a knife-

AK-74 rifle with 40mm GP-25 underbarrel grenade launcher and black plastic furniture.

bayonet or a 40mm grenade launcher, the earlier GP-25 or the later and lighter GP-30. Special versions of the AK-74 could be equipped with the so-called 'PMS' (*Pribor dlya Maloshumnoj Strelby* – low-noise, firing device), which is mounted instead of the standard muzzle brake and is intended for use with standard, supersonic ammunition.

KALASHNIKOV AKS-74U

Calibre: 5.45×39
Action: gas-operated, rotating bolt with two lugs
Overall length: 735mm (490mm with folded butt-stock)
Barrel length: 210mm
Magazine capacity: 20 or 30 rounds
Weight empty: 2.71kg
Rate of fire: 650–735 rpm

The AKS-74U short assault rifle (the 'U' suffix means *ukorochennyj* = shortened) was developed in the early 1970s from the AKS-74 assault rifle. It was officially adopted in 1979 and the first deliveries to troops were made in 1980. Surprisingly, the AKS-74U was mostly produced, not in Izhevsk (where all other Kalashnikov-type rifles were made), but in Tula, at the Tula Arms Factory. The AKS-74U was intended as a personal defence weapon for tank, gun, helicopter and other vehicle crews, and for special operations forces, who required a compact but relatively powerful, individual, automatic weapon. The AKS-74U has the size and effective range of a typical submachine gun, but has the advantage of using general issue, assault-rifle ammunition and magazines, as well as a parts interchangeability with the general issue assault rifle the AK-74. Since its introduction the AKS-74U, unofficially known as a '*Ksyusha*' (a variation of a Russian female name Ksenia), '*Suka*' (bitch), '*Suchok*' (small tree branch) or '*Okurok*' (cigarette stub), also had been issued to several police and other law enforcement

Modified AK-74M rifle, fitted with RPK-74, side-folding buttstock and silencer.

AKS-74U.

forces across the USSR and the post-USSR countries, including Russia. Interestingly, the AKS-74U is also known in the USA as the 'Krinkov', and the origins of this unofficial designation are still unclear. The AKS-74U is quite popular with its users due to its compact size, which allows it to be carried easily in vehicles and even concealed under clothes. On the other hand, its effectiveness is greatly limited by its poor accuracy at extended ranges, although the bullet itself retains its lethality at much greater ranges. The AKS-74U is also known for its tendency to overheat rapidly. A special version of the AKS-74U, developed for Special Forces (SpetsNaz), could be fitted with a quickly detachable silencer and a special, 30mm, silenced grenade launcher model BS-1 '*Tishina*' (silence). The launcher uses special HE-DP grenades, which are delivered by using special blank cartridges stored in the box magazine contained in the launcher pistol grip.

The AKS-74U has a severely shortened barrel, with the gas chamber moved back, and an appropriately shortened gas piston rod. Since the portion of the barrel after the gas port is very short, a special muzzle device was designed which is used as a flash hider and gas expansion chamber (to achieve reliable gas-operated action). The front sight base is lowered and the standard, adjustable rear sight is replaced by the flip-up

rear (marked for 200 and 400m), mounted on the receiver cover. The receiver cover is hinged to the receiver at the front and flips up when opened (the original AK-74 receiver cover is detachable). Otherwise the AKS-74U is similar to the AKS-74: it has similar controls, a folding buttstock and uses the same magazines, but the AKS-74U cannot be fitted with a bayonet. Some versions have a standard, side-mounted rail for the night or red-dot scope and are known as the AKS-74U-N. Original AKS-74U rifles were issued with shortened, twenty-round magazines, but these now are extremely rare and most rifles are used with standard, thirty-round AK-74 magazines. Another interesting and rare accessory for the AKS-74U is a special shoulder holster, designed for tank and helicopter crews. The AKS-74U is carried muzzle down in this holster and with a twenty-round magazine inserted.

KALASHNIKOV AK-101–AK-105 ('HUNDRED' SERIES)

The 'hundred' series of Kalashnikov rifles were developed at the Izhevsk state factories during the 1990s, mostly for export. The rifles are based on the AK-74M and differ mostly in the chamberings (5.56mm NATO for the AK101 and the AK102, and 7.62 × 39 for the

5.56mm AK-101.

KALASHNIKOV AK-101–AK-105 ('HUNDRED' SERIES)

	AK101	AK102	AK103	AK104	AK105
Calibre	5.56 × 45 NATO	5.56 × 45 NATO	7.62 × 39	7.62 × 39	5.45 × 39
Total length, buttstock open	943mm	824mm	943mm	824mm	824mm
Total length, buttstock folded	700mm	586mm	700mm	586mm	586mm
Barrel length	415mm	314mm	415mm	314mm	314mm
Weight	3.5kg	3.1kg	3.4kg	3.0kg	3.1kg
Magazine capacity	30 rounds	30 rounds	30 rounds	30 rounds	30 rounds
Rate of fire	600 rpm	600 rpm	600 rpm	600 rpm	600 rpm

Above *5.56mm AK-102.*

Below *7.62mm AK-103.*

7.62mm AK-104

AK103 and the AK104) and in the barrel lengths – the AK102, the AK104 and the AK105 had barrels cut down just after the gas block, making them more compact than full-size Kalashnikov rifles, yet maintaining full parts compatibility with them, unlike the smaller AKS-74U.

NIKONOV AN-94 ('ABAKAN')
Calibre: 5.45 × 39
Action: gas-operated, rotating bolt
Overall length: 943mm (728mm with butt folded)
Barrel length: 405mm
Magazine capacity: 30 rounds
Weight, without magazine: 3.85kg
Rate of fire: 1,800 and 600 rpm variable

The Russian Army and the Ministry of Internal Affairs officially adopted the AN-94 assault rifle in 1994 as a potential replacement for the venerable Kalashnikov AK-74 series of rifles; AN signifies *Avtomat Nikonova*, or Nikonov assault rifle. Much controversy surrounds the AN-94 rifle, mostly because it is advertised as a quantum leap from the Kalashnikov designs and because of its official action description, known as 'blow-back shifted pulse (BBSP)'. This unusual description could confuse anyone, especially since it is used in conjunction with the note of gas operation of the AN-94. The operation of the AN-94 will be described later, but first some of its main features will be discussed. The key 'improvement' of the AN-94 over the AK-74 is the introduction of the two-round-burst mode, added to the standard single shot and full automatic mode. The two-round bursts are fired at a very high rate and a trained shooter can virtually put both bullets into a single hole in the target at 100m.

Nikonov AN-94 with 40mm GP-25 grenade launcher.

Above *Nikonov AN-94 with folded butt.*

Right *AN-94 partial disassembly; note the pulley and cable system, which links the feed rammer to the bolt group.*

This allows for a significant increase in lethality, stopping power and body-armour penetration over the single-shot mode, with the same single-shot accuracy. The full automatic mode of the AN-94 consists of two stages: first, two rounds are fired in 'high rate', and the remaining rounds are fired at a low rate, until the trigger is released or the magazine is emptied. In the single-shot or the full automatic mode there are no significant advantages over the AK-74, except for slightly less recoil. At this point, one may well ask, 'Is all this complication of the AN-94 mechanism worth the achieved results?' There is no simple answer. The trained, professional soldier can use the two-round-burst capability of AN-94 with a great degree of success, but before this much time and resources need to be spent to train the soldier to use the AN-94 effec-

tively. Unlike more common designs, such as the Russian Kalashnikov or the American M16 rifle, the AN-94's internals are not 'user friendly' and it a lengthy process to get used to this rifle, its assembly/disassembly and maintenance procedures. It is also more expensive to make and to maintain than the AK-74. From all this it is obvious why this interesting rifle is unlikely to see widespread service, at least with the Russian Army (which is currently manned mainly by conscription and on a low budget). On the other hand, some elite units can make a good use of the major advantages of the AN-94.

The ergonomics of the AN-94 are not of the best. The shape of the pistol grip and the position of the magazine (inclined from the vertical plane) are far from being comfortable. The rear aperture sight has small apertures, is not protected from dirt and is hard to clean in battle conditions. It also has sharp edges and can snag in clothes or scratch the shooter's skin when handled roughly. The grenade launcher mount under the barrel is strange since it uses a large 'bridge' between the stock and the launcher. The folding butt interfered with the trigger when folded on earlier production guns, and the fire selector, which is separated from the safety mechanism, is hard to operate, especially with wet hands. On the other hand, in the two-round-burst mode it is very accurate and offers a great advantage in terminal effectiveness over the standard single-shot mode.

The heart of the AN-94 is the usual gas-operated, rotating-bolt, long piston stroke action. The barrel with the gas chamber above it is mounted on the receiver, which holds the reciprocating bolt carrier with a relatively short rotating bolt. The receiver is allowed to recoil inside the plastic gun shell or housing against the receiver recoil spring. This spring is located under the receiver, at the bottom of the housing and to the left, and, because of this, the magazine is offset and inclined from the vertical to the right. The rod under the barrel, which looks like the gas tube, is, in fact, a forward guide for the recoiling barrel/receiver assembly. This rod is also used as a forward mounting point for the grenade launcher. The cocking handle is attached direct to the right side of the bolt carrier. The feed system is quite unconventional since it has to transfer rounds from the stationary magazine into the recoiling receiver. To achieve this, the AN-94 uses a two-stage feed that comprises a feed tray, built into the bottom of the recoiling receiver, and a separate rammer that is used to feed cartridges from the magazine and into the feed tray.

In brief, the AN-94 works as follows. First, we assume that a full magazine is inserted and the chamber is empty, with the receiver/barrel assembly in the forward position. When the charging handle is pulled, the bolt carrier goes back, unlocking and retracting the bolt. At the same time the rammer, which is linked to the bolt carrier via the thin steel cable and a large pulley at the front of the housing, goes forward, stripping the first round from the magazine and placing it in the feed tray in the receiver. Another action that takes the place at the same time is the cocking of the hammer, which is also located in the recoiling receiver. When the charging handle is released, the bolt assembly goes forward, slamming the cartridge from the feed tray and into the chamber and locks the barrel. Now the gun is ready to fire. When the fire selector is in full automatic mode and the trigger is pressed, the following

happens. As soon as the fired bullet passes the gas port, the traditional, gas-operated action begins. Since the bolt group is relatively light and the gas pressure is carefully calculated, the bolt group rapidly goes back, unlocking the barrel and then extracting and ejecting the spent case. Due to the recoil impulse, the barrel/receiver assembly begins to recoil inside the gun housing, compressing the recoil spring. At the same time, the cartridge rammer quickly strips the next cartridge from the magazine and introduces it into the feed tray. The bolt group, under the influence of its main spring and the return buffer spring, rapidly goes forward, chambering the second round from the feed tray. As soon as the bolt group locks the barrel, the hammer is released automatically and the second shot is fired with the theoretical rate of 1,800 rpm. At this moment the receiver is still recoiling inside the housing and its recoil does not yet affect the shooter nor the position of the gun. When the second bullet is fired and leaves the barrel, the recoil cycle of the receiver/barrel group is stopped and the hammer is held in the cocked position. At this moment the shooter feels the recoil of two fired rounds simultaneously, 'shifted in time'. The reloading cycle continues as described above, but the hammer is held until the recoiling unit is returned to the forward position. If the gun were set to the two-rounds-burst mode, the hammer will be held cocked until the trigger is be released and then pulled again. If the gun were set to full automatic mode, the hammer unit will switch itself automatically to the low rate of fire and release itself only once per complete recoil cycle. It must be noted that when firing at slow rate, the receiver recoils only part of the way back, without striking the housing, and so the felt recoil in full automatic after the first two shots is somewhat lessened when compared with the AK-74. The design and the action of the trigger system of the AN-94 will not be discussed here since it is too complicated to be explained briefly.

Other features of the AN-94 include: the fibre-glass-reinforced polymer housing, integral with the handguards, and the magazine bay that can accept standard AK-74-compatible magazines with thirty- or forty-five-rounds capacity, as well as the newest, sixty-round, four-column box magazines. The sight system of the AN-94 is a step aside from all previous Russian assault rifles and consists of a protected front post, adjustable for zeroing, and an asterisk-shaped rear with fivr apertures drilled in the asterisk points. To set the distance, the asterisk must be rotated to set the desired aperture at the top of the receiver. The universal scope-mounting rail is attached to the left side of the receiver as standard. The safety and the fire selector are two separate controls. The safety mechanism is mounted inside the trigger guard and the fire selector is a small switch above the trigger guard at the left side of the receiver. The fire selector has three positions: for single shots, two-round bursts and full-automatic. There are two safety positions: safe and fire. The buttstock is made from the same high-impact-resistant plastic as the housing/stock unit and folds to the right to save space. The strange- looking, eight-shaped muzzle attachment is a special, self-cleaning muzzle brake, which is claimed to be highly effective. It can be easily detached from the muzzle if required. The front sight base carries a rear bayonet lug on its right side and so the bayonet is mounted in the horizontal plane, to the right of the muzzle. This allows for firing the grenade launcher with the bayonet attached (which is impossible with Kalashnikov-type rifles).

AEK-971

Calibre: 7.62×39 and 5.45×39
Action: gas-operated, rotating bolt, balanced
Overall length: 965mm
Barrel length: 420mm
Weight: 3.3kg without magazine
Magazine capacity: 30 rounds

The AEK971 assault rifle was developed at the Kovrov Machinebuilding Plant (formerly known as the Kovrov Machineguns Plant) by the chief designer S.I. Koksharov. It has a gas-driven, balanced action with rotating bolt locking. The balancing mean that the AEK971 gas drive has two gas chambers and two gas pistons. The first piston is linked via a gas rod to the bolt carrier and operates as usual. The second piston is linked to a balancing steel weight and moves in the opposite direction to the main piston. Both are synchronized through a simple gear. This design is intended to eliminate three of the four elements of action impulses, which cause a rifle to move during full-automatic fire. The first impulse is received when the bullet moves along the barrel – this is the basic recoil itself. The second is received when the heavy bolt carrier/bolt group moves along the receiver back and forth. The third is received when the bolt carrier/bolt group slams against the receiver in the rear position, and the fourth when this group is stopped in the forward position after a new cartridge is chambered. The synchronous and opposite movement of the balancing weight eliminates all except the recoil impulse, and thus the rifle becomes far more stable during full-automatic fire. The gain in accuracy in this mode is about 15–20 per cent, when compared to the AK-74 assault rifle in the same calibre. The newly adopted AN-94 assault rifle has a slight edge over the AEK974 only in short burst (two rounds only) mode. In full-automatic medium or long burst fire mode (three to five or seven to ten rounds per burst) the AEK974 wins hands down, being also some 0.5kg lighter than the AN-94 and much simpler and cheaper to manufacture. The AEK971 has a side-folding, plastic buttstock, a plastic forearm and fire control grip and uses standard AK-47 or AK-74 thirty-round magazines (depending on the chambering). It also features a safety switch/fire mode selector of different appearance from the Kalashnikov design. The fire selector allows three modes of fire: single shots, three-round bursts and full automatic.

Latest variant of 5.45mm AEK-971 balanced-action assault rifle.

Above *9 × 39 'Groza' OTs-14 rifle in basic version.*

Left *9 × 39 'Groza' OTs-14 rifle with modular 40mm grenade launcher.*

Below *7.62 × 39 'Groza-1' OTs-14 rifle in basic version.*

OTs-14 'Groza'

Calibre: 9 × 39
Action: gas-operated, rotating bolt with two lugs
Overall length: 497mm
Weight: 2.7kg in the basic configuration; 4.0kg with attached grenade launcher
Magazine: 20 rounds
Rate of fire: 750 rpm

The OTs-14 'Groza' (thunder) modular assault rifle was developed during the early 1990s by V. Telesh and Ju. Lebedev at the TSKIB SOO. It was intended for several Special Forces in the Russian Army and the Internal Affairs Ministry, and briefly manufactured in small numbers at the Tula Arms factory during the mid 1990s. The OTs-14 saw some action during the first anti-terrorist campaign in Chechnya in 1999, but soon felt out of favour and is apparently no longer made. The OTs-14 is based on the familiar AKS-74U receiver and action, modified for the larger 9 × 39 subsonic ammunition favoured by some SpetsNaz troops. It is fitted into a bullpup layout, with a removable trigger/pistol grip unit which could be replaced with an alternative unit integral with the 40mm grenade launcher. In the grenade-launching configuration, a single trigger controls both the 40mm GL and the rifle itself, with a separate barrel selector. The safety/fire mode selector of AK pattern is retained and in bullpup configuration is especially uncomfortable to operate. The barrel can be fitted with a quickly detachable silencer. Standard open sights are built into the carrying handle, which results in a relatively short sight base. The carrying handle also has mounting points for telescope, red dot or night sights.

AS 'Val'

Calibre: 9 × 39
Action: gas-operated, rotating bolt with six lugs
Overall length: 875mm with open butt, 615mm with folded butt
Barrel length: 200mm
Weight: 2.96kg empty
Magazine capacity: 20 or 10 rounds
Rate of fire: 800 rpm

The AS (*Avtomat Spetsialnij* = special assault rifle) was developed by TSNIITOCHMASH under the leadership of P. Serdjukov during the late 1980s, as a part of the 9 × 39 family of silenced weapons for the Special Forces. Its design is similar to that of the VSS

9 × 39 AS 'Val' integrally silenced rifle.

AS 'Val' field stripped.

'Vintorez' sniper rifle, and differs only in the design of the buttstock and the pistol grip. The AS is widely used by Russian Army reconnaissance units, as well as by MVD (Internal Affairs Ministry) and FSB (Federal Security Bureau) Special Forces. The AS is a gas-operated, integrally silenced weapon. The receiver is machined from a steel forging for improved strength. The long stroke gas piston is located above the barrel and rigidly attached to the bolt carrier. The rotating bolt has six lugs and locks into the receiver. The front part of the barrel, ahead of the gas port, has several sets of holes, drilled at the bottom of the rifling grooves. These holes are used to bleed some of the gun gas into the integral silencer. The trigger unit is somewhat similar to that of the Czech-made Sa. Vz.58 assault rifle and is striker-fired. The safety lever is similar to that on all Kalashnikov-type rifles, but the fire mode selector is a separate cross-bolt-type button, located within the trigger guard, just behind the trigger. The open sights are graduated up to 400m in 25m increments, but the actual effective range is about 200–300m owing to the rainbow-shaped trajectory of the subsonic bullets. The AS is optimized for high-performance, armour-piercing 9 × 39 ammunition, designated as SP-6 or PAB-9, but it can also fire 'ball'-type SP-5 ammunition, intended for VSS sniper rifles. The pistol grip and the short forearm are made from polymer, the skeletonized, side-folding butt is made from steel tubing. The AS rifle has a standard side-mounted rail for optical, night vision or red dot scopes. It has no provision for mounting a bayonet nor a grenade launcher.

The integral silencer can be easily detached for maintenance, repair or compact storage, but the rifle cannot be fired with the silencer removed due to safety and reliability issues.

SR-3 'VIKHR'

Calibre: 9 × 39
Action: gas-operated, rotating bolt with six lugs
Overall length: 610mm with open butt, 360mm with folded butt
Barrel length: n/a
Weight: 2.0kg empty
Magazine capacity: 20 or 10 rounds
Rate of fire: 900 rpm

The SR-3 'Vikhr' (whirlwind) compact assault rifle was developed in TSNIITOCHMASH by A. Borisov and V. Levchenko. Originally known as 'MA' (*Malogabaritnyj Avtomat* = small-size assault rifle), it was based on the silenced 9mm AS 'Val' assault rifle and intended for concealed carrying by special VIP protection teams and state security operatives. The SR-3 is widely used by several FSO (Federal Protection Service, a VIP protection organization, which guards the president and the government of the Russian Federation) and FSB (Federal Security Service) operatives, elite Russian counter-terror teams and other specialized users in the MVD and the police. The SR-3 features the receiver, machined from a bar of steel and gas-operated action with a long stroke piston, plus the same rotating bolt group from the AS. However, the SR-3 has no integral silencer nor provision to mount

9 × 39 SR-3 compact assault rifle with butt folded.

9 × 39 SR-3 compact assault rifle with butt opened.

one and thus is much shorter than the AS. Other changes include a more compact, top-folding butt and simplified flip-up rear sight. The redesigned charging handle, made in the form of dual sliders above the forearm, must be grasped by thumb and index finger and then retracted to load the weapon. The trigger unit is generally the same as in the AS, but the AK-type safety mechanism is replaced by an ambidextrous lever above the pistol grip. The fire mode selector is of the cross-bolt, push-button type and is located behind the trigger, inside the trigger guard.

9A-91
Calibre: 9 × 39
Action: gas-operated, rotating bolt with four lugs
Overall length: 605mm with open butt, 383mm with folded butt
Barrel length: n/a
Weight: 2.1kg empty
Magazine capacity: 20 rounds
Rate of fire: 600–800 rpm

The 9A-91 9mm compact assault rifle was originally developed as a part of the A-91 family of compact

9 × 39 9A91 compact assault rifle.

Early prototype of 7.62mm A-91 assault rifle; note the unusual position of the integral 40mm grenade launcher.

weapons, which included versions chambered for 7.62 × 39, 5.45 × 39, 9 × 39 and 5.56 × 45 ammunition. Of those, only the 9mm version survived and entered small-scale production at the Tula Arms Factory in 1994. Designed by the famous KBP design bureau, the 9A91 was originally intended for an Army PDW (personal defence weapon) role, but instead found favour in the ranks of MVD and Russian police troops as a less expensive equivalent of the SR-3 'Vikhr' compact assault rifle. The 9A-91 also served as a basis for a silenced 'para-sniper' weapon, the VSK-94, also chambered for 9 × 39 ammunition. The 9A-91 is a gas-operated, rotating-bolt weapon, which utilizes a long stroke gas piston, located above the barrel, and a rotating bolt with four lugs. The receiver is made from steel stampings; the forend and pistol grip are made from polymer. The steel buttstock folds up and above the receiver when not in use. The charging handle is welded to the right side of the bolt carrier. The safety/fire selector lever is located at the left side of the receiver, above the trigger guard, and allows for single shots and full automatic fire. The flip-up rear sight has settings for 100 and 200m range, but the relatively short sight base and steep trajectory of the subsonic bullet effectively restricts the 9A91 to ranges of about

100m, at which the 9 × 39 ammunition is clearly superior in penetration and hitting power to either 9mm pistol ammunition from submachine guns or 5.45 and 5.56mm ammunition from compact assault rifles such as the AKS-74U or the HK-53.

A-91

Calibre: 7.62 × 39 or 5.56 × 45 NATO
Action: gas-operated, rotating bolt with four lugs
Overall length: 660mm
Barrel length: n/a
Weight: 3.97kg empty, with integral grenade launcher
Magazine capacity: 30 rounds
Rate of fire: 600–800 rpm

The A-91 bullpup assault rifle (also known as the A-91M) was developed during the 1990s by KBP (Instrument Design Bureau) in Tula, as an offspring of the A-91 family of compact assault rifles described above. While the A-91 retains the basic, gas-operated, rotating-block action and a trigger unit design from the 9A-91, it features a bullpup polymer housing, with an integral, 40mm, single-shot grenade launcher mounted under the barrel. The earliest prototypes of the A-91 bullpup were fitted with the grenade launcher above the barrel and with a front vertical foregrip; current models are fitted with the underbarrel launcher, which also serves as a forearm. The A-91 features a forward ejection system, originally developed in Tula by designers such as Afanasiev during the early 1960s. In this system, the ejection port is located above the pistol grip and points forward. Extracted cases are fed from the bolt head through the short ejection tube to the ejection port and fall out of the gun well clear of the shooter's face, even when he is firing from the left shoulder. The controls include double triggers (front for grenade launcher, back for rifle) and a large fire mode/safety lever at the right side of the receiver, above the magazine housing. The rifle trigger is fitted with an additional automatic trigger safety. The charging handle is located above the receiver, under the carrying handle, and is easily accessible for either hand. The sights include a front post, mounted on a high base, and an aperture rear, adjustable for range, which is mounted on the integral carrying handle. The top of the carrying handle is shaped as a Weaver-type rail and can accept a vide variety of scopes. Folding grenade launcher sights are mounted at the front of the barrel. Originally developed for 7.62 × 39 ammunition and standard AK-pattern magazines, the A-91 bullpup is now also available in 5.56 × 45 NATO chambering, which uses proprietary thirty-round polymer magazines.

APS UNDERWATER ASSAULT RIFLE
Calibre, 5.66 × 39 MPS
Action: gas-operated, rotating bolt
Overall length: 823mm with retracted butt, 615mm with collapsed butt
Barrel length: n/a
Weight: 2.4kg less magazine; 3.4kg with loaded magazine
Magazine capacity: 26 rounds
Rate of fire: 600 rpm (in air)

The APS (*Avtomat Podvodnyj Spetsialnyj* = special underwater assault rifle) was developed during the early 1970s at TSNIITOCHMASH by a team lead by V. Simonov. The APS has been in active service with combat divers of the Soviet and Russian Navy since about 1975. It is designed for special underwater cartridges, which fire 5.66mm needle-like projectiles 120mm long. The projectiles are stabilized by using a hydrodynamic cavity, generated by the flat point of the projectile. The cartridges use standard 5.45 × 39 cases, sealed from water. The APS itself is a relatively crude, smoothbore arm, with a gas-operated, rotating-bolt action, fired from an open bolt. The gas system features a patented, self-adjusting, gas valve, which allows the gun to be fired both underwater and in the atmosphere. The simple trigger unit allows for single shots and full automatic fire. The rate of fire under water, as well as

Latest variant of A-91 bullpup assault rifle, in 5.56 × 45 NATO.

APS underwater assault rifle.

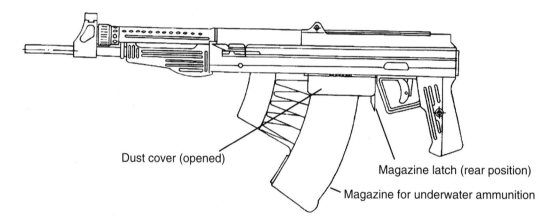

ASM-DT experimental amphibious assault rifle in underwater configuration.

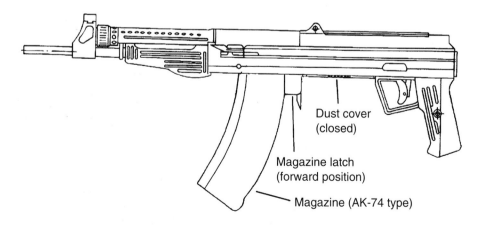

ASM-DT experimental amphibious assault rifle in surface configuration.

the effective range, depend on the actual depth. The sights are crude: a non-adjustable, open notch rear and post front. The retractable buttstock is made from steel wire. The most complicated element in the whole design is the feed system, which includes several parts to avoid double and even triple feed with the extremely long projectiles. Unusually deep (front to back) magazines are made from polymer and hold twenty-six rounds. The effectiveness of the APS in the air is extremely limited and so, during the late 1990s, a severely modified version of it appeared in Tula, in the form of the experimental ASM-DT 'dual medium' amphibious assault rifle. The key improvement in the ASM-DT is that it uses a 5.45mm rifled barrel with relatively shallow rifling, which allows it to fire both standard 5.45 × 39 spin-stabilized ammunition, and modified, underwater, hydrodynamically stabilized ammunition, which is also based on the 5.45 × 39 case, with a long projectile of about 5.4mm diameter. To achieve this, the magazine housing of the ASM-DT is fitted with a sliding magazine catch which can be positioned at the rear of the long magazine port to hold the deep underwater magazines, or in the middle of the magazine port to hold the relatively shallow (front to back) AK-74 magazines. In the latter mode, the rear, unused, part of the magazine housing is closed by a spring-loaded dust cover. To avoid problems with the remaining water in the barrel when firing the 5.45 × 39 in air, the chamber has special grooves that lead from the chamber forcing cone forward, into the rifling grooves. When the standard 5.45mm cartridge is fired, a small amount of the resulting powder gases run through the grooves ahead of the bullet, effectively blowing the remaining water out of the barrel. The rest of the action is similar to that of the APS, but the muzzle is fitted with an AKS-74U-style muzzle device/flash hider. The performance overall of the ASM-DT with underwater ammunition is similar to that of the APS, while in air and with standard 5.45 × 39 ammunition, it is roughly on a par with the AKS-74U and greatly outperforms the APS.

USA

The history of the development of the infantry rifle in the USA since the end of World War II is both turbulent and controversial. At the end of the war, most American infantrymen were armed with .30 calibre (7.62 × 63) M1 Garand semi-automatic rifles, and some with .30 calibre (7.62 × 33) M1 semi-automatic and M2 selective-fire carbines. The latter was almost suitable for a true assault rifle, being compact and

manoeuvrable, but it lacked effective range and reliability under harsh conditions. The US Army was satisfied with the ballistic properties of the full-power .30-06 cartridge, and just wanted to improve the M1 Garand with more modern features, principally a detachable magazine and a selective-fire capability. Such prototypes had been made during the latter part of the war, but did not initially succeed. The Korean War of 1950–53 was also fought mostly with M1 Garands, which performed well, and M1 and M2 carbines, which proved their lack of power, especially against enemy personnel wearing heavy winter clothes. As described in Chapter 4, there was a heated debate during the 1950s between the supporters of a traditional, full-power, 7.62mm cartridge (adopted along with the M14 rifle) and the exponents of small-calibre (including flechette) weapons, which resulted in much confusion and many false hopes before the 5.56mm cartridge and the M16 rifle largely took over from the M14 in the late 1960s. Despite several efforts to produce more effective weapons, it looks as if the M16 family may achieve its half-century in service.

While the M1 Garand performed well in World War II and in Korea, several areas for improvement were identified. The first was the feeding system with eight-round, en bloc clips that do not allow for the refilling of a partially full magazine. Others were the excessive length and weight of the rifle. The cartridge used in the M1 Garand and known as the .30-06 (7.62 × 63) was also too long and too heavy, effectively limiting the load of ammunition carried by each soldier. The first attempts to improve the M1 were made during the war and numerous experimental modifications in .30-06 were built, mostly using the twenty-round, detachable magazines from the Browning BAR M1918 automatic rifle. One such prototype was the T20 ('T' here means 'test') of 1944. The T20 was basically the M1 Garand rifle fitted with a twenty-round BAR magazine and with a selective-fire capability. With the unjustified optimism which characterized this period of American small arms development, the T20 was required to weigh less than the M1, despite being in essence the same weapon with the addition of a bipod, a folding stock and a loaded magazine. This prototype later evolved into the T37 rifle, which had the gas cylinder moved back a little and was chambered for the newest American prototype cartridge – the T65 series.

The T65s were, in effect, no more than shorter versions of the .30-06 cartridge, but retaining the original ballistic properties owing to the modern propellants used. The ultimate T65E3 is slightly lighter and cheaper to make than the .30-06 and has the long, effective range and good potential for accuracy which were desired by the Army. The idea of a truly intermediate round was not acceptable to the US military at that period because the German 7.92 × 33 was felt to lack power and range. The weapon originally conceived for the T65 was the T25, an all-new rifle designed by Earle Harvey to be made on general production tooling rather than the specialized tools needed for the M1. The mechanism was interesting and worked well, but the Army wanted to keep the same receiver as the M1 had in order to make use of the special tooling and thus the T25 was dropped in 1952. Two other competitors in the late 1940s, the T28 (based on the German StG.45) and John Garand's intriguing T31 bullpup with an unusual gas action, were never seriously developed.

In the early 1950s the T37 evolved into the T44 experimental rifle, which featured a redesigned, self-regulated gas system with short stroke gas piston. Further development and tests led to the slightly modified T44E4 and T44E5 (heavy barrelled, squad automatic weapon) prototypes, which were finally adopted by the Army as the M14 and the M15 rifle in 1957. The heavy barrelled M15, however, was never

brought into production for financial reasons. It must be noted that the T44E4 was extensively tested against the only other entry in the American trials, the T48 rifle (the Belgian FN FAL rifle made under licence in the USA by H&R Inc.). The trials took place between 1952 and 1956, with first the T48 and then the T44 gaining an advantage. Both rifles eventually passed the trials with equally high results, but the Chief of Staff of the US Army finally settled on the T44 because it was slightly lighter, similar to the M1 Garand in its manufacturing and operation, and, above all, a 'native American' design.

The M14 offered some advantages over the M1 Garand rifle it replaced, thanks to its greater magazine capacity and lighter weight. But it was still effectively a semi-automatic rifle, because the powerful cartridge generated too much recoil for any accurate automatic fire. In fact, most M14 rifles were issued to troops with the fire-mode selector blocked, they being restricted to semi-automatic mode only. M14 rifles were also plagued by production and quality control problems. The M14 has been described by the American armaments historian E.C. Ezell in his *The Great Rifle*

M1 and M1A1 (airborne, with folding stock) carbines.

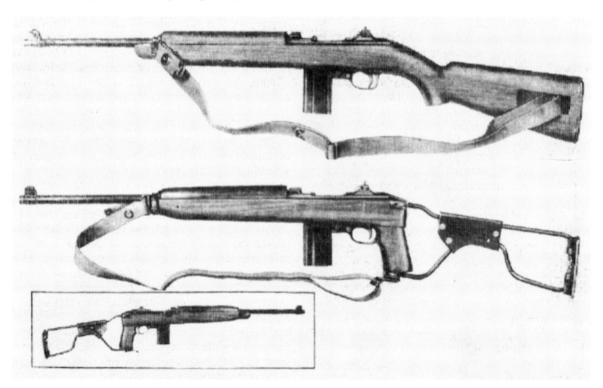

The Winchester WLAR in .224 calibre.

Controversy, as '…the proverbial racehorse created by a committee. Instead of getting a thoroughbred, the result was a cross between a donkey and a camel.'

The contracts to produce M14 rifles were issued to several American companies, such as Thompson-Ramo-Wooldridge (TRW Inc.), Harrington and Richardson Arms Co. (H&R), Winchester-Western Arms Division of Olin Mathieson (Winchester), and Springfield Armory Inc. (Springfield). Production was ended by the government in 1963, with some 1,380,000 weapons made. The termination of production was the result of a combination of factors. The M14 had been experienced production quality problems. In addition, combat experience in South-East Asia, particularly in Vietnam, had revealed that the M14 was too long and too heavy to be carried all day long in a hot and wet climate. The 7.62mm NATO ammunition was also too heavy, limiting the amount of ammunition that could be carried by soldiers on patrol. The squad automatic version, known as the M14E2, was also not very successful in its intended role. Most significant of all, however, was the prospect of the SPIW – the Special Purpose Individual Weapon – with which the Army expected to replace the M14 later in the decade (see Chapters 1 and 4).

As soon as the deficiencies of the M14 became obvious to the Army command, they started the search for lighter rifle to use in the interim before the SPIW was ready, and finally settled on the Colt/ArmaLite AR-15 5.56mm assault rifle, adopting it as the M16A1. The M14 was replaced as a first-line weapon in the late 1960s but is still used in small numbers by the US Navy. It also served as a platform to build M21 sniper rifles. Semi-automatic-only versions of the M14 have been commercially manufactured for civilian and police use by the Springfield Armory since 1974 under the name of the M1A. Some other American companies are assembling M14-type, semi-automatic rifles, using surplus M14 parts kits. Beginning in the early 1970s, thousands of M14 rifles were given to several nations under military aid programmes. In the 1990s alone over 100,000 were given to Estonia, Latvia and Lithuania. The Philippines, South Korea, Taiwan, and Turkey also received M14 rifles as military aid from the USA.

The second line of development, which led to lighter and smaller-calibre weapons, was started with the Hall and Hitchman reports described in Chapter 4. This immediately led to the next research programme, Project SALVO, which included the development and testing of a wide range of weapons and ammunition, including multiple bullet loadings, small calibre rifles and flechette-firing weapons. The first results were promising, but the Army still insisted on a full-calibre, full-power infantry rifle, which at that time was in development at the government-owned Springfield arsenal. In 1957 the Infantry Board at Fort Benning, as a result of the conclusions of Project SALVO, asked two companies, Winchester and the ArmaLite division of Fairchild, to develop a .22 calibre, lightweight, selective-fire rifle. ArmaLite responded with the AR-15, a scaled-down version of the 7.62mm AR-10 rifle, initially chambered for the .222 Remington cartridge before a longer .223 was developed. Winchester submitted the .224 calibre WLAR, an amalgam of several earlier designs.

During 1958 the US Army conducted the first comparative tests between the newly adopted 7.62mm M14, the .223 calibre ArmaLite AR-15 and the .224 calibre Winchester WLAR. Both smaller-calibre rifles proved themselves better than the M14 rifle at the proposed ranges (up to 300yd) and were favoured by the testers, but Army insisted on its own, full power weapon. Winchester rapidly lost interest in smaller calibre rifles and dropped the WLAR project. Fairchild also saw no future for a small-calibre AR-15 rifle and consequently sold all rights for it to Colt's Patent Firearms Manufacturing Co. late in 1959. At about the same time (1956–58), the Army was engaged in tests of flechette ammunition, as described in Chapter 4. By

1960 the AAI Corporation submitted for test its first subcalibre, single flechette ammunition, designed by Irwin Barr. The entire flechette concept fitted well with the SALVO project and promised many advantages over a conventional bullet, most notably the short flight time, diminutive recoil and deep penetration. By 1962 the Army Ordnance Office had prepared official specifications for a prospective flechette-firing weapon. These requirements included a burst-fire function and additional area denial capabilities in the form of a multi-shot, grenade-launching attachment. The proposed date of adoption of a new weapon, designated the SPIW (Special Purpose Individual Weapon) was rather optimistically set for 1966.

Another more conventional development, which was started in the early 1960s, was the Stoner modular system, known in 7.62mm NATO calibre as the Stoner 62 and in 5.56 × 45 calibre as the Stoner 63. Eugene Stoner, who left ArmaLite in about 1961 and joined the Cadillac Gage Corporation, known for its military armoured vehicles, developed this system. It was probably the first truly modular system and consisted of about fifteen subassemblies which could be assembled in any configuration, from an assault rifle and short carbine up to a lightweight or even a general purpose machine gun. This system, developed and promoted until the early 1970s, was extensively tested by the military as the XM22 (Stoner 63A rifle), the XM23 (Stoner 63A carbine) and the XM207 (light machine gun with belt feed). The only military application of the Stoner 63 system, however, was the Mk23 model 0, belt-fed LMG configuration, used in limited numbers by US Navy Special Forces and the Marine Corps in Vietnam. In general, the Stoner system, while having the advantages of modularity and interchangeability of parts and thus great flexibility in tactical use, is too heavy as a rifle and too expensive and somewhat over-complicated in general. It is also somewhat dirt-sensitive and requires much attention and maintenance. Despite these issues, the Stoner 63 design has been revived as the Robinson Arms M96. It is reportedly in service with some American Special Operations units, and is available in 7.62 × 39 as well as 5.56 × 45.

A further development was the AR-18 rifle, created by George Sullivan, Arthur Miller and Charles Dorchester at ArmaLite in the early 1960s. This rifle was designed for the international military market as a competitor with and potential replacement for the AR-15 project, which had been sold to Colt in 1959 by ArmaLite's parent company, Fairchild Aircraft and Engine Corporation. It could be made at a much lower cost and on simpler machinery, with a view to selling the manufacturing licence to Third World countries. The AR-18 was a successful design from a technical standpoint, but it came out too late to compete with the officially accepted and adopted AR-15/M16 and the already widely used AK-47 rifle of Soviet origin. ArmaLite made very few specimens of this rifle by itself. The manufacturing licence was consequently sold to the British company Sterling Armaments and to the Japanese company Howa Machinery, but all three produced few more than 20,000 rifles in total, and the production of the AR-18 ceased in about 1979 for some twenty years. The most interesting point about the AR-18 is that, despite being a commercial failure, it served as a platform for further development in several countries. First, the AR-18 design was obviously a starting point for the ill-fated British SA80/L85A1 bullpup assault rifle, which may be loosely described as a bullpupped and weakened AR-18. Secondly, the AR-18 served as a starting point for the Singapore SAR-80 assault rifle, designed by Chartered Industries of Singapore with the help of Sterling Armament. And thirdly, the relatively new, German Heckler & Koch G36 assault rifle bears much internal similarity to the AR-18.

In the meantime, Colt had begun an extensive promotional campaign for its new weapon, the .223 calibre[3] AR-15 rifle, resulting in sales of small batches to Indonesia and other South-East Asian countries. In 1960, after an informal demonstration, Gen Curtis LeMay of the US Air Force decided to purchase 8,000 AR-15 rifles for USAF Strategic Air Command security forces to replace the ageing M1 and M2 carbines. In 1962 the Advanced Research Projects Agency (ARPA) purchased 1,000 AR-15 rifles for live tests in South-East Asia under Project AGILE. Not surprisingly, the small-statured Asian soldiers generally preferred the smaller, lighter and soft-recoiling AR-15 rifle to the M1 Garand and the M14 rifle. ARPA also reported devastating effectiveness for the high-velocity bullet, although tests carried out in the USA were unable to replicate this.

To make matters more complex, the Secretary of Defense Robert McNamara ordered a complete halt of M14 rifle production in January 1963 owing to several production problems, and thus left the Army without any further supplies of rifles until the expected future

---

3 The new designation emerged from changed Army requirements, which extended the effective range from 300 to 500yd (274–460m); this required a new cartridge to be developed. Initially known as the .222 Remington Special, it was latter commercialized as a .223 Remington (5.56 × 45).

appearance of the SPIW. In 1963, to fill the gap, the Army ordered 85,000 5.56mm XM16E1 rifles (modified Colt AR-15s, fitted with a twenty-round magazine and a forward assist device), and the USAF ordered a further 19,000 M16 rifles (the same as the AR-15, but without a forward assist). In the following year the USAF officially adopted the M16 as its standard rifle and the Army adopted the XM16E1 as a 'Standard B'. In 1964 – 65 the Army conducted several tests of the new SPIW prototypes against the 5.56mm AR-15 and the 7.62mm M14 rifle. The AAI Corporation., Springfield Arsenal, Harrington and Richardson Arms Co. and Winchester submitted SPIW prototypes. The Army also tested the 5.56mm ArmaLite AR-18 and the Cadillac Gage 5.56mm Stoner 63. The Springfield and the AAI weapon performed the best, but the results from the SPIWs were still far from what had been desired. In 1966 Colt received a contract for 840,000 AR-15-type rifles for the American armed forces, and on 28 February 1967 the Department of Defense officially adopted the XM16E1 rifle as the 'Rifle, 5.56mm, M16A1'.

By 1968 the SPIW programme was still far from success and beginning to wind down. At the same time, the M16A1 rifles, being pressed into the service with US troops in Vietnam, began to deliver disappointing results. The best source on the subject of M16 rifle development is Stevens and Ezell's *The Black Rifle: M16 Retrospective*. To sum it up, most of the problems were inspired by the rather optimistic, to say the least, promotions by Colt, who claimed that the M16 required very little cleaning. This was partly true – as long as a proper IMR propellant was used. But the Army adopted its older ball powder for the 5.56mm ammunition, which produced plenty of fouling and had a different pressure curve, and the Stoner-designed, direct gas system of the M16 was especially sensitive to both. To add to the confusion, early M16A1 rifles

Above *The bullpup Springfield SPIW of 1964 in 5.56 × 44 XM144, with a double-box magazine.*

Below *AAI's first generation SPIW in 5.6 × 53 XM110, with a drum magazine.*

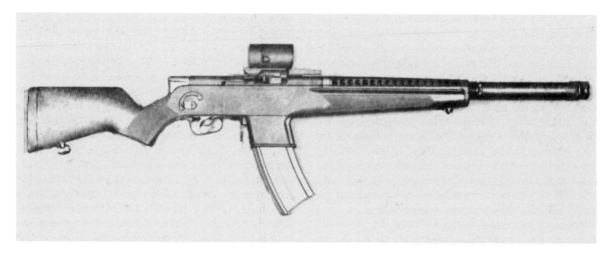

XM70, the last of the AAI SPIWs, in 5.6 × 57 XM645.

were issued to troops without cleaning kits (as a cost-saving measure) or proper maintenance training, and also without the chromium-plating of the bore and chamber. These problems resulted in degraded reliability in the hot and wet climate of South-East Asia, and the jamming of the rifles in combat caused many casualties. This caused much political argument at all levels, up to Congress. As a result, the Army quickly procured cleaning kits and started to issue these to soldiers and initiated a special maintenance training programme, improved the powder used in 5.56mm ammunition and requested Colt and the other manufacturers (Harrington and Richardson and the Hydramatics Division of General Motors) to produce further rifles with chromium-plated bolt groups and bores (an option originally offered by Colt but dropped as an economy). As a result of these changes, by the early 1970s the M16A1 had become an acceptable weapon. It outperformed its main rival, the Soviet Kalashnikov AK/AKM in terms of single-shot accuracy and better ergonomics. However, the lethality and long-range effectiveness of the 5.56mm ammunition was still questionable.

The early 1970s also saw attempts to develop a better rifle to replace the M16A1. From 1968 on, the unsuccessful SPIW programme gave way to the Future Rifle System (FRS) research and development programme. This also centred on a flechette-firing rifle, but this time without the grenade-launching ability. The AAI FRS, known as the XM19 rifle, was built around proprietary XM645 ammunition with a single flechette. The XM19 used a rare and effective, but expensive in the terms of ammunition, system of operation, based on blow-back primers. In this system the primer in the cartridge case can move back under the pressure of powder gases for about 0.1in (2.5mm), pushing the heavy firing pin rearward and thus operating the bolt-unlocking mechanism. This allowed the gun to be lightweight and simple, but the ammunition was too expensive and complicated. By 1972 the XM19 had evolved into the XM70 rifle, which fired the improved flechette ammunition with self-discarding sabots – earlier guns had required some sort of muzzle device to be used as sabot strippers, which compromised accuracy.

In 1978 the Joint Service Small Arms Program (JSSAP) proposed several directions for further R&D. First were heavier bullets for the standard 5.56mm ammunition, for improved long-range performance. Second was a saboted, subcalibre spin-stabilized projectile of 4.22/5.56mm calibre, launched at relatively high velocities (about 1,160m/s). Third was the CAWS (Close Assault Weapon System), a shotgun-type weapon that fired multiple projectiles. At the same time the Army, in co-operation with Colt, conducted the M16 Product Improvement Program (PIP), which included several modifications, such as various optical sights, rate reducers and ammunition improvements. As has already been described, during 1978–79 NATO also conducted trials for a second standard infantry cartridge to supplement the 7.62 × 51, which, not surprisingly, resulted in the adoption of the American 5.56 × 45 ammunition, albeit in the Belgian SS109 loading, with a heavier bullet.

Following the introduction of the new NATO standard, the USA faced the need to replace the existing M16A1 rifles with new weapons. It must be noted here that, until the late 1970s, 7.62 × 51 ammunition was still the NATO standard, and most American troops in Europe were still armed with older 7.62mm M14 rifles to ensure ammunition compatibility with their allies. By 1981 Colt had developed an improved M16A1E1 rifle which incorporated several options from earlier programmes, such as an adjustable rear sight instead of a simpler flip-up one, a three-round-burst mode of fire instead of full automatic and a heavier barrel, rifled with 1:7 (one turn in 7in/178mm) rifling, suitable for the new NATO-standard ammunition. Having no real alternative, the Department of Defense officially type-classified the new rifle as 'Rifle, 5.56mm M16A2' in 1982. The next year the US Marine Corps officially adopted the M16A2 as its standard rifle. The Army tried to stick with its older M16A1 rifles, but finally adopted the same weapon in 1985. But the development of the M16 continued; by the mid 1990s, Colt, at the request of the US Special Forces, produced a carbine version of the M16A2, designated the M4. This carbine traced its roots back to the 1960s vintage Colt CAR-15 carbine, but has several improvements. It was in fact the M16A2 rifle, fitted with a shorter barrel and handguards, with the gas port moved back. The fixed buttstock was replaced by a retractable, telescoping buttstock, originally designed in the mid 1960s by a Colt employee Robert E. Roy for the Colt 'Commando' carbines. The M4 was supposed to become the standard US Special Forces rifle, and could be fitted with the standard, M16A2-type bayonet and the M203 40mm grenade launcher.

By 1996, the two newest versions of the M16 had appeared: the M16A3 and the M16A4. These differ from the M16A2 by having a removable carrying handle, with the upper receiver being fitted with a Picatinny-type accessory rail. Otherwise the M16A4 is similar to the M16A2, while the M16A3 also replaced the infamous three-round-burst mode with a full automatic mode. The key advantage of both the M16A3 and the A4 rifle is the ability to mount and re-mount quickly a wide variety of optical, red dot or night vision/infra-red sights with MIL-STD 1913 (Picatinny-type) compatible mounts. The M4 carbine was also upgraded to 'flat top' configuration with the M4A1 version, which is now standard.

The M16 is still a general-issue rifle with US armed forces. It is also widely used by American law enforcement agencies, either in its military form (for example, the Los Angeles Police Department had some M16s,

retired from the Army), or in 'civilian', semi-automatic-only form. The AR-15-style rifles are made in the USA by at least a dozen large companies, such as ArmaLite, Bushmaster, Colt, FN Manufacturing, Hesse, Les Baer, Olympic and Wilson Combat, and by a number of smaller ones, many of which assemble their rifles from components made by the major manufacturers. M16-type rifles are also manufactured outside the USA, most notably in Canada, by Diemaco Co.; China also makes some AR-15-type 'CQ' rifles at the NORINCO state factories (this appears to be the version also made by Iran as the S-5.56). M16 rifles are used by many foreign military forces, most notably the British SAS, which preferred the M16 over the infamous L85A1 rifle. One of the key advantages of the M16 is the extreme flexibility provided by the method of construction. At the present, interchangeable complete 'uppers' (upper receiver assemblies with the barrel and bolt group) are available in several barrel lengths and profiles (from 7 to 24in long [18–61cm], slim or heavy), in dozens of calibres, from the tiny but fast .17 Remington up to the monstrous .458 SOCOM and .50 Beowulf rifle rounds, and from the .22LR and 9mm Luger up to the mighty .50AE pistol cartridges. Special, manually-loaded, single-shot uppers are commercially available in the extremely powerful .50 BMG (12.7 × 99) calibre. Several 'lowers' offer a broad variety of trigger units, buttstocks and other options. This advantage is obvious for military (especially special operation forces) and law enforcement and civilian applications, since it allows the tailoring of any particular AR-15-type rifle to the current situation and tactical needs. Many American – and some foreign – manufacturers make variations of the M16, including barrels as short as 105mm, upper and lower receivers in carbon fibre for a significant weight saving and bullpup conversions.

At the present time, almost all the original flaws of the M16 have been removed and it is considered among the best assault rifles in the world. While its reliability in harsh conditions cannot match that of its main rival the Kalashnikov AK-47 and AK-74, it is still a quite reliable weapon, especially when well maintained. It is also comfortable to fire and fairly accurate. But it must be noted that, during recent operations in Afghanistan and Iraq (2002 and 2003, respectively), there were several controversial complaints about the effectiveness and reliability of the M16A2 and the M4 rifle. It seems that most of the complaints about the reliability of the M16A2 rifle were the result of inadequate troop training and the resulting improper handling of the rifle. The M4 carbines are a somewhat different story, since the problems can be partly traced to the shortened gas system, which now operates at higher pressures and thus more violently. The M4 also rapidly overheated. Another general complaint was about the poor effectiveness of the standard M855 ammunition, which lacked stopping power, especially from shorter M4 carbine barrels. To cure this problem in part, the US SOCOM recently issued a new type of 5.56mm ammunition, the Mk262 mod.0, which is loaded with the heavier Sierra Match King bullet, weighing 4.99g compared with the 4.0g bullet in the M855 cartridge. The most recent experience also clearly showed the excessive length of the M16A2 rifles, which are too clumsy for motorized troops, riding in cars, armoured carriers and helicopters. At the present, many M16A2 rifles are being replaced in the hands of American troops in Iraq with more compact and manoeuvrable M4A1 carbines, probably because (unlike in Afghanistan) combat ranges tend to be short.

The early 1980s saw the rise of the next ambitious small arms programme, the Advanced Combat Rifle (ACR), initiated in about 1982, with the first contracts issued in 1985. This programme concentrated on the development of a new rifle, which should be at least 100 per cent more effective than the current issue M16A2 rifle. To achieve this goal, the Army wanted to test several new and existing technologies, including caseless, flechette and multi-ball ammunition. Several companies were contracted, but a decrease in funding resulted in only four final designs – the flechette-firing rifles by AAI from the USA and Steyr-Daimler-Puch from Austria, the caseless rifle by Heckler und Koch of Germany and the conventional rifle with duplex ammunition by Colt. All the rifles went through extensive testing, started in 1989, but, although all showed an improvement in hit probability over the M16A2, none achieved the desired 100 per cent increase in effectiveness and so the programme was ended in the early 1990s.

The failure of the ACR programme effectively underlined the view that small arms, in their present state, had reached their peak of development and to achieve any significant increase in effectiveness a quantum leap in technology was required. The first such suggestions were published around 1985 by the Infantry School at Fort Benning in a paper entitled 'Small Arms System 2000' (SAS-2000). This paper stated that a significant increase in hit probability could be achieved by small arms firing explosive, fragmentation projectiles with time-fused, air-bursting capability. These arms should also be fitted with advanced sighting devices to programme the explosive warheads automatically for detonation over the desired point on the trajectory, without any actual impact with the target. In this case, with a properly set fuse, even a miss still may result in a successful 'hit' within the blast radius. With such weapon, even a 1m miss could result in a disabled target; with a conventional bullet, even a

US Army soldier with M4A1 carbine. (image courtesy US Army)

US Army soldiers posing with ACR prototype rifles; top left Steyr ACR; top right Colt ACR; bottom left HK ACR and bottom right AAI ACR. (courtesy US Army)

1cm miss is simply a miss, a wasted bullet. The SAS-2000 rather optimistically proposed that such weapons could be developed by the year 2000.

In 1989, the US Army Training and Doctrine Center (TRADOC) published another paper, 'Small Arms Master Plan' (SAMP). The SAMP stated that the only way to achieve a significant increase in combat effectiveness would be to develop a family of 'Objective Weapons', namely, the Objective Individual Combat Weapon (OICW), the Objective Personal Defense Weapon (OPDW) and the Objective Crew Served Weapon (OCSW). The SAMP also stated that such weapons must be fitted with the latest developments in computer-based sighting and fire-control equipment and fire explosive fragmentation projectiles. The OICW should combine both a high explosive warhead and traditional bullet capabilities in a single weapon, which should be fielded around 2000. Of course, the timelines and most of the weight and cost requirements set out in this paper looked unrealistic from the start, but development of the Objective Weapons began in the early 1990s. The Americans duly started the Objective Individual Combat Weapon (OICW) programme, with the main goal being the development of a composite small arm which combined a conventional 'kinetic' weapon (5.56mm rifle component), a 20mm, semi-automatic grenade launcher with time-fused, air-bursting ammunition, and an advanced fire control/sighting unit with day/night capabilities. Contracts were signed with two companies: the AAI Corporation and Alliant

Techsystems Corp (ATK). By 2000 the team led by ATK (which also included Heckler & Koch and two other American companies, Brashear and Omega), was selected as the winner for the next stage of development. ATK is responsible for system integration and also for developing the 20mm air-burst munitions; HK is responsible for both the 5.56mm rifle and the 20mm grenade launcher; Brashear works on the sighting equipment; and Omega provides the training means. The first prototypes of the OICW system (also known as the SABR – Selectable Assault Battle Rifle) were officially designated XM29 in 2002. By early 2003 the XM29 had demonstrated successful live firing with 20mm, high-explosive, air bursting (HEAB) grenades. The M29 was supposed to enter service during 2008 in limited numbers and it was ultimately planned to issue four units per infantry squad of nine men.

However, there have been major concerns about the whole OICW system, concentrated on the excessive bulk, weight and cost of the complete weapon. The effectiveness of the 20mm ammunition has also been questioned, especially because of recent requirements for effective, 'less lethal' munitions for peacekeeping, which are hard to achieve in such a small calibre. It has not proved possible to reduce the weight to the target 15lb (6.8kg), current prototypes weighing 18lb (8.2kg). As a result, the most recent development in the development of the Objective Warrior programme (of which the OICW is a major part) is to split the 'kinetic' and the 'explosive' component for further development as separate weapons – the 5.56mm XM8 lightweight

AR-10.

assault rifle and the 25mm XM25 semi-automatic grenade launcher (the calibre of the latter being increased to match that of the 25mm XM307 OCSW automatic grenade launcher). It is still hoped to bring them together again in a single weapon, if future weight savings permit. The present plans state that the XM8 rifle (M8 after official adoption) could enter operational status in the near future, gradually replacing the M16-series rifles thereafter.

The XM8 LMCS (Lightweight Modular Carbine System) is being developed for American armed forces by the Army's Office of Project Manager for Soldier Weapons (Picatinny Arsenal), US Army Infantry Center and Heckler & Koch USA (HK-USA), the North American subsidiary of the German company. If the XM8 is adopted, HK-USA will manufacture it for the armed forces. The US Army took its first delivery of thirty prototype XM8 rifles from HK-USA on 30 October 2003, with the first tests scheduled for November or December. It will provide the replacement for M4 carbines and some M16A2 rifles now in use. In the event of the successful development of the entire XM29 system, the XM8 will provide significant parts commonality, with the kinetic part of the M29, as well as with the whole 'Land Warrior' system. The XM8 will also provide troops with an easily reconfigurable, modular weapon, available in several versions, based on the same receiver unit. It must be noted that this development has attracted some opposition within the US Army, since, in the opinion of many, the XM8 offers insufficient advantages over current M16A2 and M4A1 weapons to warrant such expensive rearmament. In particular, it fails to address one of the main complaints about current weapons – that, while the M4's barrel is too short to be effective at longer ranges, the M16 is too long to be easily manageable in vehicles and street

fighting. At present, the XM8 is advertised as a modular system, about 1kg lighter (in its basic configuration) than the M16A2 rifle, which could be easily tailored to a wider spectrum of tactical applications. For example, the XM8 could be had in a basic carbine form with a 317mm (12.5in) barrel and telescoping butt, in compact carbine (PDW) form with no butt and a 228mm (9in) barrel, in sharpshooter variant with 500mm (20in) barrel and advanced sights, as well as in a automatic rifle/light support weapon variant with a heavy 500mm barrel, integral bipod and hundred-round drum magazines. It also could be fitted with a modern, 40mm, underbarrel grenade launcher, which is also being developed by HK. Yet another proposed future development is the SCAR (Special Operations Combat Assault Rifle), which could be converted to fire 5.56mm NATO, 7.62 × 39, 7.62mm NATO, as well as the prospective 6.8 × 43mm SPC ammunition, currently being developed in the USA.

ArmaLite AR-10
Calibre: 7.62 × 51 NATO
Action: gas-operated, rotating bolt
Length: 1,016mm
Barrel Length: 508mm
Weight: 4.31kg empty, without magazine and sling
Magazine: 20 rounds
Rate of fire: 700 rpm

The AR-10 rifle, designed by Eugene Stoner at the ArmaLite division of the Fairchild Engine and Airplane Corporation, saw no significant sales success but still has some historical significance since it served as the basis for the further development of the much more successful AR-15/M16 series rifles; in essence, the earliest AR-15 prototype was no more than a scaled-down AR-10. The AR-10 was intended for the US Army trials for a new battle rifle to replace the venerable M1 Garand, but the first prototype was built only in 1955, very late for these trials, and was also too unconventional for conservative minds in the Army. It consequently lost to the T44 rifle, which was adopted in the 1957 as the M14. The AR-10 was ready for mass production by 1960, but few were made in the USA, although a manufacturing licence had been sold to the Dutch company Artillerie Inrichtingen. Only Sudan and Portugal apparently bought some AR-10 rifles for their military, and the production of the AR-10 ended in the early or mid 1960s, with only about 10,000 military AR-10s being made.

Some two or three decades later, the reorganized ArmaLite company brought the modified AR-10 rifle back to civilian and police markets. Unlike the original AR-10, the new AR-10B is a semi-automatic-only rifle and is available in four versions. The AR-10B itself is more or less a copy of the original AR-10, with similar brown plastic furniture and short buttstock, and with the trigger-like charging handle under the carrying handle. The other three models look more like scaled-up M16A2 derivatives, with the same A2-style furniture, sights and M16-type charging handles. The AR-10A2 has all the A2 furniture and options, while the AR-10A4 has the 'flat-top' style receiver, with the Picatinny rail instead of the carrying handle. The AR-10(T) is a target grade rifle, with match barrel and

trigger and A4-type flat-top receiver. Technically, the AR-10 differs little from its direct derivative, the AR-15/M16, and thus for a complete description of the weapon see the entry on it below.

M14

Calibre: 7.62 × 51 NATO
Action: gas-operated, rotating bolt
Length: 1,120mm
Barrel Length: 559mm
Weight loaded: 5.1kg (6.6kg M14A1)
Magazine: 20 rounds, detachable box
Rate of fire: 700–750 rpm

The M14 is a gas-operated, magazine-fed and selective-fire design, but it was often issued with the fire selector locked to semi-automatic only. The gas system is located under the barrel and has a short stroke (about $1\frac{1}{2}$ in, 37mm) gas piston, which operates the M1 Garand-style action rod. The gas system features an automatic gas-adjustment feature, which limits the amount of gas used to operate the weapon, as well as a manual cut-off for launching rifle grenades. The rotating bolt is quite similar to the one found in the M1 Garand, but it has a roller instead of a simple lug, which connects the bolt to the operating rod. The fire-mode selector is located at the right side of the receiver, above the trigger, and could be

M14.

Left *The unsuccessful M14A1 rifle, intended for squad automatic rifle role.*

removed to prevent the rifle from being fired in full-automatic mode or reinstalled if required. The rear receiver bridge features the stripper clip guides and thus the detachable magazine could be refilled in place by using standard stripper clips. The bolt stop device is incorporated into the left wall of the receiver and holds the bolt open when the last round from the magazine is fired. The safety switch is similar to that of the M1 Garand and is located at the front of the trigger guard. Standard sights consist of a front sight with two protective 'ears' and an adjustable aperture rear sight, mounted on the rear of the receiver. The barrel is equipped with a long flash suppressor. For use in selective-fire mode, the M14 can be equipped with a light, detachable bipod. The M14A1 squad automatic

rifle differs from the M14 in the following: the fire selector is always installed; the standard wooden, single-piece stock with semi-pistol grip is replaced by a 'straight-line' wooden stock with a separate pistol grip; there is a folding front grip under the forearm; a hinged shoulder rest is attached to the buttplate; and a special removable, muzzle jump compensator is fitted to the barrel, as is a lightweight bipod. In summary, the M14 was a somewhat outdated design at the moment of its adoption; it has the accuracy and range of an 'old time' military rifle, but it is too long and heavy and lacks the selective-fire firepower of a true assault rifle. Nevertheless, it is a reliable and powerful weapon, often favoured by users for high lethality, long range and good penetration.

Cpl Jared M. Johnson from MCRT, USMC, firing his M14 National Match rifle.

(courtesy US Marine Corps)

ArmaLite/Colt AR-15/M16

	M16A1	M16A2
Calibre	5.56 × 45 M193	5.56 × 45 NATO/M855
Action	gas-operated, rotating bolt	
Overall length	986mm	1006mm
Barrel length	508mm	508mm
Weight, empty/ loaded with 30 rounds	2.89kg/3.6kg	3.77kg/4.47kg
Magazine capacity	20 or 30 rounds standard	
Rate of fire	650–750 rpm	800 rpm

The original AR-15 rifle is a gas-operated, selective-fire, magazine-fed weapon. Every rifle from the M16 family is substantially identical, but most civilian AR-15-type rifles are semi-automatic only.

The heart of the AR-15 is the direct gas system, adopted by Eugene Stoner in the early 1950s. This system does not use a conventional gas piston and rod to propel the bolt group back after the shot has been fired. Instead, the hot powder gases are fed from the barrel and down a stainless steel tube into the receiver. Inside it, the rear end of the gas tube enters into the 'gas key', a small attachment on the top of the bolt carrier. The hot gases pass through the gas key into a hollow cavity inside the bolt carrier and expand there, acting against the carrier and the collar around the bolt body. The pressure of the gases causes the bolt carrier to move back against the originally stationary bolt. The

Above *M16A1 rifle.*

Below *M16A2 rifle with thirty-round magazine and M203 grenade launcher.*

The 'flat top' receiver with Picatinny rail replaced the integral carrying handle on the M16A3 and the M16A4 rifle.

rearward movement of the carrier is initially transferred into the rotation of the bolt via a spiral cam slot in the bolt carrier and a cam pin attached to the bolt, which follows the slot. As soon as the bolt is rotated to unlock it from the barrel, the bolt group continues its rearward movement under inertia and the residual gas pressure in the barrel, extracting the spent case and compressing the buffer return spring, located in the buttstock. The forward movement of the bolt group first strips a fresh cartridge from the magazine and, on the final stage of the movement, rotates the bolt to lock into the barrel extension. The bolt has seven radial locking lugs; an eighth lug is located on the extractor claw. Since the introduction of the XM16E1 rifle, a forward-assist device is fitted to all military and most civilian AR-15-type rifles. This device consist of a spring-loaded button with an internal claw which engages the serrations on the right side of the bolt carrier to push it forward if the pressure of the return spring is insufficient to do so (for example, due to fouling inside the receiver or chamber). The rifle will not fire unless the bolt is fully locked. The bolt carrier and the bolt itself are chromium-plated. Another feature of the AR-15-type rifles is the bolt-catch device, which locks the bolt group in the open position when the last round has been fired. To release the bolt group one must push the button, located at the left side of the receiver, above the magazine. The 'T'-shaped cocking handle is located at the rear of the receiver, above the buttstock and does not reciprocate when the gun is fired.

The trigger/hammer group basically consists of a hammer, a trigger, a disconnector, a full automatic sear and some springs. The fire selector/safety switch is located at the left side of the receiver, above the pistol grip and is easily operated by the right thumb. This switch has three positions: 'safe', 'semi' (single shots) and 'automatic' (full automatic on the M16A1 and A3) or 'burst' (three-round bursts on the M16A2 and A4). In the last case, the trigger unit also includes a ratchet device to count the shots fired. This does not reset, so that if the magazine needs to be replaced after two shots of a burst, the next 'burst' will consist of only one shot. Furthermore, the weight of the trigger pull varies if the gun is fired after one or two shots of a burst; normally, the trigger pull is about 5lb (2.3kg) but, if firing after one shot of a burst, it rises to 8lb (3.6kg) and for the last shot is 11lb (5kg).

The ejection port is located at the right side of the receiver and is closed by the spring-loaded dust cover, which automatically pops open when the bolt carrier is pulled back. The M16A2 also features a spent case deflector – a triangular bulb on the receiver, just behind the ejection port, that allows the gun to be safely fired left-handed. The M16 is fed from box magazines. The earliest magazines were made from aluminium and held twenty rounds; these were replaced by thirty-round magazines in about 1970; these remain in service.

The receiver is made from aluminium alloy and consists of two parts – the 'upper receiver' and the 'lower receiver' (sometimes referred to simply as 'upper' and 'lower'). Most receivers are made from aluminium forgings by machining, but some commercially available receivers are made from aluminium castings with final drilling and machining. The upper and the lower receiver are linked by two cross-pins – one at the front (pivot pin) and one at the rear, above the pistol grip (take-down pin). To field strip the AR-15 one must push the rear pin to the right as far as it will go and then hinge the upper receiver around the front pin. This will allow the bolt group and the carrying handle to be removed from the upper receiver. For further disassembly, the front pin must also be pushed out and the upper and the lover receiver can then be separated. The key benefit of this design is great flexibility – if all the components available are made to the same specifications (as in most cases they are), one can easily swap a variety of upper receivers on one lower receiver, and vice versa. Since the complete 'upper' module consists also of the bolt group and the barrel with the gas system, one can easily have different barrel lengths, styles (light, heavy, fluted, bull) and even calibres, for one 'lower' group, that consists of the lower receiver with the trigger/hammer unit, recoil buffer, pistol grip and buttstock.

The furniture on military rifles is made from black

plastic, hence the common name 'the black rifle'. On early AR-15 and M16A1 rifles, the handguards were of triangular cross-section and were made from two non-interchangeable halves, left and right. On the M16A2 and later rifles, the handguards are of round cross-section and have two interchangeable, upper and lower sections. The buttstock on the M16A2 is similar in design to that on the M16A1, but slightly longer. One disadvantage of the Stoner system is that it cannot be adapted for a conventional, folding buttstock because the action protrudes into the stock. Instead, if required, a telescoped stock is used which allows the shortening of the rifle, when required, by about the half of the length of the standard stock. The M16 is usually equipped with a sling and can accept a knife-bayonet, either an old style M7 or a newer style M9. The flash suppressors on the earliest AR-15s and M16s were prong-type with three open slots, but were later replaced with 'bird-cage' flash suppressors with four (M16A1) or five (M16A2) slots. Both the M16A1 and the M16A2 can be equipped with the underbarrel, 40mm, M203 grenade launcher. The M203 mount replaces the standard handguards on the rifle and requires a grenade launcher sight to be mounted on the carrying handle. The standard sights of the M16A1 consist of a protected front post, mounted on the gas block, and of an aperture flip-up rear, with two range settings. Rear sights are mounted within the carrying handle and are adjustable for windage. The A2-style rear sight also features a flip-up, dual aperture sights,

with one smaller aperture for daylight usage and another larger one for low light conditions. The rotating knob, located just under the sight, makes the range adjustments. The front sight is generally the same as on the M16A1. The M16A3 and the A4 rifle have detachable carrying handles with A2 sights, and the Picatinny-type MilStd (military standard) rail on the top of the receiver, that can accept a wide variety of sighting devices and mounts.

COLT CAR-15/XM177 COMMANDO
[Data for current production Colt mod. 933 Commando]
Calibre: 5.56 × 45 NATO
Action: gas-operated, rotating bolt
Overall length: 680–762mm
Barrel length: 292mm
Weight: 2.44kg empty
Rate of fire: 750 rpm
Magazine capacity: 30 rounds (or any other M16-type magazine)

The first carbine version of the M16 assault rifle appeared under the name of the CAR-15 in 1965, and was intended for US Special Forces who fought in Vietnam. The original M16 was simply shortened by reducing the length of the barrel by half, from the original 20in (51cm) to 10in (25cm) and by shortening the buttstock by another 3in (75mm). The butt was plastic and retractable, the handguards were triangular in shape and the flash suppressor was of the original,

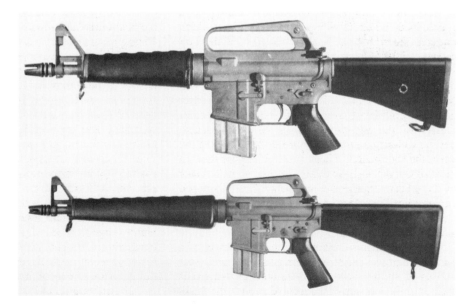

Early CAR-15 carbines made by Colt.

Modern Colt Commando carbine, factory designation RO733.

three-prong type. Based on the original CAR-15, Colt quickly developed the CAR-15 Air Force Survival Rifle, intended, as the name implied, to serve downed aircraft and helicopter pilots. This version had tubular handguards and a metallic tubular buttstock, and for some reason the pistol grip was shortened.

Early combat experience with the CAR-15 brought up some problems. First, the carbine was too loud, deafening the firing soldier quite quickly. Secondly, the muzzle flash was violent, blinding the shooter at night and giving away his position to the enemy. Colt partly solved this problem by installing a new, longer, flash suppressor. This version, known as the Colt model 609 Commando, also carried new handguards of tubular shape. The US Army officially adopted this model as the XM177. The next version, the XM177E1, had an M16A1-style receiver with forward assist button. In mid 1967 Colt slightly upgraded the Commando by lengthening the barrel to 11.5in (29cm); this version became the XM177E2. Later, with the introduction of the M16A2 and the M16A3 (flat-top) models, Colt also changed the design of its 'Commando' line, adding the three-shot-burst option and flat-top receivers with Picatinny-style rails. Current Colt Commando carbines (Colt still called these submachine guns) are based on either M16A2 or M16A3 receivers, have 11.5in (29cm) barrels with M16A2-style flash suppressors and are available in either three-round-burst or full-automatic version. Colt Commando carbines are used by US Special Forces and by some foreign forces, including the Israeli Defense Forces.

From the technical point of view, the Colt Commando is similar to the contemporary M16 rifle, having the same light-alloy, two-part receiver and direct gas-operated, rotating-bolt action, with a non-reciprocating charging handle at the rear of the receiver. The telescoping buttstock is made from metallic tubing. Since the recoil spring is located inside the butt, the Commando cannot be equipped with side or underfolding stocks without a redesign. Currently Colt Commando assault carbines are issued with standard M16-type, thirty-round magazines, but any other M16-compatible magazine may be used, including the hundred-round Beta-C dual drums. Commando carbines have no bayonet lugs and cannot be fitted with underbarrel grenade launchers.

ARMALITE AR-18
Calibre: 5.56 × 45
Action: gas-operated, rotating bolt
Overall length: 940mm (738mm with folded stock)
Barrel length: 464mm
Weight: 3.09kg with empty 20-rounds magazine
Magazine capacity: 20, 30 or 40 rounds

The AR-18 is a gas-operated, magazine fed, air-cooling, selective-fire rifle. The gas action features a short piston stroke and rotating-bolt locking mechanism. The gas chamber and piston are located above the barrel and the piston has a cupped head and its own return spring. The square-shaped bolt carrier is mounted inside the receiver on two guide rods, with each rod carrying its own return spring. The rods are linked by special end plates so that the whole bolt/bolt carrier/return springs/guide rods assembly can be

Above *The prototype 7.62 × 51 AR-16 rifle.*

Below *AR-18 rifle with standard 4× ArmaLite telescope sight.*

removed from the rifle as a single unit, which greatly simplifies field maintenance. The rotating bolt is somewhat similar in construction to the AR-15 bolt and is rotated by the bolt pin, which is engaged in the curved cam track cut into the bolt carrier. The charging handle is fixed to the right side of the bolt carrier and reciprocates when the gun is fired.

The receiver is made from stamped sheet steel and consists of two parts – upper and lower. Both parts are hinged at the front of the receiver. The upper and the lower part are interlocked by the rear ends of the bolt carrier guide rods. The AR-18 is field stripped by pressing the guide rods forward by a special lever at the rear of the receiver, then by folding the lower receiver down and forward. The controls consist of the trigger, safety/fire-mode selector at the left side of the receiver (similar to the one found on AR-15/M16-type rifles) and the bolt hold-open device. The available fire modes are single shots and full automatic, or only single shots in the AR-180 and the AR-180B.

The forearm, pistol grip and buttstock are made from black plastic. The buttstock folds to the left side to save space, if required, and the AR-18 can be fired with the butt folded. The sling attachment points are located on the barrel, just ahead of the forearm and at the butt of the pistol grip, so that the sling position is not affected by the position of the foldable buttstock. The sights consist of a hooded front post and the 'L'-shaped, flip-up aperture rear, also protected from the sides by large 'dog ears'. Each AR-18 was also fitted as standard with a scope mount at the top of the receiver.

The weapon was originally available in the military AR-18 (selective fire) and the AR-18S (selective fire, with short barrel) version, and in the AR-180 semi-automatic-only version. But in 2001 the ArmaLite company resurrected the AR-180 design, in a somewhat modified form. The new rifle, intended mostly for the civilian and the law enforcement market, features the same AR-18 layout and action, but discards the stamped steel lower receiver and replaces it with a plastic lower, with an AR-15-compatible magazine housing and AR-15-type trigger unit, which allows for a wider availability of spare parts. The original folding buttstock and flash suppressor are replaced by a plastic, fixed buttstock of the same shape and a muzzle recoil compensator, to comply with current American firearms laws. The price of the AR-180B is slightly lower than that of the similar, basic, AR-15-type rifle, and the available user reports about the AR-180B are generally positive.

STONER 63

	Stoner 63A rifle (XM22)	Stoner 63A carbine (XM23)
Calibre	5.56 × 45	
Action	gas-operated, rotating bolt	
Overall length	1,022mm	911mm; 679mm with folded butt
Barrel length	508mm	400mm
Weight, empty	3.72kg	3.67kg
Magazine capacity	30 rounds	
Rate of fire	750–900 rpm	740–800 rpm

The Stoner 63 is more than a single firearm, it is a modular kit, which contains about fifteen sub-assemblies. Different combinations of these (barrels, feed units, trigger units, sight units) allow for the assembly of several firearms on the single receiver unit. The stamped steel receiver contains a universal bolt group, with a multi-lug rotating bolt and a long stroke gas piston with gas tube. The receiver also has several sets of mounting points for the attaching of other sub-assemblies and the quickly detachable barrel. In rifle and carbine configuration, the receiver is so orientated that the gas system lies above the barrel and the feed unit mounting points are below the receiver. In all the machine gun configurations, either belt- or magazine-fed, the receiver is turned 'upside down', with the gas system being below the barrel and the feed unit being above the receiver. In rifle/carbine configuration the Stoner 63 system uses a hammer-fired, trigger unit, integral with the pistol grip and the triggerguard. This trigger unit allows for single shots and full automatic fire, and the gun is fired from a closed bolt only. In machine gun configuration, the trigger unit has no hammer, instead, its sear interoperates with the cut in the gas piston rod, allowing only full automatic fire and only from an open bolt. The magazine feed unit can accommodate proprietary, curved box magazines for thirty rounds and can be used in both the rifle and the machine gun configuration. The belt feed unit can be used only in machine gun configurations. Different rear sight units are available for several configurations, with the front sights being mounted on quickly detachable barrels.

On earlier Stoner 63 system weapons, the charging handle was located on the right side of the bolt carrier; the safety and fire selector were combined in one control, located on the left side of the trigger unit. On the modified Stoner 63A system, the charging handle was attached to the gas piston rod and projected from the top in rifle/carbine configuration, or from the bottom in machine gun/light machine gun configurations; the safety was made as a separate lever at the front of the trigger guard, with the fire-mode selector still beinglocated on the side of the trigger unit, above the pistol grip. The Stoner 63 system featured a variety

The Stoner 63A1 carbine, tested by the US Army as the XM23.

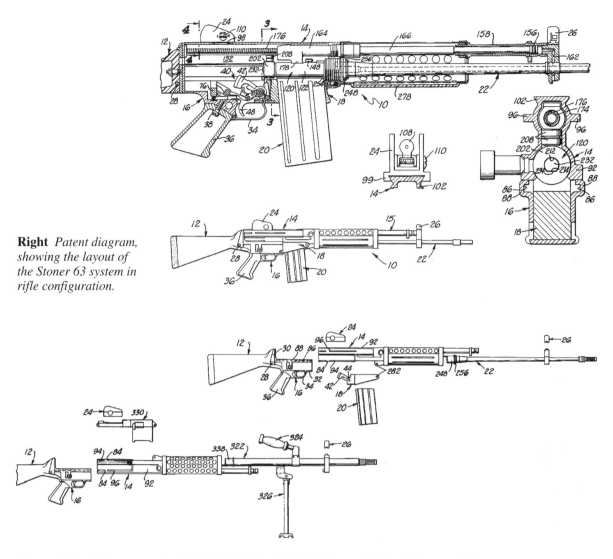

Right *Patent diagram, showing the layout of the Stoner 63 system in rifle configuration.*

Above *Patent diagram, showing the rifle and machine gun configurations of the Stoner 63 system with relevant components.*

Right *Modern reincarnation of the Stoner system: the RAV-02 assault rifle, made in the USA by Robinson Armament Co.*

(courtesy Robinson Armament Co.)

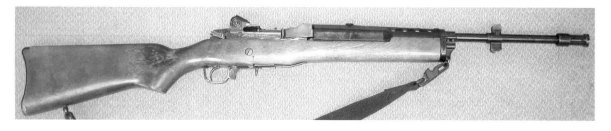

Above *AC-556 rifle, a selective-fire version of the Ruger Mini-14GB.*

Left *AC-556F assault carbine, with side-folding buttstock and shorter barrel.*

of easily detachable fixed or folding buttstocks. The latter were available in a side-folding plastic variety or in an underfolding stamped steel type, similar to the AKS-47.

STURM, RUGER & CO. MINI-14 GB/AC-556
Calibre: 5.56 × 45
Action: gas-operated, rotating bolt
Overall length: 943mm
Barrel length: 470mm
Weight: 3.06kg
Magazine capacity: 5, 10, 20 or 30 rounds in detachable box magazines
Rate of fire: 600–750 rpm (AC-556)

The Mini-14 rifle was developed by Sturm, Ruger & Co. in the early 1970s and introduced in about 1974. It was made as an attempt to imitate the popular 7.62mm M14 rifle in a smaller calibre and with a lighter weight. Original Mini-14 rifles were intended for the civilian market and so were semi-automatic only, but in the late 1970s Ruger produced two versions of the Mini-14 intended for police and military markets. One was the Mini-14GB, which was the same semi-automatic rifle but fitted with a flash suppressor and a bayonet lug. The second was the AC-556, a selective-fire assault rifle, which could be fired in three-round bursts and in full automatic mode, in addition to single shots. The AC-556 was also fitted with a flash suppressor and bayonet mount. All versions of Mini-14, including the

Mini-14/GB and the AC-556, were available either with a wooden stock with a semi-pistol grip and fixed butt, or with a side-folding, metallic buttstock and a separate, plastic pistol grip. Military versions of the Mini-14 found some favour among police units in the USA and in several other countries, because of its 'less military' look and low price.

The Mini-14 is a gas-operated, magazine-fed rifle. The gas chamber and piston are located under the barrel (much as in the M14) and hidden within the forearm. The long stroke gas piston has a cupped head and is linked to the bolt by a Garand-style operating rod, which is located to the right of the barrel and is partly enclosed by a plastic heat shield. The rotating bolt locks to the steel receiver with two large lugs. The return spring is located in the forearm, behind the gas piston, The charging handle is fixed to the operating rod, to the right side of the receiver. A Garand-style safety switch is located at the front of the trigger guard. The AC-556 rifles feature a separate, three-position fire mode selector at the right side of the receiver, behind the ejection port. The adjustable aperture rear sight is mounted at the rear of the receiver; the front sight on the military models is fixed on the gas block and on civilian models to the barrel, near to the muzzle. The AC-556F rifle was also available in a short-barrelled carbine configuration. All Mini-14 models were also offered in standard or stainless steel versions.

COLT ACR

Calibre: 5.56 × 45 duplex
Action: gas-operated, rotating bolt
Overall length: 1032mm (933mm with buttstock collapsed)
Barrel length: 508mm
Weight: 3.93kg less magazine, with telescope sight
Magazine capacity: 30 rounds, detachable box magazines
Rate of fire: 400–600 rpm

Colt's entrant in the ACR trials was the most conventional one, with the operating system and general layout similar to those of the M16A2 rifle, but with some improvements. First, the Colt ACR featured a thicker, heavier barrel with a special muzzle brake. Secondly, it featured a special recoil buffer, which decreased the cyclic rate of fire down to a manageable 400–600 rpm, compared with the 800 rpm of the M16A2. This allowed for controllable, full automatic fire instead of the fixed three-round bursts of the M16A2. Other improvements included a better shaped pistol grip and a shotgun-style, raised, ventilated rib above the barrel, which allowed for fairly accurate, short-range snap shooting in combat conditions. For longer-range fire, a telescope sight could be mounted on the top of the receiver instead of the detachable carrying handle, which also carried the rear aperture-type sight. The telescoped buttstock with four positions (from fully extended to fully collapsed) allowed for a more compact package and also gave users some degree of personal choice for length of pull.

The Colt ACR was intended to use 'duplex' 5.56 × 45 ammunition, developed by Olin/Winchester, and described in Chapter 4. The Colt ACR also retained compatibility with any NATO-standard 5.56mm ammunition. Several improvements, such as the detachable carrying handle on a universal rail, first tested on this rifle, were later incorporated into the M16 family of rifles, M16A3 and A4.

AAI ACR

Calibre: 5.56 × 45 flechette (not compatible with 5.56 × 45 NATO)
Action: gas-operated, rotating bolt
Overall length: 1,016mm
Barrel length: n/a
Weight: 3.53kg less magazine and telescope sight
Magazine capacity: 30 rounds, detachable box magazines
Rate of fire: n/a

The ACR entrant from the AAI Corporation continued the long and so far unsuccessful story of the

Right *The Colt ACR.*

Below *AAI ACR.*

*M4 carbine
with M203 grenade
launcher.*

Left *M4A1 carbine
with Aimpoint sight
and tactical flashlight
under the forearm.*

Below *The SOPMOD
kit for the M4A1
carbine.*

development of flechette-firing weapons. This saga in the USA was started by one of AAI's founders, Irwin Barr, during the early 1950s. By the late 1980s AAI had discarded most of its previous ideas, tested during the SPIW, FARC and FRS programmes, and retained only the concept of the single-saboted, flechette ammunition (see Chapter 4 for some details).

Although the AAI ACR ammunition was based on the standard 5.56mm NATO cartridge, it was incompatible with it because it produced entirely different pressure curves, hence AAI took special care to avoid the loading of standard 5.56mm ammunition into its ACR rifle. The AAI ACR is a more or less conventional, gas-operated rifle, with a long stroke gas piston. The gas port is located relatively close to the chamber. The barrel is locked by using a rotating bolt. The gun housing is made from polymer. The charging handle is located at the left side, above the forearm and the fire-selector switch at the right side, above the trigger, and the separate safety mechanism inside the trigger guard, at the front of the trigger. Standard sighting equipment includes open sights and a long, shotgun-style sighting rib on the top of the receiver and barrel shroud, as well as a 4× telescope sight on the side mount. The barrel was fitted with a relatively large combination muzzle device, which acted as a flash hider, sound moderator and muzzle brake.

COLT M4 CARBINE

Calibre: 5.56 × 45 NATO
Action: gas-operated, rotating bolt
Overall length: 838mm (stock extended); 757mm (stock fully collapsed)
Barrel length: 370mm
Weight: 2.52kg without magazine; 3.0kg with magazine loaded with 30 rounds
Rate of fire: 700–950 rpm

The Colt company developed several carbine versions of the basic AR-15/M16 rifle from the 1970s. The US military (and some other armies, most notably the Israeli) had adopted the Colt CAR-15 Commando and the XM-177 carbine during the 1970s and the 1980s. But early in the 1990s the old idea of replacing pistols with a more effective, shoulder-fired weapon, rose again within the military. This idea can be dated back to the M1 carbine of 1941, but good ideas never die. Thus in 1994 the US Army adopted the Colt Model 720 selective-fire carbine (essentially a shortened M16A2 rifle), as the M4 carbine. This weapon was intended to replace in service some M9 (Beretta 92FS) pistols, as well as some aged M3A1 submachine guns and M16A2 rifles. The new weapon was much handier

and more comfortable to carry than the long M16A2 rifle and hence the US Special Operations Command (SOCOM) was attracted to the M4 as a possible universal weapon for all the special operations community. For this purpose the M4 was later modified with the M16A3-style, flat-top receiver with an integral, Picatinny-type accessory rail instead of the M16A2/M4-type integral carrying handle. The other change to the M4A1, when compared with the M4, was that its trigger unit was modified to fire full-automatic instead of the three-shot bursts. Especially for the SOCOM M4A1s, the US Naval Surface Warfare Center developed a SOPMOD M4 kit, which consisted of the M4A1 carbine equipped with the rail interface system (RIS) instead of the standard handguards. The kit also included a variety of other accessories, such as several sights (the ACOG 4× telescopic and the ACOG Reflex red-dot, detachable, back-up, open sights), laser pointers (visible and infra-red), detachable sound suppressor (silencer) and a modified M203 40mm grenade launcher (with shortened barrel and improved sights). The kit also included a detachable front grip and tactical light. The M4 carbine differs from the M16A2 (see above) rifle only by having a shorter barrel and a telescoped, four-position buttstock. The M4A1 is a similar modification of the M16A3 rifle.

XM29 OICW

Calibre: 5.56 × 45 NATO (KE) and 20mm (HE)
Action: gas-operated, rotating bolt (KE); gas-operated, rotating bolt (HE)
Overall length: 890mm
Barrel length: 250mm (KE); 460mm (HE)
Weight: about 5.5kg empty; about 6.8kg loaded (planned)
Magazine capacity: 20 or 30 rounds box (KE) and 6 rounds box (HE)

The XM29 is a combination weapon, which has a 20mm, semi-automatic, magazine-fed grenade launcher as its primary part, and a 5.56mm compact assault rifle as its secondary part. Both are assembled into a single, one-man portable unit, with the addition of a target acquisition/fire control system (TA/FCS), which is an essential part of the whole system. The XM29 is intended to become an integral part of the future 'Land Warrior' system, capable of communicating with the other parts of this system, including tactical computers and helmet-mounted displays.

The gas-operated grenade launcher fires in semi-automatic mode only. It has a bullpup layout with the detachable box magazine located in the butt of the weapon. The rifled barrel is used to launch 20mm grenades up to a range of 1,000m with good accuracy. In the standard configuration, most of the fire controls for the grenade launcher part are located on the rifle part, including the single trigger for both firing modules. It is quite possible, however, that a separate stock will be developed for the grenade launcher part, so that it will be possible to use it without the rifle part being attached. The launcher has provision for the TA/FCS system to be mounted on top, together with the appropriate interfaces, so that data provided from the TA/FCS can be used to program the 20mm grenade fuses. These fuses, used for the 20mm HEAB ammunition, have multiple modes of detonation, including a direct impact mode and an air burst mode. In the latter, the fuse is preprogrammed to explode the warhead at the preset range, which is calculated during its flight by counting the number of grenade rotations. This allows it to defeat targets without direct impact, using the blast and fragmentation effect of the high explosive warhead. This is a major advantage over existing small arms, which, in most cases, require a direct hit on the target to be effective, since it allows for greater aiming errors and also makes it possible to defeat targets in defilade, as in trenches and behind walls. The high explosive warhead also has the advantage of not being dependent on its velocity to be effective, so, unlike bullets, its effectiveness does not decrease with increasing range.

The disadvantage of the system is the extreme complexity of the electronic fuses, which results in a high price for a single round of ammunition. Present plans state that a HEAB round must cost about US$25,

but it is still to be seen whether this can be achieved when the M29 system is fielded. It is interesting that the present design of HEAB ammunition actually has two small HE warheads, one at the front and the other at the rear of the projectile, with the fuse module located between them. The rifle, or 'kinetic energy' part of the XM29 system, on the other hand, is a fairly conventional, short-barrelled weapon, derived from the German HK G36 assault rifle. The basic 'rifle' part of the XM29 has no buttstock nor sights and thus can be used separately from the whole system only as an emergency, personal-defence weapon. While being mounted within the entire system, it can be used for close-quarters work, both defensive and offensive (the 20mm grenade launcher has a minimum range of fire of 50–100m), or as a inexpensive, low-intensity, medium-range offensive weapon. Most of the XM29 system controls are built into the 'rifle' part, around the trigger guard.

The target acquisition/fire control system (TA/FCS) is the most expensive and complicated unit of the system, since it must combine day and night vision capabilities, a laser rangefinding unit, a ballistic computer and several interfaces to the grenade launcher and external systems. It is used to find targets in any light and weather conditions, determine the range to the target, calculate and display the aiming data so that the grenade or bullet can be fired to the desired point of impact, and then supply the data to the grenade launcher so that the range can be preset into the grenade fuse. In the case of any damage to the TA/FCS, the 20mm grenade launcher still may be used in the direct impact

XM29 OICW prototype (2002).

XM8 lightweight assault rifle in basic configuration.

(courtesy Heckler-Koch USA)

mode and the rifle part of the system will still be usable. The results of current research and testing have showed that the XM29 can be up to 500 per cent more effective than existing small arms, but it is still to be seen whether all the requirements will be met in the resulting system, especially regarding the reliability of the electronic components, the weight, and, last but not least, the unit price. At present (spring 2004), the latest news has indicated a temporary halt to XM29 development, due to problems in reaching the weight target, in favour of two separate weapons: the XM25, a 25mm grenade launcher, and the XM8 rifle.

XM8

Calibre: 5.56 × 45 NATO
Action: gas-operated, rotating bolt
Overall length: 838mm (basic carbine modification, buttstock fully extended)
Barrel length: 318mm in basic configuration; also 229mm in 'Compact' or 508mm in 'Sharpshooter' and 'Automatic rifle" (LMG) configurations
Weight: about 2.59kg empty in basic configuration (objective)
Magazine capacity: 10 or 30 rounds detachable box
Rate of fire: 750 rpm

The basic action of the XM8 is mounted in the polymer receiver and consists of a short piston stroke gas system (integral with each barrel), and a rotating bolt, based on the German HK G36 rifle. The receiver has a quick-detachable barrel mounting, as well as mounting points for various handguards, sights, a carrying handle and a buttstock or butt-cap. Because of its construction, mostly from polymers, the XM8 will provide a significant weight reduction (about 20 per cent) over the current M4A1 modular carbine system, as well as improved reliability. The centrally located, ambidextrous charging handle is located at the top of the receiver and is similar to that of the HK G36 rifle. The ambidextrous fire mode/safety levers are located above the pistol grip and allow for single shots and full automatic fire. The standard sight is a battery-powered red dot type, with the built-in, infra-red laser illuminator and visible laser pointer. The XM8 features a proprietary sight mounting interface, with MIL-STD 1913 (Picatinny rail) adaptors available as options. The retractable buttstock has five positions and can be fully collapsed for reduced size or partly retracted for the best fit to any particular shooter (or when wearing flak jackets). The XM8 will feed from translucent, polymer, G36-type magazines with capacities of ten or thirty rounds, or from hundred-round, Beta-C-type, dual drum magazines in the automatic rifle (LMG) role.

Thanks to its quickly detachable barrel system, modular sighting unit and modular buttstock, the XM8 can be easily assembled in the field into the following configurations:

- Basic carbine version, with 12.5in (318mm) barrel. five-position retractable buttstock and integral red dot sight
- Grenadier's rifle, similar to the basic carbine, but with the 40mm XM320 underbarrel grenade launcher (modified HK AG-36) instead of the detachable forearm.
- Compact (personal defence weapon) version, with 9in (229mm) barrel, no buttstock and open sights.
- Sharpshooter version, with 20in (508mm) barrel and various sighting accessories, depending on the task, for designated marksmen.
- Automatic rifle (light machine gun), with heavy, 20in barrel, integral bipod and high-capacity drum magazines.

The XM8 will have a bayonet lug on both the 12.5in and the 20in barrel.

Appendix

MILITARY SMALL-ARMS CARTRIDGES

PRINCIPAL SERVICE INTERMEDIATE CARTRIDGES

Metric Calibre	Rim Diameter (mm)	Body Diameter (mm)	Country of Origin	Projectile Weight (g/gr.)
5.45 × 39	10.0	10.0	CIS	3.43/53
5.56 × 45	9.5	9.5	USA NATO USA	3.56/55 4.0/62 5.0/77
5.8 × 42	10.5	10.5	PRC	4.15/64
6 × 60	11.3	11.3	USA	7.26/112
6.5 × 50SR	12.1	11.4	J	8.94/138
6.5 × 52	11.35	11.30	I	10.5/162
6.5 × 55	12.1	12.1	S	9.0/139
7 × 49	11.9	11.9	UK/B	9.0/140
7.62 × 33	9.1	9.0	USA	7.0/110
7.62 × 39	11.3	11.2	USSR	7.97/123
7.62 × 45	11.2	11.2	CZ	8.4/130
7.92 × 33	12.1	12.0	D	8.1/125

SELECTED FULL-POWER RIFLE/MG CARTRIDGES

Metric Calibre	Rim Diameter (mm)	Body Diameter (mm)	Country of Origin	Projectile Weight (g/gr.)
7.5 × 54	12.3	12.3	F	9.07/140
7.5 × 55	12.5	12.5	CH	11.27/174
7.62 × 51	11.9	11.8	USA/NATO	9.72/150
7.62 × 54R	14.4	12.3	USSR	9.7/150
7.62 × 63	12.0	12.0	USA	9.85/152
7.7 × 56R	13.5	11.5	UK	11.27/174
7.92 × 57	11.9	11.9	D	10.0/154

Notes
1. Muzzle velocities shown are from the standard, full-length barrel. Short-length barrels will produce lower velocities
2. The 'recoil energy factor' is the cartridge recoil impulse squared. The recoil impulse is calculated as follows: (bullet weight [g] × muzzle velocity [km/s] + (propellant weight [g] × 1.2km/s). Propellant weight has been estimated where not known. The recoil impulse has been squared in order to represent recoil energy rather than momentum: in guns of the same weight (and other characteristics), the gun recoil experienced will be directly proportional to this recoil energy factor.

Sectional Density	Muzzle Velocity (m/s/ft/s)	Muzzle Energy (J/ft lb)	Recoil Energy Factor (Impulse^2)	Name/Weapons Chambered in
0.156	900/2,950	1,390/1,030	24	5.45mm Russian 7N6; AK 74
0.156	975/3,200	1,690/1,250	31	.223/5.56mm US M193;
0.176	930/3,050	1,730/1,280	32	4.0 g is NATO SS109/US M855,
0.220	832/2,730	1,730/1,280	36	5.0 g is US Mk262
0.167	930/3,050	1,800/1,340	33	5.8mm Type 95
0.280	780/2,560	2,210/1,640	75	6mm Lee USN (1895)
0.282	762/2,500	2,590/1,920	89	6.5mm Arisaka (to WWII), Fedorov Avtomat (WW1)
0.332	700/2,300	2,570/1,910	100	6.5mm Carcano (to WWII)
0.284	792/2,600	2,820/2,090	116	Swedish rifle/MG
0.246	790/2,590	2,800/2,080	107	7mm Medium
0.163	580/1,900	1,200/890	26	.30 M1 carbine
0.182	710/2,330	2,010/1,490	59	7.62 M1943: Simonov SKS, AK 47
0.193	744/2440	2,230/1,650	75	7.62mm vz52
0.171	690/2,260	1,930/1,430	55	7.92mm Kurz: StG.44

Sectional Density	Muzzle Velocity (m/s/ft/s)	Muzzle Energy (J/ft lb)	Recoil Energy Factor (Impulse^2)	Name/Weapons Chambered in
0.211	793/2,600	2,850/2,120	119	7.5mm French
0.262	780/2,560	3,430/2,540	154	7.5mm Swiss
0.226	853/2,800	3,540/2,630	142	7.62mm NATO
0.221	870/2,850	3,670/2,720	148	7.62mm Russian
0.229	837/2,750	3,450/2,560	147	.30-06 Springfield
0.257	744/2,440	3,120/2,310	141	.303in British Mk7 loading
0.212	854/2,800	3,620/2,690	154	7.9mm Mauser (typical: many others)

SOME EXPERIMENTAL ASSAULT RIFLE CARTRIDGES

Metric Calibre	Rim Diameter (mm)	Body Diameter (mm)	Country of Origin	Projectile Weight (g/gr.)
4.32 × 46	9.5	9.5	USA	1.81/28
4.6 × 36	9.0	9.0	D/E	2.7/42
4.7 × 21	–	–	D	3.4/52
4.85 × 49	9.6	9.5	UK	3.58/55
5.56 × 33	9.6	9.5	USA	2.66/41
5.56 × 38	9.5	9.5	USA	2.4/37
5.56 × 52	11.9	11.9	USA	3.46/53
5.56 × 63	12.0	11.9	USA	3.46/53
5.6 × 44	8.5	8.5	USA	0.65/10
5.6 × 48	11.9	11.9	CH	3.7/57
6 × 45	10.3	10.3	USA	6.8/105
6.25 × 43	11.9	11.9	UK	6.48/100
6.35 × 48	10.5	10.5	USA	4.54/70
6.35 × 52	11.9	11.9	USA	5.24/81
6.45 × 48	11.9	11.9	CH	6.3/97
6.8 × 43	10.7	10.6	USA	7.45/115
6.8 × 46	11.2	11.2	UK	6.5/100
6.8 × 52	11.9	11.9	USA	6.52/101
7 × 43	11.9	11.9	UK	9.0/140
7 × 51	11.4	11.4	USA	8.1/125
7.92 × 40	11.9	11.8	ESP	6.8/105

Sectional Density	Muzzle Velocity (m/s/ft/s)	Muzzle Energy (J/ft lb)	Recoil Energy Factor (Impulse²)	Name/Weapons Chambered in
0.130	1,220/4,000	1,350/1,000	18	.17 AAI Serial Bullet Rifle
0.174	850/2,790	975/720	11	HK-36 rifle
0.210	930/3,050	1,470/1,090	28	HK G11 caseless
0.204	950/3,120	1,615/1,200	31	4.85mm British: SA80 trials cartridge
0.117	950/3,120	1,200/890	17	.22 APG Carbine
0.105	1,180/3,870	1,670/1,240	34	5.56mm FABRL
0.152	1,200/3,940	2,490/1,850	60	.22 Homologous
0.152	1,200/3,940	2,490/1,850	71	.22/30 (.30-06 case)
0.285	4,000/1,220	480/360	9	XM216 SPIW flechette
0.163	1,050/3,445	2,040/1,510	51	Swiss 5.6mm Eiger
0.252	769/2,520	2,010/1,490	55	6mm SAW early 1970s
0.222	817/2,680	2,160/1,600	67	British 1970 'ideal' 6.25mm
0.151	1,020/3,350	2,360/1,750	49	1960s FA-T116 .25 (using FA-T110 case)
0.175	1,050/3,445	2,890/2,140	83	.25 Homologous
0.204	900/2,950	2,550/1,890	79	Swiss 6.45mm GP 80
0.214	808/2,650	2,430/1,800	71	6.8 Remington SPC (current)
0.187	840/2,750	2,290/1,700	67	late 1940s .270
0.187	950/3,120	2,940/2,180	96	.27 Homologous
0.246	736/2,415	2,440/1,810	90	.280/30 British EM-2
0.222	768/2,520	2,390/1,770	85	1920s .276 Pedersen
0.144	820/2,690	2,290/1,700	68	7.92 × 40 CETME

Glossary

AAI   Aircraft Armaments Incorporated

accelerator   a pivoting lever inside a short-recoil mechanism which acts to accelerate the rearward movement of the bolt

ACR   advanced combat rifle: a competition held in the USA in the late 1980s

AGL   automatic grenade launcher

air-cooled   a weapon which achieves barrel cooling by radiating heat direct to the atmosphere

ammunition   collective name for cartridges (or equivalent)

aperture sights   iron rearsights which provide a small hole through which the foresight and target are sighted; see 'peep' and 'diopter' sights

AP   armour-piercing; projectile designed to penetrate armour or cartridge loaded with such a projectile

APDS   armour-piercing, discarding sabot: subcalibre AP projectile, stabilized by the rifling, supported in the bore by a sabot or sleeve which falls away at the muzzle

APFSDS   armour-piercing, fin-stabilized, discarding sabot: similar to APDS, but a long and narrow AP projectile which stabilized in flight by fins rather than rifling

APHC   armour-piercing, hard core: standard type of AP bullet

APHHW   All-Purpose Hand-Held Weapon: USA project 1959–62

API blowback   advanced primer ignition blowback: type of automatic mechanism in which the cartridge is fired while the bolt is still moving forward

assault rifle   a military rifle offering selective fire (both full and semi-automatic) with an effective range of at least 300m and normally firing an intermediate cartridge. See 'battle rifle'

automatic   a weapon which continues to fire and reload automatically for as long as the trigger or firing button is pressed

B   added to a cartridge designation to identify a belted case (e.g., 20 × 105B)

ball (round)   small arms projectile or bullet, that is, not AP, I, HE nor T

ballistics   study of the passage of a projectile from the instant of firing to the end of its flight

ballistic coefficient   factor which measures the aerodynamic drag of a projectile and therefore the rate at which it loses velocity: the higher the number, the lower the drag

barrel tube   connected to (or integral with) the chamber, down which the projectile is accelerated

barrel extension   part of the barrel which extends behind the chamber, usually to accommodate a locking mechanism

battle rifle   a military rifle chambered for a full-power rifle/MG cartridge, e.g. 7.62 x 51

bayonet   short knife or spike fitted to a rifle barrel; may be detachable or folding

BC   ballistic coefficient

belt   (1) raised strip around a cartridge case, in front of the extractor groove

belted case (2) strip of fabric or (more usually) metal, into which cartridges are fitted to facilitate the feeding of them into a weapon; metal belts may be disintegrating, non-disintegrating or continuous loop

belted case cartridge case with a raised section in front of the extractor groove to aid in location in the chamber

belt feed use of a belt to supply ammunition to a gun mechanism

belt link piece of metal which constitutes part of a belt

bipod two-legged support fitted to the forward end of a gun, for accurate firing in a prone position

blank cartridge which has a primer and propellant but no projectile

blow-back type of automatic weapon operating mechanism which uses the pressure of gun gas pushing against the base of a cartridge case to force the bolt to the rear

bolt part of the operating system, containing the firing mechanism, which slides in line with the barrel, pushing a cartridge into the chamber and holding it there during firing

bolt carrier part of the action, which contains the bolt and reciprocates with it; it begins to move before (and finishes moving after) the bolt because its task is to unlock and lock the bolt to the barrel

bolt group bolt assembly, including the firing pin/hammer and other components which are attached to the bolt

bolt lugs protrusions from the bolt used to lock it to the barrel extension or receiver

bolt stop part of the receiver which stops the bolt's rearward movement

bore inside of the barrel

bottlenecked cartridge cartridge with a case whose diameter reduces sharply to the neck, creating a shoulder

box magazine type of magazine in which cartridges are stacked on top of each other (they may be single or double stacked)

breech opening at the rear of the chamber which allows cartridges to be loaded and fired cases extracted

breechblock alternative term for bolt, normally used when its operating movement involves pivoting, or sliding vertically or horizontally

breech face part of the barrel surrounding the breech

BRL Ballistics Research Laboratory; at US Army Aberdeen establishment

bullet *see* ball

bullpup rifle in which the action and magazine are behind the trigger

burst fire control which fires a defined number of rounds (usually two or three) for each press of the trigger

butt back face of the rifle, held against the shoulder on firing

buttstock back part of the rifle, from the receiver to the butt

calibre (1) the diameter of a projectile or of the inside of a barrel
(2) designation of the cartridge a weapon is designed for

cannelure groove around a small-arms bullet for receiving a crimp

cartridge unit or round of ammunition, normally comprising the cartridge case, projectile, propellant and primer

cartridge case part of a cartridge which contains the propellant and holds the projectile and primer firmly in place

caseless ammunition ammunition which does not have a cartridge case but uses solid propellant to hold the projectile and primer

centrefire cartridge fired by a primer located in the centre of the head or base

chamber space at the rear of the barrel in which the cartridge is positioned and supported during firing

chromium plating used to protect the barrel bore and chamber

clip piece of metal which holds together several cartridges (normally by the case heads) for feeding into a weapon; or several cartridges held together by a clip

closed bolt automatic weapon designed to commence the firing cycle with the cartridge already loaded into the chamber (*see* open bolt)

combustible case cartridge case which is designed to burn with the propellant

compensator type of muzzle attachment for hand-held weapons in which all the diverted gas is directed upwards to resist muzzle rise

cook-off unwanted ignition of a cartridge by heat in a gun chamber

cordite type of propellant

CQB close-quarter battle: especially urban fighting

crimp depression in the neck of a cartridge case, intended to hold the projectile firmly in place before firing

dark trace initial burn of a tracer, designed to give no light

deflection angle between the position of a crossing target (usually an aircraft) and the required aiming point, which will be ahead of it

delayed blow-back hybrid gun mechanism in which the bolt is locked to the barrel on firing, is then unlocked by the mechanism but relies on blow-back for the remainder of the firing cycle (*see* retarded blow-back)

diopter a type of aperture rearsight capable of being adjusted for windage and elevation (laterally and vertically) and usually with a variable aperture size'

double base type of propellant

drill round cartridge which is totally inert used to practise loading and unloading drills; always made easily recognizable

driving band strip of soft metal or plastic around a projectile intended to be gripped by the rifling in order to induce spin

drum type of circular magazine in which cartridges are held parallel to each other (sometimes used to describe a pan magazine); *see* helical drum and pan magazine

dummy round cartridge which is completely inert (no primer nor propellant)

duplex loading cartridge loaded with two full-calibre projectiles, intended to follow each other down the barrel (*see* multiball, triplex)

ejection act of throwing an extracted cartridge case clear of the gun

electric ignition method of igniting cartridges by passing an electrical current through the primer

electromagnetic gun gun which uses electromagnetic force to accelerate a projectile (also known as a rail gun)

electrothermal-(chemical) system which uses a plasma generator instead of a primer

erosion wear on the inside of a barrel caused by hot propellant gasses and friction generated by projectiles

external ballistics science of projectile flight from the muzzle of a gun (also known as exterior ballistics)

extraction act of pulling a fired cartridge case from the chamber

extractor claw hook, attached to the bolt, which fits into the extractor groove in order to pull the cartridge out of the chamber

extractor groove groove around the head of a cartridge case into which the extractor claw fits

FABRL USA ammunition project: originally Frankford Arsenal + BRL, then 'future ammunition for burst rifle launch'

FCAR full-calibre assault rifle; one firing an intermediate cartridge with a calibre the same as a full-power rifle/MG round (that is, 7.62 or 7.92mm)

feed method of delivering ammunition to the gun

fin stabilized projectile whose flight is stabilized by fins rather than by being spun by rifling

firing cycle sequence of loading, firing, extracting, ejecting and reloading

firing pin steel pin which strikes a primer to cause ignition

flash hider cone-shaped device fitted to the muzzle to screen muzzle flash from the firer

flash suppressor slotted device fitted to the muzzle to reduce the flash from burning propellant (often called a 'flash hider' but the principle is different)

flat trajectory flight of a projectile which involves

	minimal drop due to gravity; associated with high velocity
flechette	long, thin bullet; fin-stabilized and (in small arms) contained within a sabot for firing
fluted chamber	longitudinal grooves in the chamber to permit gun gas to seep back around the cartridge case to prevent it from sticking
folding stock	buttstock which can be folded to lie alongside the rifle
foot pounds	a measure of muzzle energy
fore grip	grip under the barrel for the forward (non-firing) hand
FPAR	full-power assault rifle; a selective-fire rifle chambered for the 7.62 × 51 NATO or other full-power rifle/MG cartridge
fragment	when a bullet breaks up under the stress of impact and tumbling it is said to fragment
frangible	projectile designed to break up into small fragments on hitting the target
full-calibre	projectile which fills the bore of a gun (see sub-calibre)
gas-operated	type of gun mechanism using gas tapped from the barrel to drive the firing cycle
gas regulator	valve on gas-operated weapon which regulates the amount of gas tapped to operate the action, according to circumstances
GPMG	general purpose machine gun
grain	measure of weight used in UK and USA for propellant charges and (in smaller calibres) projectiles; 1g = 15.432 gr.
grenade launcher	low-velocity gun designed to fire small HE projectiles
grooves	larger interior diameter of a rifled barrel; between the lands
gun gas	gas generated by the burning of the propellant in a cartridge
hammer	part of a trigger mechanism which pivots under spring pressure to strike the firing pin
hand grip or guard	part of the rifle intended to be held by the firer's supporting (as opposed to trigger) hand
hang fire	delay in the ignition of a cartridge

	after the primer has been struck
HE	high explosive; ammunition which relies on explosive blast for target engagement
HEAB	High Explosive Air Burst
head	rear of the cartridge (also known as the base), into which is fitted the primer
headspace	accurate location of a cartridge in the chamber ready for ignition
headstamp	information about the cartridge, stamped into the head or base of the case
helical drum	magazine in which all rounds point inwards, following a spiral track
HMG	heavy machine gun
housing	encloses part of a gun action
HV	high velocity
hybrid	mechanism which uses more than one operating principle
ignition	igniting of propellant by a primer
inert	cartridge or explosive which cannot fire nor detonate
intermediate cartridge	cartridge which is intermediate in power between the pistol rounds use in an SMG and full-power rifle/MG rounds
internal ballistics	the science of the passage of a projectile down a gun barrel (also known as interior ballistics)
iron sights	metal sights without an optical element, consisting of a rearsight close to the eye and a foresight near the muzzle
joules	a measure of muzzle energy
lands	smaller interior diameter of a rifled barrel; between the grooves
leaf sights	rearsights which consist of flat pieces of metal with a notch in the top for aiming; several flip-up 'leaves' of different heights may be provided to allow aiming at different ranges
linear action	gun mechanism in which the elements reciprocate in line with the gun barrel
link	element of an ammunition belt
LMG	light machine gun (*also see* LSW

	and SAW)
lock time	period of time between pressing the trigger or gun button and the first shot being fired
long recoil	type of gun-operating mechanism
long-stroke piston	type of gas operation in which the gas piston is attached to the bolt carrier and drives it all the way to the back of the recoil stroke (see short-stroke piston)
LSW	light support weapon (squad MG)
LV	low velocity
machine gun	automatic weapon of less than 20mm calibre
magazine	container which holds ammunition ready for loading into a gun
magazine follower	moving part of the magazine, between the spring and the ammunition, which transfers the spring pressure to the ammunition
MBR	main battle rifle
MG	machine gun (Ger. *Maschinengewehr*)
micro calibre	rifle calibre smaller than the current 5.45/5.56mm
multiball	cartridge which contains several projectiles (*see* duplex, triplex)
muzzle	end of the barrel from which the projectile emerges
muzzle blast	violent escape of gun gas from the muzzle as a projectile leaves the barrel
muzzle booster	device fitted to the muzzle to use some muzzle blast to increase recoil, to assist the action of recoil-operated guns
muzzle brake	device fitted to the muzzle which deflects part of the muzzle blast to the side or rear in order to reduce recoil
muzzle energy	calculation of the energy of a projectile as it leaves the muzzle; function of projectile velocity and weight
muzzle velocity	speed of a projectile as it leaves the muzzle
NATO	North Atlantic Treaty Organization: a military alliance of mainly western European states, but dominated by its largest member, the USA

neck	part of a cartridge case which holds the projectile
necked-down	cartridge case which has its neck reduced in diameter to accept a smaller calibre projectile than the case was designed for
necked-up (or necked-out)	cartridge case which has its neck increased in diameter to accept a larger calibre projectile than the case was designed for
obturation	sealing of a gun breech to prevent the escape of gun gas on firing (in automatic weapons, normally achieved by the cartridge case); also forward obturation achieved by the driving bands
OCSW	Objective Crew Served Weapon; US programme for a light automatic 25mm support weapon
OICW	Objective Individual Combat Weapon; US programme for a new infantry weapon combining 5.56 and 20mm calibres
open bolt	automatic weapon designed to start the firing cycle without a cartridge being loaded into the chamber (*see* closed bolt)
optical sights	sights using glass lenses, which may be of unit magnification (non-magnifying) or telescopic
optronics	combination of optical and electronic systems to provide day/night/all-weather sights
ORO	Operational Research Office (US Army)
over-bore	cartridge which has a case capacity too large for all of the propellant to be efficiently utilized
PDW	personal defence weapon: class of firearm midway between a pistol and a rifle, lighter and firing smaller-calibre ammunition than an SMG
peep sight	simple form of aperture rearsight
penetration	ability of an AP shot to penetrate armour
percussion	ignition method of igniting cartridges by striking a percussion primer with a firing pin
Picatinny rail	American type of universal mount-

pistol grip   ing rail to which can be attached a wide range of sights and accessories grip for the firing hand, immediately behind the trigger

piston primer   special primer designed to be pushed out by gas pressure on firing, in order to operate the bolt-unlocking mechanism

pivoting block   gun mechanism in which the breechblock movement is pivoted

primary extraction   act of a gun mechanism in pulling a fired case from the chamber

primer   percussion cap fitted into the head of a cartridge case, used to ignite the propellant

primer pocket   part of a cartridge case into which the primer fits

progressive rifling   rifling which commences with a gentle or zero twist, which gradually increases in twist down the length of the barrel

projectile   any bullet, shot or shell fired from a gun

propellant   chemical which burns rapidly to generate gas which accelerates the projectile up the gun barrel

pyrophoric   giving off sparks on impact and/or ignites spontaneously at high temperature

R   rimmed cartridge case (when it occurs at the end of a cartridge designation, as in 20 × 99R)

rail gun   *see* electromagnetic gun

rate of fire   frequency with which individual shots are fired in an automatic weapon, usually measured in rounds per minute (rpm)

RCAR   reduced-calibre assault rifle: with a calibre smaller than the full-calibre 7.62mm rounds

RCMG   rifle calibre machine gun, typically of 7.5–8mm calibre

receiver   body of the gun, to which the barrel and operating mechanism are attached

recoil operated   gun mechanism operated by the recoiling gun barrel

retarded blow-back   variation of blow-back mechanism in which, although the bolt is never locked to the barrel, the initial movement of the bolt is resisted by a part of the action, to give the bullet time to leave the muzzle; sometimes referred to as delayed blowback (*q.v.*) although the principles are slightly different

reticle   markings visible in an optical sight which indicate where to aim and sometimes the corrections needed for different ranges

rifle grenade   grenade intended to be fired by a rifle; it fits on to the end of the barrel and may either trap the bullet or permit it to pass through, using only the energy of the expanding gas to drive it (earlier models required a blank cartridge to fire them)

rifling   spiral grooving within a gun barrel which grips the projectile and spins it in order to ensure its stability (*see* progressive rifling)

rifling twist   angle of rifling, normally expressed as the length of barrel required for the rifling to turn the bullet through 360 degrees

rimfire   cartridge which is ignited by means of a percussion compound contained within the rim (*see* centrefire)

rimless (case)   cartridge case in which the rim is of the same diameter as the case body, separated from it by an extractor groove

rimmed (case)   cartridge case with a rim which has a larger diameter than the case body

rotary lock   locking of the bolt to the barrel extension by a rotary movement

round (of ammunition)   single cartridge (or equivalent)

RR   rebated rim (also given as RB)

rpm   rounds per minute, the usual measure of rate of fire

sabot   sleeve into which a subcalibre projectile is fitted, to enable it to be fired from a larger-calibre weapon: the sabot breaks up and falls away after the projectile leaves the muzzle

SABR   USA: selectable assault battle rifle (alternative name for OICW)

saddle drum   type of drum magazine in which the cartridges are held in two small, connected drums on either side of

	the action, from each of which rounds are fed in turn	shoulder	small pellets (as in a shotgun) part of a cartridge case where the diameter reduces sharply from the case body to the neck
salvo squeezebore	multiball system in which the projectiles are of the squeezebore type	sights sight base	devices used to aim a gun distance between the front and rear sights; the longer this is, the more accurately a weapon can be aimed
SAP	semi-armour piercing		
SAW	squad or section automatic weapon; another term for LMG		
SAWS	Small Arms Weapon Systems: 1960s US study	silencer	muzzle attachment to eliminate flash and blast
SCR/SCAR	USA: special forces combat (assault) rifle: 2000+ project to produce modular, multipurpose rifles for special forces	simplex	single-bullet loading (see duplex and triplex)
		single base	type of propellant
		skeleton butt	type of buttstock which consists of an empty frame rather than solid wood or plastic; usually designed to fold
SCHV	small-calibre high-velocity: US project post-1945		
SD	sectional density ratio; ratio between calibre and projectile weight: together with the projectile shape this determines the ballistic coefficient	sliding block	type of gun-action locking mechanism which moves across the breech face
		sling	strap used to carry and sometimes to steady a rifle
sear	part of trigger mechanism which holds back the hammer or firing pin	small arms	weapons intended to be carried by a soldier rather than fitted to a mounting
selective fire	ability to fire semi- or fully-automatically		
selector switch	control switch on a gun by the which the user can select between semi- or fully-automatic fire; usually combined with the safety catch and (on some models) a burst-fire mode	SMG	submachine gun
		smoothbored	barrel which is not rifled (used with fin-stabilized ammunition)
		SOCOM	USA: Special Operations Command
		SOPMOD	USA: Special Operations Peculiar Modifications Program
semi-automatic	rifle which automatically fires, ejects and reloads each time the trigger is pulled; also used to describe artillery in which the fired case is automatically ejected but a new round is manually loaded	spin stabilized	projectile whose flight is stabilized by being rotated by rifling
		spire point	bullet with a finely tapered nose for the optimum ballistic coefficient
		SPIW	USA: special purpose individual weapon (1960s project)
semi-rimmed (case)	cartridge case which has a rim only slightly larger in diameter than the case body, separated from it by an extractor groove; also known as semi-rimless	SPR	USA: special purpose rifle (5.56mm sniper rifle)
		squeeze bore	gun in which special projectiles are fired down a tapered barrel or fitment at end of the barrel, thereby reducing the diameter
shell	projectile which is hollow in order to contain HE or other substances		
short recoil	type of recoil-operated gun mechanism	SR	semi-rimmed (or semi-rimless); type of cartridge case
short-stroke piston	type of gas operation in which the gas piston moves back only a short distance, 'kicking' the bolt carrier to the rear (see long-stroke piston)	STANAG	standardization agreement: applies to NATO equipment
		Stellite	heat-resistant material used to line gun barrels
shot	(1) any solid armour-piercing projectile (that is, contains no HE) (2) projectile consisting of several	straight-cased cartridge	cartridge case with little or no taper between the head and the neck;

striker which therefore has no shoulder
long, spring-driven, firing pin

striking angle angle at which an AP projectile strikes armour plate; two conventions have applied: in one, a strike perpendicular to the plate is called 0 degrees, in NATO it is called 90 degrees

subcalibre projectile which is smaller than the bore of the gun, for firing, it is supported by a sabot; *see* APDS, APFSDS, flechette, sabot and full calibre

submachine gun compact, hand-held machine gun normally designed to use pistol ammunition

sub-projectiles projectiles carried by a larger projectile

suppressor muzzle attachment to reduce flash and blast

T tracer (when attached to a projectile designation)

telescoped ammunition ammunition in which the projectile is buried within the cartridge case to reduce its total length

telescoping stock buttstock which can be shortened to reduce its total length

terminal ballistics science concerning the performance of projectiles on striking their target

time of flight time taken for a projectile to reach its target

toggle joint type of elbow joint used in some short-recoil gun mechanisms

tracer chemical compound in the base of a projectile which burns slowly, giving a visible indication of the trajectory

trajectory curve traced by a projectile in flight, caused by gravity

triple base type of propellant

triplex loading cartridge containing three projectiles (*see* duplex, multiball)

tripod three-legged gun mounting used with light portable weapons

tumble when a bullet spins end-over-end, e.g., after striking the target

Warsaw Pact eastern European military alliance, set up in opposition to NATO and dominated by the USSR, which existed between 1955 and 1991

yaw when a projectile fails to fly point-first, e.g., after striking something in flight; taken to extreme, the projectile tumbles end-over-end. Most bullets yaw for a short distance after leaving the muzzle

METRIC TO IMPERIAL CONVERSION FACTORS

to convert millimetres to inches	divide by 25.4
to convert centimetres to inches	divide by 2.54
to convert metres to feet	multiply by 3.28
to convert metres to yards	multiply by 1.1
to convert kilometres to miles	divide by 1.61
to convert grams to grains	multiply by 15.432
to convert grams to ounces	divide by 28.35
to convert kilograms to pounds	multiply by 2.2

Bibliography

In addition to manufacturers' data, the following sources were consulted:

Published Books

Bolotin D.N., *Soviet Small Arms Polygon Press* (St. Petersburg, 1995)

Dugelby, T.B., *Modern Military Bullpup Rifles* (Collector Grade Publications, Toronto, 1984)

Ezell, E.C., *The Great Rifle Controversy: Search for the Ultimate Infantry Weapon from World War II through Vietnam and Beyond* (Stackpole Books, Harrisburg, PA, 1984)

Gander, T.J. (ed.), *Jane's Infantry Weapons 2003–2004* (Jane's Information Group, UK, 2002)

Hogg, I.V., *Jane's Directory of Military Small Arms Ammunition* (Jane's, London, 1985)

Hogg, I.V. and Weeks, J., *Military Small Arms of the 20th century* (Krause Publications, 7th edn, USA, 2002)

Huon, J., *Military Rifle and Machine Gun Cartridges* (Arms & Armour Press, London, 1986)

Kokalis, P.G., *Weapon Tests and Evaluations* (Paladin Press, USA, 2001)

Mullin, T.J., *Testing the War Weapons* (Paladin Press, USA, 1997)

Smith, W.H.B and Smith, J.E., *Small Arms of the World* (A & W Visual Library, 10th edn, USA, 1973)

Stevens, R.B. and Ezell, E.C., *The SPIW: The Deadliest Weapon That Never Was* (Collector Grade Publications, Toronto, 1985)

Stevens, R.B. and Ezell, E.C., *The Black Rifle: M16 Retrospective* (Collector Grade Publications, Toronto, 1994)

Wollert, G., Lidschun, R. and Kopengagen, W., *Schutzenwaffen heute: illustriette Enzyclopadie der Schutzenwaffen aus aller Welt, bild 1 und 2* (Militarverlag der DDR, Berlin, 1989)

Privately Published Sources

Labbett, P., *Assault Rifle Ammunition, 5.6mm to 11mm Calibre*

Labbett, P., *Russian Small Arms Ammunition 1972–1997*

Labbett, P. and Brown, F.A., *Die Kurzpatrone: the Development of the German 7.92 × 33 Kurz Cartridge*

Labbett, P. and Mead, P.J.F., *British 7 mm Ammunition*

Labbett, P. and Mead, P.J.F., *British 4.85 mm Ammunition*

Periodical Articles

Fackler, M.L., 'Wounding patterns of military rifle bullets', *International Defense Review* (1/1989)

Fackler, M.L., 'Wounding mechanism of projectiles striking at more than 1.5 km/sec', *Journal of Trauma* (vol.26, no.3, 1986)

Gelbart, M., 'Back to the future: the story of Britain's lost bullpups', *Small Arms Review* (vol.6, no.2, Nov. 2002)

Labbett, P., 'Cartridge development: 5.56 mm calibre and smaller', *Guns Review* (May 1979)

Labbett, P., 'Unconventional military small arms ammunition', *Guns Review* (Nov. 1979)

Labbett, P., 'Broadway Trust ammunition', *Guns Review* (Sep. 1981)

Labbett, P., '6mm SAWS ammunition', *Guns Review* (Mar. 1983)

PERIODICALS

Relevant articles are to be found in the following publications:

ARMS (Oruzhie), Russia, 1996–2003

GUN: Russian Arms Magazine (Ruzhjo), Russia, 1997–2003

Guns & Ammo, USA, 1977–2003

Guns and Weapons for Law Enforcement, USA, 2000–2003

Military Parade, Russia, 1997–2003

Small Arms Review, USA, 1999–2003

Soldier of Fortune – Russian Edition, Russia, 1996–2001

SWAT Magazine, USA, 1999–2003

The Cartridge Researcher (magazine of the European Cartridge Research Association)

WEBSITES

http://world.guns.ru/
M. Popenker's website on modern firearms and ammunition

http://www.quarry.nildram.co.uk
A.G. Williams's website on military guns and ammunition

http://www.club.guns.ru
Valery Shilin gun club

http://www.ar15.com/
comprehensive information plus discussion forums, focusing on the AR-15 / M16 and its ammunition

http://www.thegunzone.com/
compendium of information and links

http://www.cartridgesmith.com
Paul Smith's cartridge website

http://www.ecra.info/start.php
Home page of the European Cartridge Research Association

http://www.cartridgecollectors.org/
Home page of the International Ammunition Association

Index